Exclusion by El...

Exclusion by Elections develops a theory about ... under which 'class identities' as opposed to 'ethnic id... ...ne salient in democratic politics, and links this theory ... ...s of inequality and the propensity of governments to address it. The book argues that in societies with even modest levels of ethnic diversity, inequality invites ethnic politics, and ethnic politics results in less redistribution than class politics. Thus, contrary to existing workhorse models in social science, where democracies are expected to respond to inequality by increasing redistribution, the argument here is that inequality interacts with ethnic diversity to discourage redistribution. As a result, inequality often becomes reinforced by inequality itself. The author explores the argument empirically by examining cross-national patterns of voting behaviour, redistribution and democratic transitions, and he discusses the argument's implications for identifying strategies that can be used to address rising inequality in the world today.

John D. Huber's research focuses on understanding how the social, political and institutional context affects the outcomes of democratic processes. Along with numerous articles, he is the author of two previous Cambridge University Press books, *Rationalizing Parliament, Legislative Institutions and Party Politics in France* (1996), and *Deliberate Discretion? Institutional Foundations of Bureaucratic Autonomy* (2002, with Charles Shipan).

Cambridge Studies in Comparative Politics

General Editors

Kathleen Thelen *Massachusetts Institute of Technology*
Erik Wibbels *Duke University*

Associate Editors

Catherine Boone *London School of Economics*
Thad Dunning *University of California, Berkeley*
Anna Grzymala-Busse *Stanford University*
Torben Iversen *Harvard University*
Stathis Kalyvas *Yale University*
Margaret Levi *Stanford University*
Helen Milner *Princeton University*
Frances Rosenbluth *Yale University*
Susan Stokes *Yale University*
Tariq Thachil *Vanderbilt University*

Series Founder

Peter Lange *Duke University*

Other Books in the Series

Christopher Adolph, *Bankers, Bureaucrats, and Central Bank Politics: The Myth of Neutrality*

Michael Albertus, *Autocracy and Redistribution: The Politics of Land Reform*

Ben W. Ansell, *From the Ballot to the Blackboard: The Redistributive Political Economy of Education*

Ben W. Ansell, David J. Samuels, *Inequality and Democratization: An Elite-Competition Approach*

Leonardo R. Arriola, *Multi-Ethnic Coalitions in Africa: Business Financing of Opposition Election Campaigns*

David Austen-Smith, Jeffry A. Frieden, Miriam A. Golden, Karl Ove Moene, and Adam Przeworski, eds., *Selected Works of Michael Wallerstein: The Political Economy of Inequality, Unions, and Social Democracy*

Andy Baker, *The Market and the Masses in Latin America: Policy Reform and Consumption in Liberalizing Economies*

[continued after Index]

Exclusion by Elections

Inequality, Ethnic Identity, and Democracy

JOHN D. HUBER

Columbia University

CAMBRIDGE
UNIVERSITY PRESS

CAMBRIDGE
UNIVERSITY PRESS

University Printing House, Cambridge CB2 8BS, United Kingdom

One Liberty Plaza, 20th Floor, New York, NY 10006, USA

477 Williamstown Road, Port Melbourne, VIC 3207, Australia

4843/24, 2nd Floor, Ansari Road, Daryaganj, Delhi – 110002, India

79 Anson Road, #06-04/06, Singapore 079906

Cambridge University Press is part of the University of Cambridge.

It furthers the University's mission by disseminating knowledge in the pursuit of education, learning, and research at the highest international levels of excellence.

www.cambridge.org
Information on this title: www.cambridge.org/9781107182943
DOI: 10.1017/9781316863497

First published 2017

Printed in the United States of America by Sheridan Books, Inc.

A catalogue record for this publication is available from the British Library.

Library of Congress Cataloging-in-Publication Data
Names: Huber, John D., author.
Title: Exclusion by elections : inequality, ethnic identity, and
democracy / John D. Huber, Columbia University.
Description: Cambridge, United Kingdom ; New York, NY :
Cambridge University Press, [2017]
Identifiers: LCCN 2016049749 | ISBN 9781107182943 (hardback) |
ISBN 9781316633977 (pbk.)
Subjects: LCSH: Minorities–Suffrage–United States. | Ethnicity–Political
aspects–United States. | Income distribution–Political aspects–United States. |
Democracy–Economic aspects–United States.
Classification: LCC JK1846.H83 2017 | DDC 324.6/20973–dc23
LC record available at https://lccn.loc.gov/2016049749

ISBN 978-1-107-18294-3 Hardback
ISBN 978-1-316-63397-7 Paperback

Contents

Figures

Tables

Acknowledgments

This book project grew from a narrow initial ambition, which was to develop an argument about how different identities emerge in electoral competition. But the project grew and developed in unanticipated directions, and ended with a rather sobering theme, which is that through its role in shaping identity politics, inequality itself often constrains the extent to which democracies can be expected to address inequality. I hope that by sketching the logic of how inequality can impede redistribution in democracies we can think in new ways about how to address growing inequality in the world today.

The unanticipated trajectory of the project was due in large part to the constructive suggestions that my early efforts drew from others. I am grateful to seminar participants at the American Political Science Association meetings, at the University of Bocconi's Innocenzo Gasparini Institute for Economic Research, the University of Cagliari, Cornell University, the University of Geneva, Harvard University, the Institute for Economic Analysis in Barcelona, New York University, the University of Paris I, the Institute of Political Economy and Governance at the University of Pompeu Fabra, the University of Lausanne, the London School of Economics, Sabanci University, Sciences Po-Grenoble, and the University of Wisconsin. I received helpful research assistance from Lucas Leemann, Ben McClelland, and Camille Strauss-Kahn. Macartan Humphreys, Kimuli Kasara, Nolan McCarty, and Mike Ting gave me helpful comments on portions of the manuscript, and I received very useful suggestions from the reviewers at Cambridge University Press. And

Columbia grad students in the political economy working group gave great advice on what has become Chapter 6: thanks to Abhit, Anna, Ebie, Erin, Gosha, Kolby, Matt and Tara. Finally, thanks to Jane, Ben, and Lucy for providing welcome distractions from the book and to Lucy for her not-so-subtle prods to get back to it.

I

Introduction

Since the mid-1980s there has been a marked increase in inequality across most democratic countries around the world. The super-rich now earn a much greater proportion of income and hold a much greater proportion of wealth than they did in the 1970s. The well-known Gini coefficient has steadily increased. The wages of rich individuals have increased much more quickly than those of poorer individuals, and the middle class has been hit hard, with the relative wage of the median earner steadily declining. Measured in any of a number of ways, the distribution of income across societies has become increasingly skewed toward the rich.

One might expect the competitive electoral process to create incentives for parties and candidates to adopt policies that redress economic inequalities: if economic advantage is concentrated in the hands of a few, the disadvantaged masses should elect parties committed to redistributive policies. This dynamic does occur in varying degrees across many democracies, but it is often striking how weak the democratic response is to inequality. As income and wealth in the United States become increasingly concentrated among the very rich in the United States, for example, so has the prominence of right-wing policies that call for a sharply limited role of government. Similar dynamics unfold in other countries, rich and poor. This frequently tepid response to the concentration of wealth presents a puzzle: Why do voters, faced with rising income disparities, often elect parties that oppose policies that could address these disparities? Or, put differently, why does it often seem so challenging for "class politics" – where an important element of electoral

politics concerns the role of government in aiding the nonrich – to emerge
in democratic polities?

An important part of the answer to this question can be found by
considering a second puzzle, one that is typically treated as unrelated to
concerns about inequality. In many countries, an "ethnic identity" with
which one is born – by which I mean not only ethnic identities, but also
racial, religious, linguistic, or tribal identities, depending on the context –
becomes a salient element of electoral competition. When this happens,
parties explicitly or implicitly try to win votes by competing for support
from specific groups, and voters view their relevant electoral identity more
in terms of their ethnicity than their class. In US elections, for example,
there is considerable emphasis on the role of race. In Bangladesh there
are electoral divisions between Hindus and Muslims. In India there are
electoral divisions based on religion and caste. In Nigeria, Housa, Yoruba,
and Ibo often support different parties. At times, things can go badly
awry when group identity becomes central to electoral politics. Iraq, for
example, descended into chaos after the American invasion in large part
due to sectarian divisions between Shias and Sunnis. And civil conflict in
Ukraine has been centered on tensions between Russians and Ukrainians.

But there is substantial variation across countries in the extent to
which ethnic identities become central to electoral politics. The salience of
"Catholic" and "Protestant" identities, for example, is much different in
Northern Ireland than in Germany. The salience of racial identity is much
more central to electoral politics in the United States than in Brazil. When
Georgia has had democratic elections, "identity politics" has been much
less salient than in Ukraine, even though these countries have similar
levels of ethnic diversity. In Estonia, ethnic divisions in voting are more
apparent than they are in Latvia, even though ethnic diversity is greater in
Latvia. India and Indonesia have similar levels of ethnic diversity, but the
salience of identity in elections is much greater in India. These examples
suggest a second puzzle: Why does ethnicity become more important to
electoral politics in some contexts than in others?

We can gain insights into these two puzzles by developing a theory
of how various identities become salient in electoral competition. Individuals typically have multiple identities. One identity that is ubiquitous
in all societies is economic "class" – a term used narrowly in this book
to refer to an individual's level of economic well-being. Individuals also
have at least one "ethnic identity" that is inherited at birth. Ethnic and
class identities frequently become salient in democratic politics because
they create an efficient means for politicians to organize the quest for

votes and for voters to understand the link between vote choice and access to government resources. But if people have multiple identities, how do particular identities become salient in electoral politics?

The answer to this question is intrinsically important. Substantial levels of inequality are often regarded as unjust, and regardless of one's normative position on distributive justice, high inequality can contribute to a range of other outcomes that most would agree are best to avoid. Similarly, when ethnic divisions becomes salient in politics, a variety of bad outcomes can follow. Thus, to the extent that class politics leads to policies that redress inequality and ethnic politics can lead to bad governance outcomes, it is important to understand conditions that encourage ethnic versus class identities by parties and voters.

This book has two related goals. The first is to offer a theory of electoral competition and voting behavior that describes how ethnic diversity and economic inequality can interact to influence the salience of class and ethnic identities in elections. The second is to consider how the role of different identities in electoral competition should influence expectations about the extent to which democracies should produce policies that redress inequality.

The central theme that emerges from the analysis is that inequality will often make it *more difficult* for electoral competition to elect parties committed to addressing economic disparities. Rather than encouraging redistributive class politics, inequality often fosters the success of parties that focus on creating electoral coalitions based on noneconomic identities, such as ethnicity. And when winning electoral coalitions are based on such noneconomic identities, the democracy does less to redress inequality than would be the case if class politics could prevail. The remainder of this chapter describes in broad strokes this argument and its implications.

I.I THE ARGUMENT

Electoral competition is shaped by myriad factors, including the personalities of the candidates, policy debates about economic and noneconomic issues, patronage commitments, historic ties between various groups and political parties, and mobilization efforts, among other things. The argument in this book seeks to isolate and understand one such factor: distributive commitments by parties to voters. To this end, I make the stark assumption that voters care only about how their vote choice affects their economic well-being, and that they support the party that can *credibly* offer them the most material benefits. This focuses our attention on trying to understand what types of credible commitments parties can make to voters.

If parties compete for votes by making commitments to voters about how government resources should be distributed, how do parties make it clear which specific voters will benefit from a given party's victory, and how do they make these commitments credible, so voters will believe that parties will follow through on their commitments? One important strategy can be to make commitments to specific groups that have boundaries of membership that cannot be easily changed. Such commitments will be clear insofar as voters recognize the group boundaries, and they will be credible insofar as voters understand that if parties renege on promises to groups, they will lose the support of the entire group.

Ethnic and class identities are particularly useful in electoral politics in large part because they often define group boundaries that parties can exploit in efforts to win votes. When a party makes a commitment to a particular class – say the nonrich – and this party wins, a rich voter cannot easily change his or her "class identity" to obtain policy benefits from the government. Similarly, when a party commits to providing benefits to a particular ethnic group, a voter in the losing ethnic group cannot decide after the election to change his or her ethnic identity to that of the winning group. For this reason, ethnic identity is also often salient as an exclusion device. Class and ethnic identities can thus be exploited by parties trying to win votes: class parties can form by making commitments to income groups, while ethnic parties can form by making commitments to ethnic groups.

But though ethnic and class identities make possible credible commitments by parties to groups, they also constrain the types of commitments that parties can make. Given that the boundaries between groups make commitments credible, when parties ignore these boundaries, for example, by making commitments to random subsets of groups, their promises become less clear and credible. Thus, if we think about electoral competition from the perspective of group-based commitments, the size of groups will influence the types of commitments that parties can make, and in particular the amount that parties can promise to voters.

Consider a bare bones model of how this could work. Suppose there exists some government pie and that parties compete for votes by making promises to groups about how the pie should be distributed in society. A class-based party can promise to distribute the pie to a particular income group and an ethnic-based party can promise to distribute the pie to a particular ethnic group. Voters have two identities, their class and their ethnicity. The identity that becomes relevant to them at election time depends on the type of party they support. A voter emphasizes his or her "class identity" by supporting a class-based party and "class politics" prevails in society when the government pie is distributed to individuals based on their income. A voter emphasizes his or her "ethnic identity" in elections by supporting a party committed to his or her ethnic group, and "ethnic politics" prevails in society when the government pie is distributed to individuals based on their ethnic identity.

As voters wish to receive as much as possible, the amount they can receive from a particular party will be constrained by the number of voters the party represents. It is easy to depict the logic in a simple framework where there are two class identities (rich and nonrich) and two ethnic identities (majority and minority), as in Figure 1.1. The columns depict the ethnic identity of individuals, with members of the majority group on the left and the minority group on the right. The rows depict the class identity of individuals, with rich individuals on the top and nonrich individuals, who represent a majority, on the bottom. The cells describe the number of individuals in a hypothetical 100-person society. Parties can represent a column (e.g., there can be a party of the majority group or a party of the minority group) or a row (e.g., there can be a party of the rich or a party of the nonrich). What is the most that any party could offer to voters?

Consider the electoral dynamic under plurality rule. As the party representing the rich could always be defeated by a party representing the nonrich, a winning class party will represent the nonrich. Similarly a winning ethnic party will represent the majority ethnic group. Electoral competition therefore boils down to a contest between the party of the nonrich and the party of the majority ethnic group. In the top panel of Figure 1.1, the party of the nonrich represents 70 individuals and the party of the majority group represents 63 individuals. Thus, the most that the class-based party could offer to each of the nonrich is $\frac{\pi}{70}$ where π represents the government pie. By contrast, the most that the ethnic party could offer to members of the majority ethnic group is $\frac{\pi}{63}$. The rich in the majority group obviously prefer the ethnic party (because they receive nothing if class politics prevails) and the nonrich in the minority group obviously prefer the class party (because they receive nothing if ethnic politics prevails). The nonrich in the majority group receive benefits regardless of whether class or ethnic politics prevails and in this example they prefer ethnic politics because $\frac{\pi}{63}$ is greater than $\frac{\pi}{70}$. Thus, the ethnic party could defeat the class party and government policy

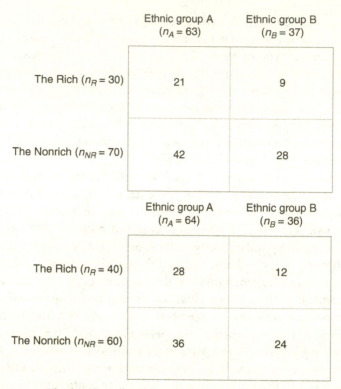

	Ethnic group A (n_A = 63)	Ethnic group B (n_B = 37)
The Rich (n_R = 30)	21	9
The Nonrich (n_{NR} = 70)	42	28

	Ethnic group A (n_A = 64)	Ethnic group B (n_B = 36)
The Rich (n_R = 40)	28	12
The Nonrich (n_{NR} = 60)	36	24

FIGURE I.I. The number of nonrich voters and incentives for class politics.

would distribute to individuals based on their ethnicity. In the bottom panel, the dynamic would be different. An ethnic party must spread the pie among 64 individuals and a class party must spread the pie among 60 individuals. Thus, the class party can offer more to voters than can the ethnic party, giving class politics an advantage.

The ideas developed in this book derive from this basic logic about group size and minimal winning electoral coalitions. If group identities make possible credible commitments, then parties representing larger majorities will be disadvantaged because they can offer less to their supporters than can parties representing smaller majorities. When the number of nonrich is "too large," for example, it is more difficult for a class-based party to win. But what it means for a group to be "too large" depends on the size of alternative electoral coalitions. In the preceding example, if the majority ethnic group is very large, then class politics can prevail even if the number of nonrich voters is relatively large. As the size of the majority ethnic group becomes smaller, the definition of "too large" changes, and becomes smaller. Expectations about whether class politics or ethnic politics prevails in electoral competition should therefore be influenced by the interaction of two variables: the number of nonrich and the number in the majority ethnic group. As the number of nonrich grows smaller relative to the number in the majority ethnic group, class politics should be more likely to prevail. As the number in an ethnic majority grows smaller relative to the number of nonrich, ethic politics should be more likely to prevail. In Chapter 3 I develop these ideas about the role of social structure, and address the possibility that parties could form to appeal to any subset of voters who can be defined by their multiple identities (such as voters on the diagonal in Figure 1.1).

Party Competition and Social Structure

To understand the role of social structure in shaping party competition, we should not assume that group size will lead automatically to the election of particular types of parties. Party formation is costly, and a theory of how social structure matters in electoral competition should describe why parties form and what types of platforms they offer given the social structure. In the distributive framework here, there is always an advantaged party (the one that represents the smallest majority), so we might ask why losing parties would ever form. And if losing parties have no incentive to form, why do leaders of winning parties have incentives to distribute anything at all to voters? To answer such questions, we need to be explicit about how political parties emerge endogenously from social structure.

To this end, the argument rests on two assumptions about the motivations of party entrepreneurs. The first is that potential party entrepreneurs care about the rents from office, that is, about the private gain they can reap from keeping a slice of the government pie for themselves. Rents from winning create incentives for individuals to form parties that represent the advantaged (smaller) majority, but they also create incentives for such entrepreneurs to maximize their rents by distributing as little as possible to the group members they represent. The second assumption is that potential party entrepreneurs care about policy outcomes, that is, about how the government pie is distributed to voters, and in particular about the policy benefits that winning parties give to the group to which the entrepreneur belongs. Losing parties therefore form to ensure that the rent-seeking incentives of winning parties do not allow such parties to keep excessive rents. The entrepreneurs for the losing parties benefit from paying the cost of party formation because they benefit directly from the policies that their losing party forces the winning party to adopt. In the top panel of Figure 1.1, for example, a nonrich individual from group A would have an incentive to form a class-based party that would lose because doing so can force the winning party representing group A to offer more to group A members, and the individual forming the losing class party is a member of group A.

These assumptions lead to clear predictions from the theoretical model about how many parties should form, about what types of policies they should offer to voters, and about which identities become important to individuals when they vote. And group size remains central. When the number of nonrich individuals is small relative to the number in the majority ethnic group, a class party representing this group will form and win the votes of the nonpoor, who vote their class identity. The winning class-based party will distribute as much of the government pie to the nonrich that is necessary in order to win against the other party that forms, which represents the majority ethnic group. By contrast, when the number in the majority group is small relative to the number of nonrich, an ethnic party representing the majority group will form, and will win the votes of the members of this group, who vote their ethnic identity. The winning ethnic-based party will distribute to members of its group as much of the government pie as it needs to in order to win against class-based party that forms to influence policy. This argument about social structure and party competition is developed in Chapter 4.

Empirical Implications

To go from the abstract theory to specific empirical implication requires linking the key variables in the model – the number of nonrich and the number in the majority group – to substantive variables that can be measured. I take up this task in Chapter 5. Some might be concerned at the outset that it makes little sense to take the size of income groups as exogenously given. Instead, it may make more sense to assume that governments can determine who is "nonrich" through policy, for example by giving benefits only to those below the median income in society. Chapter 5 begins by considering this issue, pointing out limitations of such a median voter framework but also pointing out how the theoretical framework employed here could be integrated into a median voter model. The chapter then argues that income inequality – and specifically the

Gini coefficient – is a good measure of the size of nonrich, one that emerges directly from the parameters of the model and also from the median-voter framework for thinking about the number of nonrich. The chapter also argues that ethnic diversity – and specifically, a measure of ethnic polarization – is a good measure of the size of the majority group. As ethnic polarization increases, the expected size of the ethnic majority decreases. Thus, the model suggests that inequality and ethnic polarization should interact to influence the nature of electoral politics in democratic systems.

The theoretical model has a number of empirical implications related to inequality, ethnic polarization, and their interaction, which I take up in Part II. One empirical implication involves the salience of class versus ethnic identity in elections, which are the focus of Chapters 7 and 8. When should a person's class versus ethnic identity be most strongly related to his or her voting behavior? If inequality is low relative to ethnic polarization, class parties can offer the most to nonrich voters, and thus we should see individuals' "class identities" – that is, voters' incomes – being more important to predicting vote choice than is the case when inequality is high relative to ethnic polarization. Thus, the role of class and ethnic identity in predicting voting behavior across different societies should depend on the interaction of ethnic polarization and inequality.

I present several tests of the argument. In Chapter 7, to test the relevance of class identity, I examine the relationship between individual income and vote choice, finding that this relationship is strongest in societies in which the conditions for class politics are strongest – that is, where inequality is low relative to ethnic diversity. In Chapter 8, to test the relevance of ethnic identity, I examine a measure of ethnic voting that taps the degree to which the bases of support for parties are ethnically homogeneous. I find that when the conditions for ethnic politics are strongest – that is, where inequality is high relative to ethnic diversity – political parties have stronger ethnic bases of support. Thus, voting behavior is related empirically to social structure in the way that the theory predicts.

The second empirical implication concerns policy outcomes, and in particular the degree to which government policy reduces inequality. If class politics prevails in the theoretical model, the ensuing government policy targets only the nonrich. By contrast, if ethnic politics prevails, government policy targets some individuals who are rich (those in the winning group) and excludes some individuals who are not rich (those in the losing group). Thus, government policy should do the least to redress inequality when inequality is *high* given the level of ethnic diversity. Chapter 9 provides evidence regarding this empirical implication of the argument.

Finally, the argument has implications for studies of transitions from autocratic to democratic rule. Scholars who examine the strategic incentives of autocratic elites to democratize emphasize the redistributive effects of democracy (e.g., Boix 2003 and Acemoglu and Robinson 2005). Autocratic elites are typically rich, democracy is a credible institutional commitment to redistribution, and thus autocratic elites will lose economically if they accept transitions to democracy. But how do autocratic elites form expectations about the economic cost of democracy? Existing studies typically invoke a class-based tax-and-transfer model to argue that democracy is most costly to elites when inequality is highest (because high inequality leads to more redistribution through its influence on the preferences of the median voter). The argument here is quite different. The redistributive effects of democracy will depend on whether class politics emerges as dominant in political competition, and inequality will make class politics less likely if there is sufficient ethnic polarization. Thus, if autocratic elites care about the effect of democracy on redistribution, their expectations about the cost of democracy should depend on the interaction of inequality and ethnic diversity. That is, inequality should discourage democratization only when ethnic polarization is low. Chapter 9 provides evidence for this implication of the mode by examining the conditions associated with democratic transitions themselves.

1.2 SOME ILLUSTRATIVE OBSERVATIONS AND EXAMPLES

African democracies are often notorious for the intensity of their ethnic politics. By contrast, if we look at Scandinavian countries, class politics rules and there is substantial redistribution from rich to poor. Why might this difference between Africa and Scandinavia exist?

These countries are obviously different in many, many ways, which may make the comparison of Africa with Scandinavia seem strange. But the framework here would simply remind us to observe that in Africa, where inequality is typically high and the vast majority of people often have low incomes, it would be very challenging for a class party to form. If a party says "We're the party of the poor," it can be easily undercut because it can promise very little to individual voters given that such a large proportion are poor. This opens the door to parties that can offer more to smaller coalitions, and given the presence of ethnic diversity in many African countries, ethnicity provides a pathway to supporting some poor voters at the expense of others. In most of Scandinavia, by contrast, ethnic politics is virtually impossible. Ignoring some recent changes brought about by immigration, it would be very difficult, for example, for a party in Norway or Sweden to stand up and say "We are the party of the white people!" This opens the door to class-based parties that redistribute income from the rich to the nonrich.

This comparison of Africa to Sweden illustrates how high inequality with high ethnic diversity can undermine the emergence of redistributive class-based parties. The central argument of this book, however, is not that inequality and ethnic diversity always undermine class politics, but rather that they can *interact* to influence the role of ethnicity and income in elections. Consider, then, several countries within Africa that have similar levels of ethic diversity but quite different levels of ethnic politics. Are these differences related to the level of inequality? Figure 1.2 plots the level of ethnic voting in democratic African countries against the Gini coefficient (with relevant details of these variables given in Chapter 8) after removing the effect of ethnic polarization. That is, the figure plots the residuals of a regression of ethnic voting on ethnic polarization. The positive relationship between ethnic voting and inequality is clear and suggests that the relative salience of ethnic politics across African countries may indeed be related to underlying levels of economic inequality.

Voting and Naturalization by Immigrants in Nineteenth-Century American Cities

Consider the effect of group size on ethnic voting in a context in which all groups are relatively poor. Shertzer (2013) provides a useful example from municipal elections in four large American cities at the turn of the twentieth century. Local politicians in the wards of these cities had substantial power to influence the neighborhoods in which to make infrastructure investments (such as those related to sanitation and transportation) and they could provide access to municipal jobs, protection from gangs, access to public works contracts, and even inside tracks to jobs in the private sector. Whether a particular politician was responsive to the needs of particular immigrant groups depended on their electoral value, and for the new immigrants from places such as

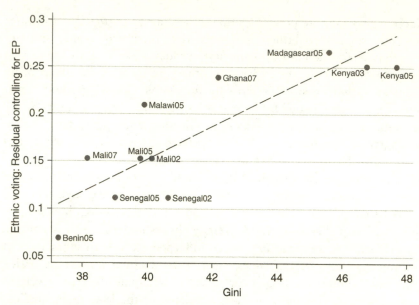

FIGURE I.2. Inequality and ethnic voting in Africa.
Note: Ethnic voting on the *y*-axis is measured as the residual from regressing Party Voting Polarization (PVP) (see details in Chapter 7) on ethnic polarization (EP). Multiple points exist for some countries because of the availability of multiple surveys.

Italy, Russia, Czechoslovakia, Hungary, and Poland that were flooding into these cities at the time, they could become politically valuable to politicians only if they undertook a costly naturalization process. Thus, the propensity of immigrants to naturalize is an important indicator of political mobilization of ethnic groups by politicians at that time.

What determined whether immigrants from a particular group would in fact be willing to pay the price of naturalizing in a given political ward? Shertzer focuses on group size: immigrants who belonged to groups that could become pivotal to the Democratic Party's ability to form minimal winning electoral coalitions would have been the most likely to be the subject of mobilization efforts by a politician in a ward, and thus would have been the most likely to naturalize. Whether a group could be pivotal depended on the group's own size (was it large enough to facilitate a victory?), which had to be considered relative to the size of the Democratic Party's core level of support in the ward (something that Scherzer could measure by examining the number of Germans and Irish in a ward at the time).

Scherzer finds convincing support for the importance of group size. The number of naturalizations by a particular ethnic group increases substantially when the conditions suggest the group could be electorally pivotal. In addition, the effect is nonlinear, with naturalizations diminishing once a group surpasses a particular size. This is consistent with the idea that when politicians can influence group size – as they can, for example, by mobilizing individuals to naturalize – they have incentives to create electoral coalitions that are as small as possible while winning. It also illustrates that individuals from particular groups see the benefits from group membership declining as group size becomes "too large."

The Bumiputera in Malaysia

Malaysia has held regular elections since independence in 1957, although it is not the kind of "democracy" on which one would typically want to base generalizations, with clear limitations on political and individual liberties.[1] Nonetheless, the dynamics of political competition and policymaking illustrate elements of the argument emphasized here. At the time of independence, there were myriad ethnic groups among indigenous Malaysians, with more than thirty-five ethnic categories in the 1960 census. There was also a relatively large population from two immigrant communities: the rich, urban Chinese, who worked primarily in commerce, industry, and services, and the Indians, who were less rich than the Chinese, and who often were employed on public works projects or on rubber plantations. The indigenous Malaysians often lived in rural areas and earned their livelihood by cultivating rice and working on rubber plantations.

After independence in the 1960s, a coalition of parties ("the Alliance") created a consociational power-sharing arrangement that essentially preserved the economic status of Malaysia's groups. During this time, there were strong efforts to create radical class-based parties or movements that would have addressed the concerns of the many individuals who were poor. And although a large proportion of the individuals who would have benefited from such class-based politics were from indigenous groups,

---

[1] The Polity2 score for Malaysia has typically been between 1 and 4 since 1970, and Freedom House continues to identify strong limitations on freedom of expression and other political rights.

there were also a nontrivial number of less well-off Chinese and Indians. In 1970, for example, 58 percent of the population earned less than 1,199 RM, and of these 28 percent were Chinese or Indian. Of the 84 percent of the population that earned less than 400 RM, 35 percent were Chinese or Indian. But these class-based movements were suppressed and gained no traction. Instead, following ethnic riots on May 13, 1969 in Kuala Lumpur, Malaysia entered a rather extreme form of ethnic politics when a coalition of parties endorsed the "New Economic Program" (NEP).

The NEP created a system that conferred government benefits on individuals who were members of the "Bumiputera," an ethnic category that existed prior to this time and that referred to a wide range of indigenous ethnic groups, but excluded the Chinese and Indians.[2] These benefits included financial assistance for buying housing, quotas for places in universities, quotas for jobs in the public sector, privileged access to government public works contracts, and preferential treatment in the purchase of shares in companies. Importantly, all of the benefits were available to individuals from the Bumiputera, independent of their economic status, and many of the programs specifically benefited the wealthiest from among the indigenous groups. Since its creation, the NEP has been supported by the ruling Barisan National (BN) coalition, a central member of which is the United Malays National Organization.

From the perspective of the argument here, it is not surprising to see the emergence of this ethnic policy. In 1970, the Bumiputera constituted 56 percent of the population, making it an attractive "group" on which to base an ethnic division of government spoils in a relatively poor country. But the effect of the NEP has been to change the ethnic composition of Malaysian society, with many ethnic Chinese leaving Malaysia, increasing the proportion of the population who are Bumiputera. In 2010, the Bumiputera share of the population rose to 67 percent.[3] Thus, the argument developed here suggests that this should make the NEP quite fragile, as such a large group must divide the spoils of government thinly.[4] Indeed, a 2008 survey found that 71 percent of Malaysians thought the

[2] The Bumiputera included Malays, as well as Kadazan, Murut, and Bajau in Sabah, and Iban, Bidayuh, and Melenau in Sarawak, as well as assorted smaller groups.
[3] See Teik (2005) and www.statistics.gov.my/portal/index.php?option=com_content& id=1215.
[4] On the possible end of this sort of ethnic politics in Malaysia, see Pepinsky (2009).

NEP was "obsolete" and in that year, opposition parties vowing to roll back the NEP-won control of Panang, an economic hub in Malaysia.[5]

1.3 ORGANIZATION OF THE BOOK

The remainder of the book develops and tests the argument sketched in this chapter. Chapter 2 situates the argument in the existing literature. The chapter also underscores the importance of understanding the emergence of class and ethnic politics by describing many of the social problems that can result when ethnic politics prevails, and when inequality goes unaddressed.

The theoretical argument is developed in Part I, which consists of Chapters 3 through 5. Chapter 3 describes how social structure – and in particular the distribution of ethnic and class identities – should advantage and disadvantage particular types of parties. Chapter 4 describes the central theoretical argument about social structure and the distributive commitments of parties in a model in which party competition emerges endogenously. In addition, the chapter takes up the question of "theoretical robustness." Are the central intuitions about social structure robust to different assumptions about electoral law, the source of government revenues, and the number of groups? The appendix to this chapter provides the game theoretic model that is the foundation for the theoretical argument. Chapter 5 describes how the abstract model of group size motivates testable arguments about the interaction of inequality and ethnic diversity.

I examine the empirical implications of the argument in Part II. Chapter 6 addresses the issue of causal identification. I argue that techniques that have been developed to address limitations with traditional approaches to observational data are ill suited for testing the argument in this book. I also argue that carefully linking a clear theoretical framework to empirical research creates possibilities for learning about causality even when we are limited to traditional methods with observational data.

Chapters 7 to 10 present the empirical evidence based on cross-national comparisons. Chapters 7 and 8 focus on electoral behavior. Does the strength of the relationship between income and voting behavior vary across countries with the levels of inequality and ethnic polarization as predicted by the theory? Do the ethnic bases of support for parties become

5 See www.economist.com/news/briefing/21576654-elections-may-could-mark-turning-point-never-ending-policy and http://news.bbc.co.uk/2/hi/asia-pacific/7342052.stm.

stronger when the conditions for class politics become weaker? Do the answers to these questions differ in old and new democracies?

Chapter 9 tests the implications of the theory for macropolitical outcomes. The first concerns redistribution. Is redistribution highest when the conditions for class politics are strong? The second concerns democratization. Does the theory help us to understand the relationship between inequality and democratic transitions?

The implications of the theoretical argument and evidence are contrary to what is typically assumed about democracy and inequality, and they are discouraging for those concerned about the ill effects of inequality. Given electoral incentives to exclude, inequality often makes class politics and the redistributive policies that go with it less viable. Thus, democracy might be expected to do the least to redress inequality when inequality is high. The book concludes with a brief summary of the argument and evidence, and discusses some pathways that might foster class-based policies that redress inequality and discourage ethnic politics.

2

Why Worry about Inequality and Ethnic Politics?

The central argument of this book is that economic inequality and ethnic diversity interact to influence the importance of class and ethnic identities, and thereby influence the extent to which democracy can be expected to redress inequality. This chapter draws on the existing literature to motivate and situate the research in two respects. The first is to describe the substantive consequences of an electoral dynamic that fails to address inequality and instead encourages ethnic politics. Why do we care if democracy fails to redress inequality, or if electoral competition fosters ethnic identities? The second is to situate the argument in two existing literatures. How have scholars previously studied the salience of ethnic identity in electoral politics, or the politics of redistribution? How does the argument here contribute to these previous approaches?

The chapter has four sections. Section 2.1 reviews arguments about the problems associated with leaving inequality unaddressed, and Section 2.2 discusses problems that can ensue when ethnic identity becomes salient in politics. The remaining two sections situate the argument in the literature on ethnic politics (Section 2.3) and redistribution (Section 2.4).

2.1 PROBLEMS WITH INEQUALITY

Economic inequality is often viewed as intrinsically unjust, and normative theorists have articulated a number of frameworks for thinking about how to evaluate different distributions of economic well-being, and of policies that change these distributions. A Rawlsian perspective, for example, encourages us to consider the "fairness" of economic outcomes, in which the notion of "fairness" emerges from thinking about choice from behind Rawls' veil of ignorance. Rawls argues that from behind such a veil, people would agree on a distribution of welfare that satisfies a maximin principle, in which society is structured so as to maximize the well-being of the least well-off individual (see Rawls 1971). This perspective does not preclude economic inequality: it may well be that the social structure that maximizes the well-being of the least well-off individual will also lead to inequality of outcomes. Taxes on the rich, for example, could be used to obtain revenues that are redistributed to the poor, but if such taxes are set so high that they substantially discourage economic activity, they may not maximize the welfare of the least well-off. Such taxes would be unjust from the perspective of Rawls' "fairness principle." The normative objective, then, is to choose policies that maximize the welfare of the least well-off, not to eliminate inequality.

A normative alternative to Rawls' fairness principle, to take a second example, criticizes Rawls' emphasis on economic outcomes for ignoring the activities and efforts that generate these outcomes. Dworkin (1981a, 1981b), for example, incorporates the notion of "personal responsibility" into a framework for thinking about distributive justice. He points out that individual well-being is due both to factors that are inside a person's control (e.g., individual effort) and factors outside a person's control, or "brute luck." Individuals might be disadvantaged by their ethnic identity, by the types of schools to which they have access, or by physical disabilities that they suffer through no choice they have made. Inequality due to such (bad) luck is undesirable because it unfairly affects opportunities for individuals to advance their own well-being. Such inequalities can therefore justify policies that remedy differences in economic opportunities. Other outcomes, however, are due to differences in individual effort. Some people, the argument goes, choose to work hard, or to take more risks, and the normative justification for redistributive policies that redress inequalities due to differences in effort or risk-taking are unfounded. From this perspective, it is important to distinguish between inequality of opportunity, which invites policies that level the playing field, and inequality due to individual choices about work, which can and should be embraced.[1] From the perspective of the argument here, government distribution that targets particular ethnic rather than income groups is unjust both because it violates the maximin

---

[1] Related treatments of justice that focus on personal responsibility include Arneson (1989), Cohen (1989), and Roemer (1993, 1998).

principle and because it targets based on a characteristic with which one is born (ethnicity) rather than on effort.

If one wishes to describe the degree to which particular distributions of economic well-being are just, one needs to embrace a normative theory like one of those described previously to guide measurement. A framework that embraces a Rawlsian theory of justice would need to consider economic well-being of individuals after government redistributive policies take effect, and in so doing would focus on the well-being of the least well-off. To this end, Atkinson created a famous measure (now called the Atkinson Index) that was motivated in large part by the effort to capture Rawls' notion of fairness in a single number, one in which different weights can be applied to different parts of the income distribution.[2] By contrast, a Dworkian approach asks that we disentangle inequality of opportunity from inequality due to differences in effort (Roemer et al. 2003; see also Bourguignon, Ferreira, and Menéndez 2007; Ferreira and Gignoux 2011; and Ferreira, Lakner, and Berk Özler 2014).

We do not, however, care about the salience of ethnic versus class politics solely on normative concerns for just income distributions. If inequality is allowed to increase unchecked, a range of negative repercussions can follow. Consider how inequality can create incentives that lower economic development. Inequality can be linked to inefficiencies in investment decisions (including investments in schooling and occupational choice) and in decisions regarding debt repayment (e.g., Banerjee and Newman 1993; Galor and Zeira 1993; Aghion and Bolton 1997).[3] And inequality can undermine economic development by contributing to financial crises that in turn lead to stagnating purchasing power by the lower and middle classes (Piketty 2014).

There can also be a political channel through which inequality influences economic development. Some scholars argue that governments should be expected to respond to inequality with redistributive tax schemes (e.g., Meltzer and Richard 1981; Alesina and Rodrik 1994; Persson and Tabellini 1994), which in turn can harm economic development. Others have argued that inequality can harm growth by empowering the rich, leading to taxes that are too low for optimal public investment (e.g., Bénabou 2000) or to harmful rent-seeking by the rich (Esteban and Ray 2000).

---

[2] See Atkinson (1970, 1975).
[3] For reviews of the theoretical and empirical literature, see Ferreira et al. (2014) and Voitchovsky (2009).

Inequality can also have socially corrosive effects unrelated to economic development. Scholars, for example, have found a link between social inequality and health. One pathway that may contribute to this link is psychological stress that is inherent to dominance relationships, while another is that inequality may lead to a lower provision of public goods, which in turn affects health outcomes.[4] Higher levels of inequality are also linked to higher levels of crime. This may be true because the payoff from crime to low-income individuals may increase with the level of inequality in society (e.g., Becker 1968; Freeman 1999). There can also be sociological pathways linking inequality to crime. Inequality, for example, can lead to feelings of deprivation, and relative deprivation theory might then lead us to expect that poorer individuals will have increased incentives to commit acts of violence even if there is no material gain (see, e.g., John Braithwaite 1979 and the critical review in Stack 1984). The empirical evidence for this hypothesis is mixed, but a recent paper by Enamorado et. al. (2014) provides causal evidence from Mexico of a positive effect of inequality on crime.

Social mobility is also negatively related to inequality. The "Great Gatsby curve," a term coined by Alan Krueger, shows that countries with the highest levels of inequality are also those where economic advantages and disadvantages persist most strongly across generations. Children, for example, often inherit the social networks of their parents, which can aid the children of richer parents and hurt those of poorer parents. And if there are strong economic returns to education, itself a measure of inequality, then inequality will reduce social mobility because richer parents have a greater ability to invest in education, and they have the greatest incentives to do so when inequality is high.[5] And inequality may hinder social mobility by dampening the aspirations of the least advantaged.[6] Kearney and Levine (2014) provide recent evidence, for example, linking inequality to higher dropout rates in US high schools.

It is clear, then, that even if we disagree about how to think about inequality normatively, when it reaches certain levels, inequality creates problems we might all agree should be avoided. This makes it important to understand when political conditions create incentives that discourage policies that redress inequality. The discouraging implication of the argument here is that inequality itself can create political obstacles to

---

[4] See collection of essays in Kawachi, Kennedy, and Wilkinson (1999).
[5] For a recent and very useful review of this literature, see Corak (2013).
[6] See the theoretical model by Genicot and Ray (2014).

inequality-reducing policies, creating a sort of trap from which it can be difficult to emerge. And if this is not discouraging enough, if a main alternative to class-based politics is ethnic politics, this invites a new set of problems, which I take up next.

2.2 PROBLEMS WITH ETHNIC DIVERSITY

As described previously, scholars have developed clear normative frameworks for thinking about the justice or fairness of particular distributions of economic well-being, or of policies that change these distributions. The same is not true, of course, for evaluating the distributions of ethnic identities in a society. Indeed, historic efforts to do so, such as Nazi efforts to argue for the superiority of non-Jewish whites, are not only patently unscientific, they are also deeply disturbing and morally repugnant. This moral repugnancy is almost certainly connected in part to the widely embraced idea that individual well-being should not be tied to identity markers with which one is born. Normative opposition to a political dynamic that systematically favors particular group identities at the expense of others can therefore be rooted in Dworkin's critique of inequalities of opportunity: to the extent such dynamics reinforce rather than reduce such inequality, they should be opposed. And programs like affirmative action, which are designed with the intent to address inequality of opportunity, even though they target individuals based on traits with which they are born, should be embraced insofar as they reduce inequalities of opportunity.

Thus, except when they are intended to redress inequalities of opportunity, we should be concerned on normative grounds when the benefits and advantages that individuals receive from government are tied to ethnic markers. But when ethnic politics is rife, we often observe precisely this connection between ethnic identity and government benefits. Burgess et al. (2013), for example, studied the location of road construction in Kenya, finding that regions dominated by the president's ethnic group receive the most investment, suggesting "ethno-favoritism" – an ethnic bias in the allocation of state resources – in Kenyan politics.[7] Similarly, in a study of education and infant mortality across a wide range of sub-Saharan African countries over time, Franck and Rainer (2012) show that having a coethnic as the head executive in a country during one's primary school age increases the likelihood of having attended school.

---

[7] Jablonski (2014) also find evidence of ethno-favoritism in the distribution of foreign aid.

The findings are further supported by a case study of Congo–Brazzaville, in which plausibly exogenous variation in the ethnicity of the president and the cabinet resulting from a presidential death and subsequent coup correlates with an increase in educational attainment in citizens from the new president's ethnic group and a decrease in the former's group.[8] Ethno-favoritism is not universal across policies. Kasara (2007) studied the relationship between ethnicity and government tax policy in agriculture across a wide range of African countries. Taking advantage of the fact that particular crops are raised by particular ethnic groups, she provides convincing evidence that groups supporting the president receive less favorable tax treatment than groups that are not in the president's coalition. Kramon and Posner (2016) provide a comprehensive review of empirical studies of distributive ethnic politics, a review that emphasizes that the conclusions we can draw depend strongly on the types of policies and outcomes that we study.

In addition to concerns about ethno-favoritism, scholars have identified a number of problems related to governance in ethnically diverse societies. Consider economic performance. In theory, ethnic diversity could increase economic output for reasons that are outside of politics. Alesina and La Ferrara (2005), for example, argue that if members of ethnic groups have complementary skills, then this can increase economic output in a diverse society (see also, e.g., Prat 2002; Page 2008). But the implications for growth could also be expected to be negative. If members of different groups have differing preferences for public goods, this can lower the production of public goods, which in turn hurts economic development. Whether the net effect of diversity on economic performance is positive or negative depends on the tradeoff between these two mechanisms, and may depend on the overall level of development in society (with richer countries better able to cope with the negative effects).

The evidence suggests that the net effect is typically negative. In an early pathbreaking paper on the topic, Easterly and Levine (1997) showed that economic growth is lowest in countries that have high levels of ethnic diversity, which they argue contributes to low levels of growth. In subsequent research with new measures of ethnic diversity, Alesina et al. (2003) provide further evidence of a negative relationship between ethnic diversity and economic development, as do Alesina and La Ferrara (2005). This negative relationship, however, may be mitigated by "good

---

[8] Further evidence regarding ethno-favoritism can be found in Alwy and Schech (2004), Posner (2005), and Kramon and Posner (2016).

institutions" – such as capable bureaucracies and rule of law (Easterly 2001), or by economic development itself (Alesina, Michalopoulos, and Papaioannou 2003).[9]

This raises the possibility that ethnic diversity might also have an indirect effect on economic development through its effect on institutional quality. La Porta, Lopez-de-Silanes, Shleifer, and Vishny (1999) were perhaps the first to offer a comprehensive empirical investigation of the topic, and they found in cross-national regressions that on many issues related to governance – such as property rights protection, corruption, tax compliance, and public employment – there is little relationship between the governance outcome and ethnic diversity. But they did find that public goods are produced at lower levels in ethnically diverse societies. Alesina et al. (2003) also studied the relationship between ethnic diversity and governance outcomes and found stronger evidence of a negative relationship between ethnic diversity and the quality of governance.

More generally, scholars have emphasized that ethnic diversity diminishes the provision of public goods. In addition to some of the broad cross-national studies mentioned earlier, the literature is huge and it suffices to note a few examples: higher ethnic diversity is associated with weaker maintenance of public infrastructure in northern Pakistan (Khwaja 2009), lower provision of a very wide range of public goods in India (Bannerjee, Iyer, and Somanathan 2005), weaker provision of transportation infrastructure, trash collection and educational expenditures across US cities (Alesina, Baqir, and Easterly 1999), and lower levels of financial support for education in communities in Kenya (Miguel and Gugerty 2005).

This persistent finding of a negative relationship between ethnic diversity and public goods provision has led to efforts to uncover mechanisms that link ethnic diversity to weaker levels of public goods provision. Some argue that ethnic differences diminish trust across groups, and that such distrust can limit public goods provision (e.g., Alesina and La Ferrara 2002; Bannerjee et al. 2005). Others emphasize the preference differences for public goods that may exist across groups (e.g., Alesina and Spolaore 1997; Alesina et al. 1999; Luttmer 2001; Baldwin and Huber 2011). And others emphasize how ethnic homogeneity can make it easier for

---

9   Ager and Brückner (2013) used changes in immigration patterns in the United States to examine the effect of economic diversity on development and found that ethnic fractionalization is positively related to growth but that ethnic polarization is negatively related.

individuals to sanction others for failure to cooperate in public goods provision (e.g., Greif 1993; Fearon and Laitin 1996; Miguel and Gugerty 2005). Habyarimana, Humphreys, Posner, and Weinstein (2007, 2009) used experiments in a poor neighborhood of Kampala to disentangle the relevance of these and other mechanisms. In this setting, they found that shared ethnicity facilitates cooperation because it provides a clear means for adopting strategies of reciprocity: coethnics encounter each other more often, can identify each other more readily, and are embedded in social networks that allow coethnics to locate and punish each other more easily. Although it is almost certain that different mechanisms might be at play in different contexts, the evidence for a negative effect of ethnic diversity on public goods provision is quite strong.

Ethnic politics is also associated with the problem of violence. In the last fifty years, most civil wars have been largely ethnic or religious in nature (e.g., Doyle and Sambanis 2006).[10] And in the context of elections, elites often foment ethnic violence to win votes (e.g., Bates 1983; Offe 1992). Wilkinson (2004), for example, provides a compelling argument about how the nature of electoral competition can encourage violence. When there exists multiparty competition, or two-party competition when minority groups are crucial, elites have incentives to suppress outbreaks of violence and protect minorities. But when two-party competition exists and minority ethnic groups are not crucial to government success, there is little incentive to suppress violence, and indeed can be incentives to encourage violence against minorities to activate voter sentiments based on majority identity rather than on some other ideological basis. And Brancati (2008) shows that incentives for secession by regions, which typically represent particular ethnic groups, are increased when political institutions encourage the formation of regional parties that represent these ethnic groups.

2.3 ETHNIC IDENTITIES AND ETHNIC POLITICS

It is widely accepted that ethnic identity is not strictly primordial, but rather is "constructed," emerging, often instrumentally, from the social context. At the same time, ethnic categories into which individuals are born – such as race, language, ethnicity, tribe, caste, and in some cases religion – are intrinsically important because they provide a menu

---

[10] See Montalvo and Reynal-Querol (2005); Esteban, Mayoral, and Ray (2012); and Arbatli, Ashraf, and Galor (2013) for recent evidence on the connection between ethnic structure and conflict.

from which politicians can choose as they target voters for inclusion or exclusion in efforts to build winning electoral coalitions (e.g., Bates 1983; Horowitz 1985; Laitin 1998; Chandra 2004; Posner 2005). Indeed, a central reason that targeting votes based on "ethnicity" can be attractive to voters and parties is that ethnicity often provides a clear marker that makes it possible to understand who is included and excluded from an electoral coalition. This is true because individuals usually cannot choose to belong to any specific ethnic group. They cannot decide, for example, that they are dark skinned if they are light skinned (though there are exceptions, such as when Chinese convert to "Thai" in Thailand or Russians convert to "Lithuanian" in Lithuania). But individuals are often born with multiple group identities – they may have both a tribal and a language group, for example – and thus it is important to understand when particular identities emerge.

Scholars therefore often examine how politicians use ethnicity to target voters. Chandra (2004), focusing on India, emphasizes that ethnic parties are most likely to succeed in patronage democracies when there are competitive rules for intraparty advancement and when the ethnic group they seek to mobilize is large enough to win. Other research focuses more explicitly on individual-level calculations that transcend the electoral context. Laitin (1998), for example, emphasizes the size of groups and the expectations that individuals have about the behavior of others. Posner (2004, 2005) also focuses on the strategic choice of identity, describing ethnic electoral politics as a sort of "ethnic head count" where the challenge politicians face is to form a minimum winning coalition of ethnic groups. Parties strategically employ appeals to particular group identities, and voters invoke the particular identities that give them access to the highest levels of government resources.

The theoretical framework adopted here lies squarely in this constructivist tradition. Agents in the theory have multiple but exogenous identities with which they are born, and identities that become salient to their electoral behavior emerge from social processes, and specifically from the dynamics of electoral competition. Economic considerations lie at the center of the argument: the emergence of particular types of identities cannot be attributed in the argument here to cultural or religious or other noneconomic considerations. Voters in the theory, however, do not consciously or strategically choose a social identity during the election to gain economic advantage, and they do not do any sort of headcount. Instead, voters simply consider their options at election time and vote for the party that offers them the most. It is party elites who exploit the fact that voters care about economic well-being by emphasizing the identity categories in campaigns that will be most effective at winning votes. Importantly, however, voters are not like sheep who can be willy-nilly manipulated to respond to ethnic political appeals. Rather, a central idea advanced here is that there are specific conditions related to ethnic diversity and inequality that determine when particular types of electoral strategies will be credible.

In developing this idea, the argument builds on Fearon (1999) and Posner (2004, 2005), who link identity politics to the logic of minimum winning electoral coalitions. A key difference, however, is the role played here by economic class. Like most research on identity politics, this previous research focuses on instrumental choices among possible "ethnic" identities, and thus does not examine the possibility that lower income individuals could band together to support parties that represent all the poor rather than parties that represent specific groups. The focus here on the trade-off between ethnic and class politics makes it possible to explore when ethnic markers should become salient in electoral competition in the first place, and to introduce the importance of inequality in shaping the salience of ethnic politics. In addition, a goal here is to advance this "small majorities" framework by developing a theoretical argument that explores the endogenous formation of different types of parties, that examines the robustness of the argument to alternative assumptions about electoral competition, that develops testable arguments about the conditions under which ethnic identity or income becomes central to electoral behavior, and that relates these conditions to redistributive outcomes.

Integrating the study of ethnic and class politics to understand when ethnicity becomes salient in elections represents perhaps the biggest departure of this study from previous research on ethnic politics. This is not to say that we have lacked ideas about why ethnicity becomes salient in electoral politics. Previous research, for example, has emphasized that ethnicity helps clearly communicate party commitments to voters (e.g., Bates 1983; Fearon 1999; Chandra 2004; Birnir 2007). In addition, scholars have emphasized that geographic concentration of ethnic groups makes it easy to target voters, and that ethnicity brings voters together based on their cultural or kinship ties. The organization of parties themselves can also be important: as noted earlier, Chandra (2004) argues that ethnic parties are most likely to succeed when they have competitive rules for intraparty advancement. And Dunning and Harrison (2010), focusing on Mali, find that ethnicity is most salient in politics when the cleavage structure of society is reinforcing rather than cross cutting. In the spirit of many of these studies, the goal here is to develop arguments about the salience of ethnicity in politics, but with a focus on linking this question to the study of class politics and to the implications for electoral dynamics that emphasize redistributive policies.

2.4 REDISTRIBUTIVE POLITICS

Drawing on classic works by Romer (1975) and Meltzer and Richard (1981), scholars often argue there should be a link between inequality and redistribution in democracies. The idea is advanced in a variety of related models that observe that when inequality increases, the voter with the median income prefers greater taxes and transfers. Because democratic competition must respond to the median voter, democracies should do the most to reduce inequality when inequality is highest (e.g., Acemoglu and Robinson 2000, 2005; Boix 2003).

Empirical support for the standard tax and transfer arguments about inequality and redistribution has been quite uneven. Kenworthy and Pontusson (2005) found a positive relationship in a small sample of developed countries between changes in inequality and changes in redistribution, a finding that may be due to how modern welfare states respond automatically to changes brought be economic shocks that affect inequality. And Lupu and Pontusson (2011), also focusing on advanced democracies, found that inequality matters for redistribution, but only a particular kind of inequality: redistribution is highest when the distance between low- and middle-income voters is small relative to the distance between the middle-income and rich voters. Perotti (1996) did not find in cross-national data a link between inequality and redistribution, nor do many other studies (see reviews in Persson and Tabellini 1994, 2002 and Bénabou 1996). Some scholars found a negative relationship, with more inequality leading to less redistribution.[11]

At the individual level, studies of voting behavior look for support for the tax-and-transfer framework by examining the relationship between income and the vote. If party competition is focused on redistribution and class, then poorer voters should support more left-wing parties and richer voters should support more right parties, and this relationship should become stronger as inequality increases. Perhaps the most careful and supportive research on this issue is found in McCarty, Poole, and

[11] See, for example, Ramcharan's (2010) study of American counties in the early twentieth century.

Rosenthal (2006), who seek to understand empirically the link between inequality and party polarization in the United States. They find that as inequality has increased over time, so too has the strength of the link between income and voting behavior. From the perspective of the tax-and-transfer model, this should lead to greater redistribution, something that does not occur in the United States. The authors attribute this to the fact that much of the change in inequality is driven by poor immigrants who cannot vote, and that poor individuals often do not vote. If one focuses on the median *voter* rather than the median *income* in applying the tax-and-transfer framework, then policy responses (or a lack thereof) to rising inequality in the United States can be seen as generally consistent with the median voter models. In addition, McCarty et al. emphasize that for policy to respond to changes in inequality, new legislation must be adopted, something that is very difficult to achieve in the United States given the strong division of power across branches of government.

But other research often finds a weak link between income and the vote. de la O and Rodden (2008) attribute this weakness in advanced democracies to the salience of religion, and Huber and Stanig (2011) explore the circumstances under which religion can drive a wedge between poor secular voters and poor religious voters. In developing democracies, the weak link between income and the vote may be due to some combination of the salience of personalistic, patronage, and ethnic appeals, which may be more effective in situations where voter education levels are low and parties are weakly institutionalized (see review in Hagiopan 2007). The role of patronage-oriented appeals is the focus of Stokes, Dunning, Nazareno, and Brusco's (2013) study of Argentina, as well as the contributions in Kitschelt and Wilkinson (2007). And Thachil (2014a, 2014b) argues that poor support for right-wing parties in India stems from the material interest of the poor. The right-wing Bharatiya Janata Party (BJP) is able to attract poor voters not by making explicit ethnic appeals or by distracting them with other issues such as religion, but rather by working with grass-roots organizations to provide poor voters with material support. The argument here is related to Thachil's research in that I seek to develop a theory of when it might be in the economic interest of poor voters to support parties that oppose class-based redistribution.

To explain the weak empirical support for the tax-and-transfer framework, scholars focusing on advanced democracies have emphasized that government policies undergirding the welfare state are often less about redistributing income per se than about insuring against risk. Moene and Wallerstein (2003), for example, emphasize that richer individuals will have a higher demand for insurance against lost income, so when the median income declines relative to the mean (i.e., inequality increases), the median voter will prefer less insurance. Consistent with this idea, they find that as inequality increases, there are decreases in demand for policies that protect against employment risk but little effect on demand for more universal policies (e.g., health care).

Other theoretical arguments for why the link between inequality and redistribution could be weak focus on the dominant power of rich elites. Bénabou (2000), for example, focuses on unequal participation, which can allow elites to limit redistribution, leading to nonlinearities in the relationship between inequality and redistribution. The ease with which rich elites can solve collective action problems can also empower them in ways that undermine incentives for winning parties to redistribute when inequality is high (e.g., Acemoglu and Robinson 2008). And Bourguignon and Verdier (2000) describe a model in which education can enhance participation by the powerful, increasing the link between inequality and redistribution, but thus creating incentives for the rich to limit access to education, thereby undermining the link between inequality and redistribution.

The research here emphasizes a different way to understand how democracy can condition the relationship between inequality and redistribution. The classic median voter models assume that the only identity relevant to electoral competition is "class," which implies that voter preferences are a function of the voters' income, and party strategies are a function of the distribution of incomes in the electorate. The argument here emphasizes that policy can target voters based on income, as well as other "identities," such as ethnicity. In the theoretical model here, where electoral identities emerge endogenously from party competition, as inequality increases, class politics is displaced by ethnic politics (when there is sufficient ethnic diversity), and ethnic politics diminishes the redistributive effects of government policies. We might observe what looks like elite power – for example, where little redistribution occurs and elites keep high rents – but this "power" stems from the underlying social structure, which can make it difficult for parties who would like to use redistributive policy to attract votes.

The argument developed in this book also departs from previous arguments emphasizing how redistribution in democracies can be undermined by noneconomic preferences of voters. Alesina and Angeletos (2005), for example, describe how underlying attitudes toward fairness, as well as attitudes toward individual responsibility, can lead to a negative relationship between inequality and redistribution. Shayo (2009) explicitly models whether individuals identify with their class or their nationality. Thus, like in the model here, individuals have multiple identities that they can tap at election time, one of which is class (they are rich or poor). But for Shayo, the other "identity" is not an ethnic group but rather is a single national identity to which all individuals can adhere. Thus, "identity politics" in the Shayo model does not create a basis for exclusion of particular groups (as it does here) and is not driven exclusively by individual interest in material gain (as it is here). Instead, his model focuses on the fact that national identity is something like a second dimension (as in Roemer 1998), the importance of which is influenced by exogenous factors. Nationalist identity can distract the poor from their economic self-interest, leading to lower levels of redistribution. Similarly, Penn (2008) examines how the institutional context affects whether voters will identify with their ethnic group rather than with their national identity, using a framework where voters choose identity instrumentally to maximize well-being, and where voters have an intrinsic attachment to their group. And scholars have argued that intergroup antipathies undermine support for redistribution. Members of one group do not like to support programs that are perceived to benefit members of other groups. They therefore are willing to accept worse economic outcomes in order to satisfy their racial animosities (e.g., Luttmer 2001; Alesina and Glaser 2003), or at least to avoid providing benefits to what they view as undeserving groups (Gilens 1999).

In all of these models, poorer voters are essentially distracted from the economic interest by a second dimension. The argument here is different because voters have no intrinsic attachments to any group or nationality and no preferences on dimensions other than their economic well-being. This assumption is not of course motivated by a conviction that group-based loyalties or cultural attributes are unimportant, but rather by the goal of isolating a feature of identity politics that is perhaps underappreciated, and to show that we do not need to assume that when poorer voters support parties that do not advocate redistribution, they are acting against their economic interest. Instead, such actions are economically motivated, and in some contexts, subsets of nonrich voters can do best by forming coalitions with the rich rather than with all the nonrich.

The theory proposed in this book therefore shares features of existing models of electoral competition that examine how class coalitions can be disrupted by offering subsets of the nonrich an opportunity to form coalitions with the rich.[12] Most closely related is that of Fernàndez and Levy (2008), who model elections under plurality rule where individuals are either rich or poor, and where (only) the poor can have a group identity (i.e., the poor can have particular preferences for a group-specific good). Fernàndez and Levy's general focus, however, is on how the diversity of group interests among the poor affects the propensity for class politics to emerge. Their model suggests that ethnic diversity has a nonmonotonic effect on the amount of general (rich to poor) redistribution that occurs, with increases in diversity diminishing redistribution at low levels of diversity and increasing redistribution at high levels of diversity. The model here, by allowing rich and poor to have a shared ethnic identity, explicitly focuses on the tension that can exist between group-based and class-based electoral politics. So doing makes it possible to describe how ethnic diversity and economic inequality interact to influence identity politics and redistributive outcomes.

2.5 NEXT STEPS

High levels of inequality can be viewed as intrinsically unjust, and can result in other normatively undesirable outcomes, such as lower economic development, crime and limited social mobility. Similarly, ethnic politics is intrinsically unjust, and can lead to other undesirable outcomes, such as low public goods provision, low economic development, and higher levels of violence. Scholars have not, however, provided clear arguments about when we should expect ethnic politics to prevail over class politics (or vice versa), and have not considered how inequality and ethnic diversity influence redistribution through their impact on electoral incentives. In what follows, my goal is to develop and test such an argument.

---

[12] Examples include Levy (2004), Austen-Smith and Wallerstein (2006), Huber and Stanig (2011), and Huber and Ting (2013).

PART I

THE THEORETICAL ARGUMENT

I develop the theoretical argument in three chapters. Chapter 3 describes the distributive framework that is central to what follows. A central feature of electoral politics is "distributive" promises – that is, electoral commitments by parties to voters regarding who should benefit from government policy. But in such a framework, without something like group identity, it is very difficult for parties to make commitments that voters will view as credible. Ethnic and class identities can be very useful in addressing this problem parties face: these identities create a pathway by which parties can make credible commitments about government distribution, though a pathway that also constrains the types of promises that parties can make. By focusing on the nature of these constraints, we can gain insights into how social structure – and in particular the distribution of ethnic and class identities – should advantage and disadvantage particular types of parties.

Chapter 4 takes up the question of how social structure should map onto party strategies and voting behavior. If social structure confers advantage on parties that represent particular types of groups, what should we expect with respect to party competition? In particular, why should disadvantaged parties form if they know they are going to lose? And what influences the nature of electoral promises that parties make to voters? The argument in Chapter 4 emphasizes the interaction of rent-seeking and policy incentives of party leaders, and describes how if party leaders have both such incentives, we can expect a clear mapping from social structure to electoral and policy outcomes. In addition, the chapter takes up the question of "theoretical robustness." Are the central intuitions about social structure robust to different assumptions about electoral law, the source of government revenues, and the number of groups? The game theoretic model on which the argument is based is found in the appendix to the chapter.

Finally, Chapter 5 moves from the abstract model of group size to testable arguments about the interaction of inequality and ethnic diversity. I take up the issue of whether it makes sense to treat the number of nonrich as exogenous, when in fact we might expect the government to determine through policy who benefits from redistributive policy. The chapter also argues that the Gini coefficient of inequality is an appropriate measure of the number of nonrich and that ethnic polarization is an appropriate measure of the majority group size. This mapping from model parameters to explicit variables makes it possible to form expectations about how voting behavior and government policy will vary with social structure.

3

Group Identity and the Politics of Exclusion

Democratic elections are notoriously complicated and noisy events about which it can be difficult to generalize. It is nonetheless important to develop theories that isolate particular aspects of electoral processes, and the goal of this chapter is to begin laying the groundwork for a theory that can describe how class and ethnic identities can influence electoral competition. The argument is based on the assumption that voters care only about maximizing their share of the "government pie," and voters and candidates invoke "class" and "ethnic" identities instrumentally to this end. Although no one should deny that material considerations are important in elections, it should also go without saying that this assumption does not come close to fully describing the ways that voters and parties behave, or the role that class and ethnicity play in social interactions. The goal is simply to see if the assumption can aid the development of useful intuitions. To this end, I focus in particular on how social structure can impose limits on the types of promises that parties can make to voters motivated by material concerns.

The chapter is organized as follows. The next section reviews the basic distributive politics model of elections and describes its limitations for generating intuitions about electoral politics. Section 3.2 then describes why it makes sense to consider how class and ethnicity can be used to make credible distributive promises to voters. Using the assumption that class and ethnicity constrain party promises, Section 3.3 explains how social structure – the distribution of voter incomes and ethnic identities – can shape which types of parties should be advantaged in electoral competition. The framework, however, raises important questions about the formation of party systems and the nature of party promises to voters.

35

If social structure, for example, creates advantages for particular types of parties, why do parties that are not advantaged bother to form? And what types of platforms should advantaged parties offer to voters? I address such questions in Chapter 4, when I develop an explicit argument linking social structure to party competition.

3.1 ELECTIONS WITH APPEALS TO ATOMISTIC VOTERS

In democratic elections, parties (or candidates supported by party organizations) make promises about who will get what if the party wins. Voters make choices and their votes determine which party or parties can make policy. The winners then make policy, knowing that they will be held accountable at the next election.

Parties obviously make promises about revenues (how they will raise money) and about distribution (who will get what from the government). Although both types of promises can be important, at this stage, we can convey important intuitions about elections and motivate central intuitions from the argument without worrying about where government revenues come from. (Below, we will consider this issue directly.) That is, we will focus on electoral competition over distribution.

Consider a standard distributive politics model describing such electoral competition with plurality rule. Assume there exists some government resource, call it the pie ("π"), that the government can distribute to citizens. Parties compete by making promises – or offering platforms – describing how π should be distributed, and voters support the party that offers them the most. What will be the winning platform?

Because voters will support the party that gives them the largest share of π, in order to win, parties want to exclude as many voters as possible: spreading the pie across a larger number of individuals leaves less pie for each supporter. But parties need to win a majority to gain power. Parties must therefore adopt platforms that pledge to divide the entire pie among the *smallest majority* possible. For example, if there are N voters, then a party promise to divide the pie equally among $\frac{N+1}{2}$ individuals can defeat a promise that does not divide the pie in this way. If a platform proposes to give the pie to more than a bare majority, it will give each person less than a platform that distributes the pie to a bare majority (because the platform appealing to the larger coalition must spread the pie more thinly). And if a platform proposes an unequal distribution within the bare majority, there will always exist another platform that distributes the pie equally and that can defeat the unequal one.

This simple framework drives home an important logic: there is a powerful force in democratic elections to form exclusionary electoral coalitions. Elections therefore often revolve around identifying who is "in" and who is "out" if a particular party or candidate wins. If any parties promise to be highly inclusionary (i.e., to spread the pie thinly across a large number of voters) they are likely to lose to a party that is more exclusionary (i.e., to a party that appeals to a smaller number of voters). Of course, with majority rule, the smallest possible winning coalition must represent a majority of voters.

Though intuitive, this simple framework is quite limited in its ability to convey precisely how we might expect electoral politics to unfold, for example, by describing which specific parties will form or which individuals will receive benefits. The central problem is that there are a large number of minimal winning electoral coalitions, all of which are completely interchangeable. Consider the top left panel in Figure 3.1. In the figure, there are 100 voters, each represented by a square. If a voter's square is colored, this means that the party promises to give the voter a share of the pie. A bare majority consists of any 51 voters, and in the top-left panel, these are voters in the top five rows, along with the right-most voter in the sixth row. So a party that promised an equal distribution to this majority could defeat any party that proposed a larger, more inclusionary platform. Of course, all of the other bare majorities depicted in the other three panels also satisfy the requirements for a winning platform, as do the many bare majority electoral coalitions that are not depicted.

From an equilibrium perspective, this problem is not insurmountable – game theoretic models have described equilibria that rely on complicated mixed strategies in which parties offer different platforms with different probabilities (e.g., Myerson 1993; Laslier and Picard 2002). For example, a party platform in the 100-person example might declare that individuals 1 to 51 get x with some probability, some other 51 individuals receive x with some other probability, and some other 51 individuals receive x with some other probability, and so on.

Of course, such equilibria have little intuitive appeal as descriptions of electoral campaigns. What would a campaign look like in such a model? Would parties publish lists of voter coalitions and probabilities that the party would select a particular list if it won? How would they communicate these lists and probabilities? And how would parties implement probabilistic promises if they win?

And consider the credibility problems parties would face in such electoral competition. Why would an individual voter believe that the

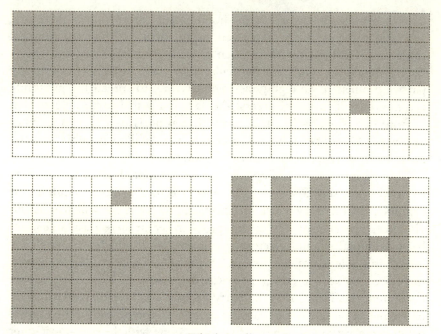

FIGURE 3.1. Which smallest majority?

politicians would actually reward him or her – rather than some other individual who can be part of a bare majority – if elected. After all, if voters are identical and interchangeable in quests to build bare majorities, then they have little reason to believe that politicians will in fact follow through if they win. They can pick any bare majority and then expect that majority will support them again at re-election time. And for any majority that a particular politician or party picks, there is another majority that could defeat it.

In addition, why would parties ever form? Parties are organizations composed of individuals who must pay a cost to contest elections. They might pay this cost because there are rents – private goods for the politician or her party – associated with success. Or they might pay this cost because they care about the nature of final policy outcomes. But there are no rents in this example: the parties must distribute the entire pie in order to win, leaving no private benefits for party entrepreneurs.

Models with atomistic voters, then, have limitations for understanding the emergence of particular electoral coalitions or particular parties. This is not to say the models have little value – they provide crucial insights, for example, into how the characteristics of any equilibrium party platform (such as how may voters receive benefits) should differ under different electoral laws. But if the goal is to develop testable arguments about party systems or voting behavior, the arguments come up short. Thinking about the limitations of the pure distributive model with atomistic voters, however, can help us gain insight into the substantively important role of "identity" in electoral politics.

3.2 GROUP IDENTITY AND ELECTORAL COMPETITION

Group identity can play an important role in addressing these issues parties face in efforts to win votes. If individuals belong to groups that can be targeted, group identity provides a means for conveying which voters will receive government benefits if the party wins. That is, group identity becomes a means for describing inclusion and exclusion. Using group identity is efficient because parties merely need to clarify which groups they support. And group-based commitments should be viewed as credible by voters because if a party pledges to give resources to a particular group and then reneges, the party loses the confidence of the entire group, which is much more costly than losing the confidence of a specific individual in the atomistic framework. So links between parties and groups can help solve the commitment problems that emerge in efforts to fashion electoral coalitions.

What must be true about group identity in order for it to play this role in electoral competition? If group identity becomes a means for articulating the composition of electoral coalitions, a crucial feature of identity must be *excludability*, a feature of ethnic identity Fearon (1999) emphasizes. That is, it must be possible to describe who is in the group and who is not, and for this description to remain valid after the election. Suppose, for example, a party commits to supporting any individual who votes for the party. This cannot be an effective "group-based" strategy because with a secret ballot, parties cannot know who is in their coalition and who is not, and everyone has incentives to claim ex post that they voted for the winning party. This will drive down the value of belonging to the group because no one can be excluded. Similarly, suppose a party pledges to support all individuals who wear green shirts. If this party wins, everyone will have an incentive to wear a green shirt, the size of the coalition will grow to the entire population, and thus the value of competing in elections by appealing to green-shirted voters will be minimal. Thus, the most credible groups in electoral competition will be those from which it is relatively easy to exclude individuals.

A second related criterion for viability in group-based electoral politics is *identifiability*. There may be some objective criterion for classifying individuals by groups, one that creates clear possibilities for exclusion. But this criterion may not create a viable opportunity for vote-seeking because it is difficult to know who is in the group and who is not. In principle, for example, it may be possible to identify how smart people are, perhaps by giving some sort of intelligence test. One could then appeal to the "smartest" (or "dumbest") "50%+1," but this would be a highly inefficient way of appealing to groups because administering the test would be essentially impossible. Similarly, in principle it might be possible to know an individual's beliefs about something (such as the existence of God, the role of humans in global warming, or the importance of marital fidelity) and to promise the government pie to those with particular beliefs. But the practical problems of identifying these beliefs are enormous, which makes it very difficult to exclude individuals from receiving the government pie based on some sort of "beliefs" litmus test.

Finally, if electoral competition is about distributing a government pie, which creates incentives to distribute to small majorities, then for a particular group identity to be viable, it is important that a large proportion of group members are *unwilling to share outside their group*. The importance of this criterion comes from thinking about why it might be difficult to appeal only to women, or only to men. Gender is usually highly identifiable and politicians could easily exclude individuals from benefits based on gender, so it could be a good candidate for an identity politics of exclusion, but we seldom see such gender-based parties. One reason might be that the importance of families would encourage both men and women to share if their party wins. Suppose, for example, that 51 percent of society are women, and that society is also divided by race, with 60 percent green and 40 percent orange (and gender evenly distributed within each group). A party that appealed to women should be able to defeat a party that appealed to the greens because women represent a smaller majority. But if the pie is distributed to women and not men, then women with families will share their pie with the male partners, effectively reducing the pie by up to half. A similar dynamic might exist for "age-based" parties. It might be possible to target only individuals over (or under) a particular age. But families exist and certainly have incentives to share. So promising benefits to only the old, for example, dilutes these benefits if the old have incentives to share with the excluded young (or vice versa).

One can think of a variety of group-based identities that might satisfy these criteria more or less well, and individuals typically have multiple identities to which a party could appeal. One possibility, for example, is the geographic location of voters. Although individuals can move – and indeed they might well do so to get benefits – the costs of doing so might be high, so parties might compete for votes by targeting individuals in particular areas. Another possibility might be employment-related groups, like unions. Again, individuals can make choices that affect union membership, but these choices can have high costs, and union members have incentives to exclude nonunion members from benefits.

Although there are a wide range of groups to which parties appeal, it is worth considering why "class" and "ethnic" identity might be so central in many analyses of electoral politics. "Class" – an individual's level of economic well-being or income in this study – is probably the most commonly exploited identity in electoral competition. Indeed, one could argue it is nearly ubiquitous, and that electoral competition in almost any democracy involves a significant class-based component pitting the least well-off against the most well-off. Class is likely widely invoked in large part because it is usually possible to identify the general economic well-being of individuals and to include or exclude them from particular policy benefits based on their economic well-being. In many situations it may even be the case that individuals have incentives to reveal their class identity in order to claim government benefits. And although citizens can clearly have incentives to hide their class identities, governments are very creative at devising structures that can make this difficult and costly.

"Ethnicity" – a group-based attribute with which one is born[1] – is also extremely important in electoral competition, with parties seeking to gain support by promising benefits to individuals who belong to particular language, racial, tribal, ethnic, caste, or even religious groups. There can be limits in this regard. Horowitz (2001) and Habyarimana, Humphreys, Posner, and Weinstein (2007, 2009), for example, provide evidence that it can be difficult for individuals to identify the ethnicity of others, particularly in contexts where there are many such identities and the differences between them are somewhat limited. But when clear ethnic identities exist, ethnic memberships can be used to mark inclusion and exclusion. Using ethnicity as an electoral strategy will therefore be most effective when individuals find it difficult to hide their ethnic identities,

[1] I provide a more precise definition of ethnic identity in Chapter 5.

and when it is particularly costly for an individual to change her ethnic identity, for example, by adopting a new language and its corresponding cultural customs.

I hope it is clear that I am using "identity" in a rather narrow way – as a marker that can be used as a basis for targeting. When I use the term "class identity," for example, I am referring to the fact that individuals can be targeted for benefits based on their economic well-being, and when a person's class identity is salient, I am arguing that his or her economic status is decisive for his or her vote. The term "class" can of course refer to a richer range of phenomena that are more integrated than anything I am considering here. It is possible that some of the sociological elements of "class" would be more likely to arise under the conditions that I describe here, but that is not my focus. It is also important to bear in mind that I am focused only on identity in electoral behavior. As others have argued (e.g., Thachil 2014c), different identities can be salient in different contexts. Finally, I should underline that identities are not clear cut in the real world as they are in a theoretical model, and both class and ethnic boundaries will have gray areas. I hope, however, that the discussion here gives us a sense of what we want to look for in any identity if we want to consider identity politics through the lens of inclusion or exclusion.

3.3 SOCIAL STRUCTURE AND ELECTORAL POLITICS

To describe the role that class and ethnic identity can play in a distributive model of elections, it is useful to begin with a framework that is as simple as possible. Assume that there are two different incomes in society, the majority "nonrich" and the minority "rich." Also assume there are two different ethnic groups, the majority ethnic group and the minority ethnic group. The left panel in Figure 3.2 depicts a population in which individuals are sorted based on their income. Rich individuals (represented by white squares) are above the solid horizontal line, and nonrich individuals (represented by gray squares) are below the solid horizontal line. In this example, 70 percent of the population is nonrich.

For ethnic identity, label the majority group *A* and the minority group *B*. The right panel in Figure 3.2 depicts a population in which individuals are sorted based on their ethnic identity. Individuals in the majority group (represented by gray squares) are to the left of the vertical line and individuals in the minority group (represented by white squares squares) are to the right of the vertical line. In this example, 80 percent of the

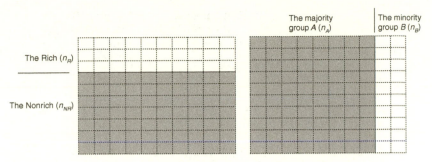

FIGURE 3.2. Class and ethnic identity in a population of 100 voters.

population is in the majority group. Each individual therefore has two identities: he or she belongs to an ethnic and an income group.

How can identity politics constrain the sort of atomistic cherry-picking of individuals that occurs in the pure distributive model described earlier? Individuals are in one of four subgroups, so one possibility is to assume that parties cannot discriminate against members of the same subgroup – that is, to assume that if a party supports one member who is nonrich in A, it must support all individuals who are nonrich in A. The incentive discussed above to create the smallest majority coalition would always yield a unique winning electoral coalition: a party representing the smallest winning coalition of subgroups could defeat any other party. Consider Figure 3.3, which is the same as Figure 1.1 from Chapter 1. In the top panel of Figure 3.3, a party that pledges to represent the nonrich in A and the rich in B, who together represent 51 percent of voters, could defeat any other majority coalition of subgroups because all other majority coalitions of subgroups represent more individuals. In the bottom panel of Figure 3.3, to take another example, a party representing the nonrich in B and the rich in A would win because it represents the smallest coalition of voters (52 percent).

But there is something rather peculiar about the winning electoral coalitions in both examples: they transcend the two identity dimensions that are supposed to clarify electoral communication and ensure commitment. In both examples the winning party represents the rich, but only some of the rich; the nonrich, but only some of the nonrich; the majority group, but only some of the majority group; and the minority group, but only some of the minority group. As in the case of atomistic voters, it is hard to understand what a clear and credible campaign message would be like in these examples, and indeed, an assumption that parties can credibly

	Ethnic group A $(n_A = 63)$	Ethnic group B $(n_B = 37)$
The Rich ($n_R = 30$)	21	9
The Nonrich ($n_{NR} = 70$)	42	28

	Ethnic group A $(n_A = 64)$	Ethnic group B $(n_B = 36)$
The Rich ($n_R = 40$)	28	12
The Nonrich ($n_{NR} = 60$)	36	24

FIGURE 3.3. Societies in which individuals have a class and ethnic identity.

commit to any coalition of subgroups is strikingly close to the example of purely atomistic voters described earlier. This parallel perhaps becomes even more stark as the number of groups increases. In Figure 3.4, for example, there are three income groups and three ethnic groups, and the smallest winning coalition of subgroups would include the support of the rich in A, the middle class in B and the nonrich in C, which combine to account for 51 of 100 individuals. How would a party campaign for the support of these groups? What role would identity or class play in credibly communicating party platforms to voters?

For each of these examples, one could expect there to be problems of trust. In the top panel in Figure 3.3, for example, the nonrich in the majority group would reasonably worry that a party representing them and also the rich in the minority would work against the nonrich in the majority, either on the class dimension (serving the interests of the rich once elected) or on the ethnic dimension (serving the interest of

	Group *A*	Group *B*	Group *C*
Rich	17	10	10
Middle class	5	17	5
Poor	10	9	17

FIGURE 3.4. A society with three incomes and three ethnic groups.

the minority group once elected). And the rich in *B* may have the same worry. Similar issues of trust should arise in the other two examples. In addition, one can imagine difficult problems in implementing policies that transcend group and class. In Figure 3.4, for example, the party would have to devise a credible policy for discriminating against the nonrich in two ethnic groups, against the middle class in two ethnic groups, and against the rich in two ethnic groups. And in each case of discrimination, the two excluded ethnic groups would be different. Policies would therefore lack coherence on the two dimensions that can be used to organize electoral competition. This reality underlines the difficulties parties might face in communicating the platform that will serve, say, the rich in one ethnic group and the nonrich in another. Parties would have to argue for a policy that discriminated within the very class and ethnic dimensions that are supposed to serve as a basis for inclusion and exclusion.

Parties almost surely do at times try to promote policies that transcend group and class, but it is clearly more difficult to articulate and implement such policies than it is to articulate and gain the trust of voters for policies that do not force them to accept cooperation with the "other" class or ethnic group. Indeed, if parties can willy-nilly choose subsets of groups, one is essentially back to the problems of the distributive models with atomistic voters. This observation motivates a central simplifying assumption in the theory developed here, which is that political parties can credibly commit only to representing a particular class or a particular ethnic group. Parties cannot credibly commit to representing arbitrary coalitions of subgroups, but instead are constrained to representing voters on the class or ethnic dimension. To readers who feel that this assumption is too strong, it is perhaps worth noting that it is not nearly so strong as the assumption of median voter models that assume only "class" can be used to target voters.

Four types of parties could form under this assumption. There are two potential class parties (one representing the rich, which I will label P_R, for party of the rich) and one representing the nonrich (P_{NR}). There are also two possible ethnic parties, one representing a majority group (P_A) and one representing a minority group (P_B). I will also assume that parties cannot discriminate within the groups that they represent. If P_{NR} wins, for example, it must treat all the nonrich the same.

This framework for developing a theory of party competition provides a clear way to think about which identities become salient in electoral politics. Each voter could in principle support a party that represents his or her ethnic group or class. A nonrich voter in group A, for example, might have to choose between a class party representing the nonrich or an ethnic party representing group A. The dimension of identity that becomes salient in elections to a voter depends on the type of party he or she supports. Ethnic identity becomes salient if the voter supports the party pledging to distribute the pie to group A, and class identity becomes salient if the voter supports the party pledging to distribute the pie to the nonrich. After the election produces a winner, the society will be characterized by "ethnic politics" if the winning party represents an ethnic identity and distributes the government pie based on ethnic group membership. Class politics dominates in society if the winning party distributes based on income.

Returning to Figure 3.3, what type of politics should we expect to emerge in the two examples? The answer to this question should include an argument about how parties form and contest elections, a task for the next chapter. At this point, however, it is useful to highlight the constraining role played by social structure, that is, by the distribution of class and ethnic identities that were described in Chapter 1. Note that with plurality rule, the party of the minority group could always be defeated by the party of the majority group, and the party of the rich could always be defeated by the party of the nonrich. Thus, for now we will focus on a contest between the party of the nonrich (P_{NR}) and the party of the majority group (P_A).

One of these two parties will have a clear advantage, and it will be the one that represents the smallest majority. In the top panel of Figure 3.3, this is P_A, which distributes the pie to 63 voters, which is less than the 70 represented by P_{NR}. And if P_A were to win, there would be a relatively weak link between voter income and vote choice (because the nonrich in A support an ethnic party), parties would have a relatively clear ethnic basis of support (because all in the majority group would support P_A) and there would be a relatively low level of redistribution (because P_A would distribute to the rich in A and exclude the nonrich in B). In the bottom panel, the social structure advantages P_{NR} (because it represents 60 voters as compared with the 64 represented by P_A), and if this party were to win, we would expect a relatively strong link between income and the vote (because all the nonrich support P_{NR}), a weak ethnic basis of support for parties, and a relatively high level of income redistribution (because P_{NR} distributes to all nonrich and to no rich).

This example provides the core intuition for the main argument in the book. If individual markers that are difficult to change – such as class or ethnic identity – provide an attractive way for parties to make credible commitments about distribution, then social structure should influence whether class or ethnic politics prevails. This is true because this structure determines the size of the winning electoral coalitions. If the number of nonrich is very large, it becomes more difficult to convince nonrich voters that a class-based party is in their interest because a class-based party will be constrained in how much it can offer to lower income voters. Ethnicity can provide a clear pathway for parties to commit to smaller coalitions, and if the ethnic composition of society allows an ethnic coalition that is smaller than a class coalition, the ethnic coalition has an electoral advantage.

3.4 FROM SOCIAL STRUCTURE TO PARTY SYSTEMS

This chapter has argued that distributive commitments by parties to voters are core elements of democratic politics, and that if we treat all voters as identical and interchangeable, a standard distributive politics model has clear limitations for generating insights about party formation and electoral behavior. Thinking about these limitations encourages us to focus on the challenges parties face in making credible commitments to voters, and about the role group identity can play in addressing these challenges. If individuals have group identities that can form the basis for inclusion and exclusion from government benefits, parties can use these identities to make credible commitments about distribution. But in so doing, parties cannot select some individuals within groups but not others, as such "cherry-picking" would diminish the clarity and credibility of group-based distribution. The logic of group-based distributive politics therefore imposes constraints on the types of commitments that group-based parties can make to voters, which implies that social structure should confer advantages on particular types of parties: a party that represents a smaller majority should have an advantage over a party representing a large majority because it can offer more to each voter.

The theoretical challenge is to turn this observation about social structure into a clear argument about party systems and voting behavior. Why would parties disadvantaged by social structure ever form? What types of commitments can winning parties make? Does the answer to these questions depend on the nature of electoral law, or the source of government revenues? These questions are the focus of the next chapter.

4

A Theory of Social Structure, Electoral Identities, and Party Systems

Chapter 3 described a framework for thinking about how social structure can constrain party competition, but it also left unanswered important questions. What ensures that a party will form to represent the smallest majority? What will this party propose for its platform and why? What other parties might form and why would they form if they are disadvantaged by the social structure? Answering such questions is important in order to complete the argument about social structure and politics. The goal of this chapter is therefore to form the ideas from the previous chapter into an explicit theory of party formation and party competition.

4.1 SOME PUZZLES ABOUT PARTY COMPETITION WITH IDENTITY POLITICS

Individuals create and operate the political parties that contest elections. We can call such individuals "party entrepreneurs," and it is important to recognize that a party entrepreneur pays a personal cost to operate a party. Why would an entrepreneur pay any cost of forming a party that the entrepreneur knows will lose? Suppose, for example, that a party of the nonrich, call it P_{NR}, could defeat a party representing the majority ethnic group and could also defeat any other ethnic or class party (i.e., $n_{NR} < n_A$). Then why would a potential entrepreneur pay the cost to form any party other than P_{NR} given there is no chance of winning?

What about party platforms? If a class-based party could defeat any other party, what should be the party's platform? Answering this question requires more specificity about the motivations of party entrepreneurs,

49

and two motivations are particularly salient. The first motivation is policy. In the distributive theory here, this would mean that a party entrepreneur would be motivated to distribute as much as possible to the group she represents. Thus, a nonrich person would be an entrepreneur for P_{NR}, and the policy-oriented entrepreneur would pay the cost of forming P_{NR} to ensure that the party distributed as much as possible to the nonrich. Thus, the platform would distribute $\frac{\pi}{n_{NR}}$ to all nonrich voters.

But this is not a satisfactory story about parties or party competition for several reasons. First, the assumption of "pure policy" incentives – of party entrepreneurs paying the personal costs of forming a party simply because they want to help their group as much as possible – does not resonate in many contexts. In reality, individuals are often drawn to politics for selfish reasons that may have little to do with the public good. Policy platforms that serve the public good may be instrumental to winning office, but political entrepreneurs often want to win office in order to benefit themselves personally. Second, if it were true that the party entrepreneurs are motivated to distribute the entire pie to their group, as only the winning party can influence policy, only one party entrepreneur – the one that represents the smallest majority– should form for any given social structure. This is obviously far from the empirical reality of competitive electoral politics. Finally, if party entrepreneurs pay a cost to form a party and care only about the policy platform, there should be a collective action problem for party entrepreneurs. Continuing with the example in which P_{NR} can win, why would any particular nonrich person pay the costs to be the party entrepreneur that offers the platform that distributes the entire pie – why not leave it to some other policy entrepreneur to do the hard work that benefits everyone who is nonrich?

Suppose instead of pure policy motivations that party entrepreneurs were motivated exclusively by personal enrichment, or rents. One straightforward way to incorporate this idea into the argument is to make party entrepreneurs "residual claimants" – party entrepreneurs adopt platforms and if they win, they distribute the amount promised in the platform to their constituents, keeping the rest for themselves. Losing entrepreneurs keep nothing. If this "personal enrichment" assumption captured all motivations of party entrepreneurs, could we say anything about the party system and equilibrium platforms? An entrepreneur obviously has an incentive to make the smallest possible winning platform because doing so maximizes her rents. And one party's entrepreneur will be advantaged because her party represents the smallest winning majority, and thus she can offer a platform that can defeat any other. What could be an equilibrium party system under this assumption? Suppose $n_{NR} < n_A$, which means that even if the party entrepreneur for P_A proposed to distribute the entire pie to the members of A, the entrepreneur for P_{NR} could defeat P_A by offering more to the nonrich (given $n_{NR} < n_A$).

If P_A is going to lose for any platform and if P_A's entrepreneur is motivated by the rents associated with winning, she will have no incentive to pay the cost of forming a party, and thus she will not form. But if P_A and other parties do not form because they only care about the rents of winning and they cannot win, then the entrepreneur for P_{NR} has an incentive to maximize her rents by offering the smallest possible platform, one giving near zero to her supporters. But if the entrepreneur for P_{NR} offers the smallest possible platform (because she leads the only party that has formed), then it cannot be optimal for the other entrepreneurs not to have paid the cost of entering the electoral competition. They must enter and beat P_{NR}. In short, there is no equilibrium prediction.[1] If the other parties stay out, the rent-seeking entrepreneur for the winning party must offer the smallest possible platform, but then it cannot be an equilibrium for the other parties to not form, but then the smallest possible platform cannot be an equilibrium, and so forth.

This digression reminds us that in developing arguments about how social structure influences party competition, we need to consider explicitly the dynamics of party formation and party competition. In so doing, it is useful to focus on individual party entrepreneurs to gain a deeper understanding of how social structure matters to electoral politics.

4.2 PARTY COMPETITION UNDER PLURALITY RULE

One reason losing parties might form could involve uncertainty about which party will win. Some party entrepreneurs may know they are likely to lose because another party is advantaged by social structure, but because elections are uncertain events that turn on much more than social structure, these entrepreneurs might also believe there is some chance that random events will allow them to win. Thus, even if the odds of winning are long, if the costs of forming parties are low, a party entrepreneur might as well form a party and see what happens. Uncertainty can clearly capture an element of electoral politics that is important, but in the context here it does not lead to strong intuitions

---

[1] As noted in the appendix, we are focused on pure strategy equilibria in this model.

about which parties will not form (because if any party could win due to random events, all parties could form given low formation costs). It also makes it difficult to know what the optimal platform for losing parties might be. Does an entrepreneur maximize her party's chance of "winning by mistake" by offering to distribute the entire pie to voters (i.e., by offering the most competitive platform possible)? If it does so, there would be no rents for the entrepreneur, so we would be back to the original question of why the entrepreneur would pay the costs of forming. Theoretical predictions would therefore have to rest on an assumption about the relationship between platforms and "winning by chance," raising the question of whether an assumption about uncertainty has sufficient intuitive appeal to underpin a theory of party system formation in the distributive framework central here.

Instead of invoking uncertainty, I make two specific assumptions about the motivations of party entrepreneurs. The first is that party entrepreneurs care about the rents from winning. The second is that party entrepreneurs can about policy outcomes, and specifically about the share of the pie that the entrepreneur will win by virtue of the entrepreneur's identity and the policy enacted by the wining party. These two assumptions make it possible to derive intuitions about social structure and party competition.

The game theoretic argument about party politics, developed in detail in the appendix to this chapter, works as follows. First, any voter can pledge to pay a small cost to form a party that represents her group, and if more than one voter pledges to form a party, one is randomly selected to be the group's party entrepreneur.[2] The cost is the same for all voters and can be arbitrarily small – the role of the costs is to ensure that a party does not form if there is not some benefit, however small, to the entrepreneur.

Party entrepreneurs are motivated by both policy motivations and rents. Party entrepreneurs are citizens, and thus if a party entrepreneur belongs to a group represented by the winning party, the entrepreneur receives the amount proposed in the winning platform. There might therefore be a benefit to the entrepreneur of forming and losing if so doing drives up the policy payoff from the winning party to the entrepreneur's advantage. Party entrepreneurs who win elections also can receive rents: they are residual claimants, keeping the share of the pie that is not

---

[2] An alternative formulation to the "random selection" might be to have different costs of party formation, advantaging the individual with the lowest costs. This assumption would help us to explore the dynamics of intraparty competition.

distributed to voters. This assumption encourages winning parties to offer as little as possible to voters. With these assumptions, it is possible to gain intuitions about what types of parties and party systems will emerge in response to social structure. Here I focus on the case of plurality rule.

Under plurality rule, the party system in equilibrium is always characterized by two parties, and the party platforms "converge" with respect to the amount offered to voters. But the two parties pledge government resources to different constituents. Specifically, the party system will have the following characteristics:

- There will always be two parties, one for the majority ethnic group (P_A) and one for the nonrich (P_{NR}).
- The class party will win when the number of nonrich is less than the number in the majority group, and the ethnic party will win otherwise.
- The two parties will always offer the same platform in terms of size: each platform will pledge to give its party's constituents the amount they would receive if the *losing* party distributed the pie to all its constituents.
- The entrepreneur for the winning party therefore always obtains positive rents, and these rents increase as the size of the group represented by the losing party increases (holding constant the size of the group represented by the winning party).

The formal model is found in the appendix, but here I describe key elements of this logic. First consider why the model predicts two-party systems and the specific platforms described earlier. An individual will pay the cost to become a party entrepreneur only if she can either win or influence the platform of the winning party to her advantage (because she cares about policy and will be represented by the winning party). This implies that under plurality rule there can be at most two parties. For any social structure, there will be an advantaged party – a party that can pay the most for votes because it represents the smallest majority. But there can only be one such party (because there are no exact ties in the underlying social structure). Thus, the reason for other parties to form is to influence the winning platform, and since the winning party platform responds only to the next smallest platform, an entrepreneur for a third party can never influence the policy of the winning party. Thus, no individual would pay a cost to become an entrepreneur for this third party. There also cannot be only one party, for reasons described earlier: that is, given the rent-seeking motivations of party leaders, if there were only one party, its entrepreneur could win with a platform that gave its constituents near zero. If this occurred, another party would want to form, so there must be two parties in any party system. But which two parties?

The two parties must be those that represent the two majority groups. It could never be possible for a party representing a minority – that is, the party of the rich or the party of the minority ethnic group – to form and win if there are only two parties. This is true because if the minority party wins, then the party representing the majority of that group must not have formed (because it would have won had it formed). But this could not be optimal behavior because if it had formed, it would have been able to win. And it could never be possible for a party representing a minority to form and lose when there are two parties. If it is a minority party, it represents fewer voters than the winning party, and thus its platform could not influence the platform of the winning party. Thus, the entrepreneur for this party would both lose and have no impact on policy, implying the entrepreneur would not want to pay any cost of forming. Thus, the only party system with plurality rule is one in which the only two parties that form are those representing majorities.

Because one of these two parties representing a majority of voters will certainly lose, why will an entrepreneur pay the cost of forming the losing party? Policy motivations are central. Suppose $n_{NR} < n_A$ so that that the entrepreneur for P_{NR} can win with certainty. P_{NR} must adopt a platform that defeats P_A and if P_A does not form, P_{NR} can push its platform toward zero. If P_{NR} is going to win no matter what, the only incentive a voter in A might have to form P_A would be to influence the policy of P_{NR}, which means that only the nonrich in A have incentives to form P_A: the rich in A receive nothing when P_{NR} wins, and thus would never pay to influence P_{NR}'s platform, but a nonrich person in A has an incentive to form P_A because so doing allows her to offer a platform that maximizes the policy payout to the nonrich. In particular, the party entrepreneur can propose to distribute the entire pie to the members of A, forcing the entrepreneur for P_{NR} to offer at least this much to the nonrich. Thus, there is a clear policy benefit of forming a losing party for the nonrich in A, and this policy benefit dictates the type of platforms that must be adopted in equilibrium and thus the rents that accrue to party entrepreneurs.

The general intuitions from Chapter 3 about social structure and identity politics therefore emerge from a theoretical model in which party competition arises endogenously, self-interested party entrepreneurs pay a cost to represent their groups, and voters support the party that gives them the greatest material gain. When the number of nonrich is low relative to the number in the majority ethnic group ($n_{NR} < n_A$), a class-based party representing the nonrich will win because such a party can offer a bigger payoff to voters than can the ethnic party that represents a majority. Nonrich voters therefore vote their class identity and government resources are distributed based on income. When the number of nonrich voters is high relative to the number in the majority group, the opposite occurs: the party of the majority ethnic group can offer the most to voters, rich and nonrich voters in the majority ethnic group vote their ethnic identity and government resources are distributed based on ethnic identity.

4.3 THEORETICAL ROBUSTNESS

The intuition about group size is based on a model in which electoral competition is by plurality rule, where there exists an exogenous government pie, and where there are only two groups and income classes. Does the main intuition survive when we change some of these assumptions? This section considers this question. Specifically, I consider three possible changes to the model. The first concerns the electoral law: if elections are contested under proportional electoral law, how does this affect our intuitions about the role of n_A and n_{NR}? The second concerns the source of government revenue. If government revenues are generated by taxes on the rich, what are the implications for the theory developed here. Finally, if there can be more than two ethnic groups, does the main intuition about group size survive?

Proportional Representation

Under plurality rule with endogenous party formation, only two parties will form and the relationship between n_A and n_{NR} determines which party can offer the most to its supporters. Would this same logic hold if party competition occurred under proportional representation (PR), which may allow more than two parties to form, and which might then result in coalition politics?

To analyze the model under the assumption of PR, I assume that the number of seats won by a party is proportional to the number of voters who support it. Elections might therefore produce no majority winner, resulting in coalition bargaining. I analyze this process with the following model (with technical details in the appendix):

- Parties form endogenously, under the same structure and set of assumptions used in the plurality rule case.
- If no party wins a majority, a coalition formation process begins, whereby any party can make a proposal describing the specific amount that all individuals represented by the parties in government will receive.
- The coalition that emerges must be supported by parties representing a majority in the assembly.
- Voters are fully strategic, voting for the party that will give them the largest share of the pie, while taking into account the dynamics of coalition politics.

If a party wins a majority, it obviously will not form a coalition but instead will form a single-party majority government and implement its policy as under plurality rule. If no party wins a majority, then some sort of coalition process must unfold. I assume that in this coalition bargaining process, party leaders must agree on how much they will give to each person represented by the parties in the coalition, and that they will treat each of these represented individuals in the same way. Thus, if P_R and P_B negotiate a coalition, they will decide on some amount x that will be distributed to each of the n_R and n_B individuals who are rich and/or in B. The entrepreneurs will then split any of the pie that is not distributed to voters.

What possible coalitions could form? Because party leaders cannot discriminate within their group, it can never be optimal for any party that represents a majority group to enter into a coalition with another party because such a coalition would lead to sharing the pie with a larger number of voters than necessary. To see this, suppose the party of the nonrich, P_{NR} were to enter a coalition with the party of the minority group, P_B. Then the coalition would have to distribute the pie to $n_{NR} + n_B$ individuals, and the entrepreneurs would have to share any residual. But all of the nonrich would prefer to support P_{NR} and have it win a majority than to have voting strategies lead to this large coalition because the coalition shares the pie with more voters. And the entrepreneur for P_{NR} would have preferred this as well because the entrepreneur would not want to share rents with the leader of P_B. So this coalition could never be the outcome of equilibrium behavior. In general, if a party representing a majority group ends up trying to form a coalition, it would have preferred to have adopted a strategy that would have allowed voters in this group to give it a majority. Because coalitions with parties representing majority

	Ethnic group	
	A	B
Rich	10	13
Nonrich	43	34

$$n_A < n_{NR}$$

	Ethnic group	
	A	B
Rich	10	13
Nonrich	47	30

$$n_A < n_{NR}$$

	Ethnic group	
	A	B
Rich	30	13
Nonrich	35	22

$$n_{NR} < n_A$$

	Ethnic group	
	A	B
Rich	30	13
Nonrich	47	10

$$n_{NR} < n_A$$

FIGURE 4.1. Elections under PR.

groups cannot emerge in an equilibrium, there are only three possible outcomes: the party of the nonrich wins, the party of the majority group wins, or there is a coalition of P_R (the party of the rich) and P_B (the party of the minority group).

We can see the logic of the equilibria from the PR model in Figure 4.1. Consider the top two panels, where the majority ethnic group is smaller than the number of nonrich (i.e., $n_A < n_{NR}$); so under plurality rule we would expect ethnic politics to prevail. By the same logic discussed with respect to plurality rule, P_{NR} could never win a majority (because this could never be preferred by the members of group A to a victory by P_A). The only possible outcomes are therefore either a victory by P_A or a coalition victory by $P_R + P_B$. The rich in A are part of the winning coalition for either scenario, and thus are pivotal. In the top-left panel, a victory by P_A will distribute the π to 53 voters and a victory by a $P_R + P_B$ coalition will distribute the pie to 57 voters. The rich in A prefer to support P_A, which will win in any equilibrium, just as under plurality rule, and P_{NR} will be formed by a member of A to limit rent-seeking by P_A's entrepreneur. By contrast, in the top right panel, if ethnic politics prevails (P_A wins), the pie is shared with 57 voters, whereas if a coalition between P_R and P_B prevails, the pie is shared by 53 voters. The rich would vote for P_R, ensuring no party wins a majority and that a coalition between P_R and P_B prevails. And P_A would be formed by an entrepreneur from the rich in the majority group in order to curtail rent-seeking by the two minority parties. Thus there would be three parties contesting the election.

Now consider the bottom two panels, where the majority ethnic group is larger than the number of nonrich (i.e., $n_A > n_{NR}$); so under plurality rule we would expect class politics to prevail. In this case P_A could never win, so the outcome must be a victory by P_{NR} or a coalition between P_B and P_R, making the nonrich in the minority party pivotal (because they are included in the winning coalition for either outcome). In the bottom left panel, if P_{NR} wins, the pie is shared among 57 voters, whereas if the coalition prevails, the pie is shared among 65 voters. Thus, the nonrich in B prefer supporting P_{NR} and class politics will prevail (with P_A also forming to curtail rent-seeking). In the bottom right panel, if the coalition of the rich and the minority prevails, the pie will be shared by 53 voters, whereas a victory for P_{NR} would lead to sharing the pie among 57 voters. Thus, the nonrich in the minority would prefer supporting their ethnic politics, ensuring coalition politics (and P_{NR} would form to curtail rent-seeking).

There are three observations about the PR model worth underlining. First, as under plurality rule, the number of nonrich and the number in the majority group interact to influence the salience of particular identities and voting outcomes under PR. Class politics can emerge under PR only when n_{NR} is sufficiently low (where "low" is determined by n_A), and ethnic politics can emerge only when n_A is sufficiently low (relative to n_{NR}). The opposite is never true: ethnic politics can never emerge when the majority group is large relative to the number of poor, and class politics can never emerge when the majority group is small relative to the number of poor. Second, PR makes it possible for party entrepreneurs to break up both group and class politics by dividing the majority ethnic group or the nonrich against themselves. Thus, although the relationship still exists among n_A, n_{NR}, and electoral competition, it may be weaker under PR. Third, consistent with our understanding of electoral laws and party systems, two parties form (endogenously) in equilibrium under plurality rule and more than two parties can form under PR (depending on the underlying social structure).

It is useful to recognize that any difference that can occur between PR and plurality rule is driven by the assumption in the model that under plurality rule, parties cannot credibly commit to supporting both ethnic and class groups. If hybrid parties – that is, parties that represent both a class and a group – can form under plurality rule, there would be no difference in the model between outcomes under plurality rule and outcomes under PR. In particular, with plurality rule, a hybrid party representing the rich and group B could win under the same conditions that the P_R and P_B coalition wins under PR because this hybrid party would represent the smallest possible majority coalition. It is reasonable to assume that it is more difficult for the same party to commit credibly to both an ethnic group and a class than it is for such coalitions to emerge after coalition bargaining. The nonrich in B, for example, might reasonably worry that if they support a P_{BR} party under plurality rule and it wins, then the rich within this party might adopt policies that are disadvantageous to the nonrich. Such a nonrich voter might reasonably expect that if it supports P_B to bargain on its behalf in the coalition politics of PR, there will be less risk. The results and this discussion therefore suggest that the effects of electoral laws on identity politics and party systems might be driven principally by the ability of parties to commit credibly to multi-identity governing coalitions before elections (as they must under plurality rule) as opposed to after elections (as they can under PR). The greater the problems of ex ante commitment, the greater should be the differences between PR and plurality rule.

Government Revenues from Income Taxes on the Rich

In some democratic contexts, substantial government revenues come from taxes on income, and these taxes affect government revenues directly (because they are the source of government revenues) and indirectly (because they affect labor decisions, and thus the amount of income that can be taxed). What if government revenues in the model come from taxes on the rich? Does this affect the central intuition about the interaction of n_A and n_{NR}? I explore this question focusing on the case of plurality rule, although the logic will apply under PR as well.

In the formal details of the model described in the appendix to this chapter, the rich pay taxes and make labor decisions based on the utility of consumption versus the utility of leisure. As taxes go up, the rich will work less, and there will be lower government revenues. In addition, following standard assumptions about the diminishing marginal utility of consumption (and thus of income), if the rich are given payments from the government, they will work less (consuming more leisure). The first intuition from the model follows from this standard assumption about work and leisure: consistent with literature reviewed in Chapter 1, there is an economic cost of ethnic politics. Under ethnic politics, the rich in A receive transfers, which reduces their incentive to provide revenue-generating labor. Since the rich in A work less when P_A wins than when P_{NR} wins, total economic output from labor will be less when ethnic politics prevails than when class politics prevails. This also means that total government revenues from taxes will be less when P_A wins, which is consistent with the literature discussed in Chapter 2 regarding the economic cost of ethnic politics.[3]

Although raising government revenues from taxes rather than windfalls has implications for labor decisions and the size of the government pie under ethnic versus class politics, it does not alter the logic of group size. That is, under plurality rule, the party of the rich and the party of the minority group can never win, and thus the emergence of class politics (i.e., victory by the party of the nonrich) depends only on whether the number of nonrich is sufficiently low relative to the number in the majority group.[4] What does change is the minimal size threshold that n_{NR} must go below for P_{NR} to win. In general, taxes make ethnic-based politics less attractive to the nonrich in A because of the differential effect of taxes on revenues under ethnic-based as opposed to class-based politics. As just noted, ethnic politics affects the size of the government pie by reducing the incentives of the rich in the majority group to work. The pivotal nonrich in A, then, care not simply about the size of the winning coalition if P_{NR} or P_A wins; they also care about how big the pie will be under the two possible election outcomes. It could be that n_A is smaller than n_{NR} (making P_A more attractive), but that the negative effect of a P_A victory on π is sufficiently large that the nonrich in A prefer the class-based politics associated with a P_{NR} victory.[5]

Although it does not alter the logic of group size, the model does add an additional intuition about the emergence of ethnic politics. When government revenues come from taxes rather than for exogenous sources (such as natural resources or foreign aid), ethnic politics becomes less attractive to the pivotal nonrich because of its negative effect on government revenues. Thus, all else equal, it will be more difficult for ethnic politics to prevail when government revenues come from taxes rather than from exogenous sources. We might therefore expect to see a relationship between tax-based revenue generation and class-based electoral politics.

---

[3] See Lemmas 6 and 7 in the appendix. Note under PR the effects could be even larger because all the rich are included when coalition politics prevails.

[4] See Proposition 3 in the appendix.

[5] A similar logic would obviously make it more difficult to satisfy the conditions for ethnic politics under PR. But because there are more rich who receive transfers under coalition politics than under ethnic politics, it will undermine even more the value of the P_R and P_B coalition, thus bringing the PR model even closer to the plurality rule model.

Some might find it unconvincing to argue that the negative effect of ethnic politics on economic output is through its effect on labor output by the rich receiving benefits based on their ethnicity. On one hand, this is a very standard way to think about the effect of government policy on labor decisions, and many would find it unconvincing to assume otherwise. But on the other hand, it is important to note that given the assumption about rent-seeking parties, the model would produce the same intuitions about groups size (but not about total government revenues under ethnic versus class politics) if we did not assume a diminishing marginal utility from consumption. No matter which party is advantaged by social structure, it will have an incentive to set taxes to generate the maximum revenues possible in order to maximize rents.[6] Thus, the logic of group size is quite robust to different assumptions regarding the sources of government revenues.

More than Two Ethnic Groups

The assumption of two ethnic groups makes it very simple to convey intuitions, but are the intuitions about group size robust when we assume that there can be more than two groups? The results from any model with more than two groups will depend on specific assumptions about how bargaining occurs across parties and about whether multiethnic parties can form. But for any assumption about such bargaining processes or party formation, the logic of group size should extend to any number of groups because the constraint imposed by the number of nonrich is unaffected by the number of groups.

Consider Figure 4.2, where in the top panel the number of nonrich is 70 and the number of rich is 30, and there are three groups: *A* (45 voters), *B* (30 voters), and *C* (25 voters). The smallest ethnic coalition that could form would be between *B* and *C*, and if a coalition formed among parties representing these groups, or if a multiethnic party representing both *B* and *C* formed, it could clearly defeat a class-based party. Without more explicit assumptions and a formal model, it is difficult to say which specific parties would form to limit rent-seeking, but we can say that there is nothing that could be done to make the class party competitive against the ethnic alternative.

---

[6] This would be consistent with research finding little relationship between partisan control of the government and the size of government (e.g., Garrett and Lange 1991; Cusack 1997).

Ethnic group

	A	B	C
Rich	5	15	10
Nonrich	40	15	15

n_{NR} **large**

Ethnic group

	A	B	C
Rich	14	18	14
Nonrich	18	20	16

n_{NR} **small**

FIGURE 4.2. Three ethnic groups.

In the bottom panel, there are 54 nonrich individuals and A has 32 members, B has 38 members, and C and has 30 members. Thus, the smallest ethnic coalition would represent 62 voters, which could be defeated by the class party representing the nonrich. Again, without further assumptions, it is difficult to say which specific parties would form to limit rent-seeking, but it is clear that one could not form an ethnic coalition that could dislodge the class party. The key idea, then, is that if a potential party entrepreneur wants to pay the cost of creating a class party, the distribution of income in society will affect the likelihood of success, independently of the number of ethnic groups.

4.4 CONCLUSION

Chapter 3 argued that relatively rigid identities can play a central role in efforts by political parties to make credible commitments to voters about the distribution of government resources. Thus, a party representing a relatively small majority should have an advantage over a party representing a relatively large majority. But that chapter left unanswered the theoretical question of how party competition might be expected to unfold in response to the social structure describing group size. This chapter has addressed this question by examining a model of party formation and party competition.

A key puzzle about party formation that emerges from any group-size argument about social structure concerns why losing parties would ever form if they represent a group that is too large to win. And if parties that are sure to lose do not have incentives to form, what should we expect the winning party to offer voters? The argument developed here focuses on the fact that party entrepreneurs can be motivated both by the desire for rents (some sort of private gain from holding office) and for beneficial policy (the distributive consequences of the winning party's commitments). Losing parties form because if they do not, rent-seeking incentives allow a winning party to give little or nothing to voters. Thus, losing parties form essentially to keep the winning party honest – to force the winning party to distribute government benefits to voters. This benefits the entrepreneurs of the losing parties because they are from groups that the winning party represents.

This framework for studying party competition leads to a straightforward map from social structure to party systems and electoral outcomes. The winning party represents the smallest majority group because it can offer the most to voters. It is important to recognize, however, that "smallest majority" is relative. Whether the number of nonrich is small enough to trigger class politics, for example, is a function of the size of alternative ethnic coalitions. Thus, our expectations should be shaped by the interaction of n_{NR} and n_A. The framework also suggests that losing parties should form in order to influence the platform of winning parties. The size of the group represented by the losing party determines how much of the government pie must be distributed to voters, and how much can be kept as some form of rents.

This theoretical argument is robust to alternative assumptions about electoral competition. The reason is straightforward. No matter our assumption about the electoral law, whether government revenues come from exogenous windfalls or taxes on the rich, or whether there are two groups or more, the number of nonrich will always pose a constraint on the value of class politics to voters. As this number grows large relative to the number in alternative electoral coalitions, such as ethnic ones, it is more difficult for a class-based party to win.

4.5 APPENDIX

This appendix presents the formal model on which the theoretical argument is based. As noted in the chapter, in the model, voters are either rich or nonrich (their "class" identity) , and they belong to either the majority or the minority ethnic group (their ethnic identity). Party entrepreneurs are voters who can pay a cost to form a party representing a class (e.g., a party of the rich or a party of the nonrich) or an ethnic group (e.g., a party of the majority group or a party of the minority group). If they pay this cost, they make credible campaign promises about how government resources will be distributed to the individuals they represent. The entrepreneur for the party of the nonrich, for example, makes a promise regarding how much each nonrich person will receive from the government if the party of the nonrich wins. The winning party distributes the promised government resources to the members of the group the party represents, and the entrepreneur keeps any residual that is not distributed.

Formally, consider a population n of measure 1. Let A denote the majority group, which has a size of n_A, and let B denote the minority group, which has a size of n_B, so that $n_A + n_B = n$ and $n_A > n_B$. Individuals are rich (R) or nonrich (NR).[7] Let n_{NR} denote the number of nonrich individuals in society and n_R denote the number of rich individuals. The nonrich are a majority, with $n_{NR} > n_R$ and $n_R + n_{NR} = n$. The number of individuals in ethnic group j and class k is denoted by n_{jk} and the set of individuals in ethnic group j and class k is denoted by j_k (so, e.g., n_{AR} is the number of individuals in group A who are rich and A_R denotes this set of individuals). Thus, individuals belong to one of four subgroups: A_{NR}, A_R, B_{NR}, or B_R. I ignore the substantively uninteresting case where any subgroup has a majority (which means that $n_{ANR} < \frac{1}{2}$). In large electorates, the probability that the groups or subgroups are identical in size obviously goes to zero. It therefore simplifies the analysis to eliminate substantively uninteresting ties by assuming that no subgroups or groups are exactly the same size: that is, for any $r,s \in M = \{A, B, NR, R\}$, $n_r \neq n_s$, and for any $r,s,w,u \in M$, $n_{rs} \neq n_{wu}$ and $n_{rs} \neq n_u$.

---

[7] Fernàndez and Levy (2008), Esteban and Ray (2011), and Huber and Ting (2013) are recent examples of models that classify voters as rich or nonrich.

I begin by assuming that parties compete for votes by offering platforms that describe how exogenous government revenues, $\pi > 0$, will be distributed to voters. This assumption makes the model simple to analyze, and also captures a reality in many democracies in the developing world, where direct taxes on income or wealth represent a small proportion of government revenues. Instead, revenues often come from "exogenous" sources, such as natural resources, foreign aid, sales from state-owned farms or industries, or taxes on imports or exports.

Because parties can form to represent a class or a group, there are at most four parties that can form: P_{NR} (representing the nonrich); P_R (representing the rich); P_A (representing the majority group A); and P_B (representing the minority group B). Each party therefore represents two subgroups – P_A, for example, represents subgroups A_{NR} and A_R.

As in Feddersen, Sened, and Wright (1990), party formation occurs in two stages. First, in the party entry stage, voters can nominate themselves to become party entrepreneurs for a group to which they belong. A nonrich voter, for example, can nominate herself to become the party entrepreneur for a party that represents the nonrich. From the set of individuals who self-nominate, one is randomly chosen to lead the party. This entrepreneur is obligated to pay a cost $\delta > 0$ (which can be arbitrarily small) to form the party representing her group. As members of a subgroup are identical, I will treat them as a single actor in the party formation stage. Each ethnicity-class subgroup, jk, is represented by two potential parties, so voters make party formation decisions about two different parties. The nonrich in A (subgroup A_{NR}), for example, must decide about forming P_A and P_{NR}. For all $j, k = m$, let $e_{jk}^m = \{0, 1\}$ be the formation strategy of subgroup jk regarding party P_m, where 0 denotes that members of the subgroup jk will not pay δ to form P_m and 1 denotes that these member will pay δ to form the party. For example, $e_{ANR}^A = 1$ denotes that members of A_{NR} will pay δ to form P_A and $e_{AR}^A = 0$ denotes that members of A_R will not pay δ to form P_A. Let $e^m = max(e_{jk}^m)$ for all $j = m$ and $k = m$, so that $e^m = 1$ if any voter represented by P_m is willing to pay δ to form P_m. Then the vector $e = (e^A, e^B, e^{NR}, e^R)$ defines the parties that form. If voters from two subgroups seek to form the same party – for example if members of A_R and A_{NR} seek to form P_A – then one is randomly chosen to be the party's entrepreneur. Below I show that this assumption about random selection has no substantive implications because the entrepreneur for a given party always has the same incentives and thus adopts the same platform regardless of from which subgroup the entrepreneur is selected.

In the second stage, party entrepreneurs, having observed which parties have formed, adopt platforms. Party P_m's platform is $p_m > 0$, and it describes the amount of π that will be paid to each individual the party represents if the party wins. If an entrepreneur pays δ to form P_A, for example, then p_A describes how much each member of A will receive if P_A wins. Let $\mathbf{p(e)} = (p_A, p_B, p_{NR}, p_R)$ be the vector of party platforms given party formation decisions represented by e. If $e^m = 0$ then $p_m = 0$. Where it creates no confusion, I will refer to the set of party platforms from which voters choose simply as $\mathbf{p}$.

If a party representing m ultimately adopts $p_m = x$ and P_m wins, then each voter in m – no matter how they vote – receives x. Parties therefore cannot discriminate against particular members of the group they represent but instead must treat all group members the same. This implies that the maximum platform for a party representing group m is $\frac{\pi}{n_m}$, which occurs if the party entrepreneur proposes to distribute the entire π to the group her party represents. The amount that parties can "pay" for votes therefore varies with the size of the group the party represents.

Agent Utility Functions

After a party system forms and voting takes place, a voter receives the amount promised to his or her group in the platform of the winning party. Thus a voter receives the promised amount if the voter belongs to one of the two subgroups that the winning party represents and receives zero otherwise. Formally, let $p_m^*(\mathbf{p})$ be the platform of the winning party, P_m, which represents individuals from group or class m, and let $u_{jk}(p_m^*)$ be the linear utility of a voter of ethnic group j and class k given p_m^*. Then

$$u_{jk}(p_m^*) = \begin{cases} 0 & \text{if } j \neq m \text{ and } k \neq m \\ p_m^* & \text{if } j = m \text{ or } k = m. \end{cases}$$

The utility function of party entrepreneurs has three components. First, as noted previously, an entrepreneur pays a cost $\delta > 0$ of offering a platform. Although the cost can be arbitrarily small, its presence ensures that parties will not form unless there is some benefit of doing so. Second, entrepreneurs can obtain personal rents from forming parties and winning control of the government. Specifically, if the entrepreneur offers the winning platform, she keeps any government resources that are not distributed to voters after honoring the platform. This residual for the entrepreneur of the winning party, P_m, is $r_m = \pi - (p_m * n_m)$, which we can think of as the political rents that accrue to party entrepreneurs. Politicians therefore have an incentive to offer the smallest possible winning platform so as to maximize the rents they receive. Finally, party entrepreneurs are voters and thus receive the policy utility resulting from the winning platform.

Let $p^*(\mathbf{p})$ be the winning platform given party system $\mathbf{p}$ and equilibrium voting strategies. Suppose a voter from subgroup jk has proposed to pay the cost of party formation and has been selected to be P_M's entrepreneur. The utility for this entrepreneur is given by

$$u_{jk}^m(p^*(\mathbf{p})) = \begin{cases} u_{jk}(p^*(\mathbf{p})) - \delta & \text{if } P_m \text{ loses (i.e., if } p_m \neq p^*(\mathbf{p})) \\ u_{jk}(p^*(\mathbf{p})) + r_m - \delta & \text{if } P_m \text{ wins (i.e., if } p_m = p^*(\mathbf{p})). \end{cases} \tag{4.1}$$

Definition of an Equilibrium

Given a party system, $\mathbf{p}$, voters will choose the party that results in the highest payoff. Voters from each subgroup are identical and vote in the same way. Voters in subgroup jk can be represented only by one of two parties. Let these parties be P_m (with platform p_m) and $P_{m'}$ (with platform $p_{m'}$) and let $v_{jk} = P_m$ denote that subgroup jk supports P_m. Define $\mathbf{v}_{\neg jk}(\mathbf{p})$ as the vector of voting strategies for the three subgroups other than jk given the party system $\mathbf{p}$. Define $p^*(v_{jk} = P_m | \mathbf{v}_{\neg jk}(\mathbf{p}))$ as the winning platform that results for party system $\mathbf{p}$ if subgroup jk supports P_m and other subgroups have voted as specified in $\mathbf{v}_{\neg jk}(\mathbf{p})$. A Nash equilibrium voting strategy for subgroup jk is given by

$$v_{jk}^*(\mathbf{p}) = \begin{cases} \emptyset & \text{if } p_m = p_{m'} = 0 \\ P_m & \text{if } p_m > 0 \quad \text{and} \quad p_{m'} = 0 \\ P_m & \text{if } u_{jk}\left[p^*(v_{jk} = P_m | \mathbf{v}_{\neg jk}(\mathbf{p}))\right] > u_{jk}\left[p^*(v_{jk} = P_{m'} | \mathbf{v}_{\neg jk}(\mathbf{p}))\right] \\ P_m & \text{if } u_{jk}\left[p^*(v_{jk} = P_m | \mathbf{v}_{\neg jk}(\mathbf{p}))\right] = u_{jk}\left[p^*(v_{jk} = P_{m'} | \mathbf{v}_{\neg jk}(\mathbf{p}))\right] \\ & \text{and } r_m > r_{m'}. \end{cases}$$

$$\tag{4.2}$$

A Nash Equilibrium at the voting stage exists if the vote choice of all subgroups satisfies Eq. 4.2.

Equation 4.2 states that if no party represents a voter, the voter abstains (line 1). If there is only one party that represents the voter, the voter plays the weakly dominant strategy, which is to support this party (line 2).

Finally, there may be both a class and an ethnic party that represent a voter. In this case, the voter chooses the party that yields the highest expected utility given the strategies of other voters (line 3). If a voter is indifferent between his class- and ethnic-based parties, the voter supports the party whose entrepreneur has the largest surplus (i.e., who has the largest r_m, line 4). This tie-breaking rule makes it possible to avoid requiring party entrepreneurs to choose platforms that maximize on an open set. Suppose, for example, that a voter is pivotal in choosing between P_j and P_k and that $p_j = p_k$. By assumption, $n_j \neq n_k$, so assume $n_j < n_k$. This implies that it is always possible for P_j to offer more to its voters. If P_k proposes to distribute all of π to voters, for example, its platform is $\frac{\pi}{n_k}$. But then since $n_j < n_k$, P_j could propose $\frac{\pi + \epsilon}{n_k}$ and win against the larger group. Of course, as $\epsilon \to 0$, $\frac{\pi + \epsilon}{n_k}$ converges to $\frac{\pi}{n_k}$. The tie-breaking assumption rules out the need to make such "ϵ" proposals.

A Nash equilibrium exists in party strategies if members of each subgroup make optimal entry and platform decisions. Consider the platform stage. Let $\bar{p}_m(\mathbf{e})$ be a platform for P_m conditional on the vector of entry strategies, and let $\bar{\mathbf{p}}_{\neg m}(\mathbf{e})$ be the vector of platforms for parties other than P_m. Together, $\bar{p}_m(\mathbf{e})$ and $\bar{\mathbf{p}}_{\neg m}(\mathbf{e})$ define a party system, $(\bar{p}_m(\mathbf{e}), \bar{\mathbf{p}}_{\neg m}(\mathbf{e}))$. Voters will choose optimally given this party system, producing the outcome $p^*(\bar{p}_m(\mathbf{e}), \bar{\mathbf{p}}_{\neg m}(\mathbf{e}))$, and yielding for P_m's entrepreneur the utility defined in Eq. 4.1, which we can label $u_m(p^*(\bar{p}_m(\mathbf{e}), \bar{\mathbf{p}}_{\neg m}(\mathbf{e}))$. Suppose P_m's entrepreneur is from jk. Then $\bar{p}_m$ is optimal if

$$u_{jk}^m(p^*(\bar{p}_m(\mathbf{e}), \bar{\mathbf{p}}_{\neg m}(\mathbf{e})) \geq u_{jk}^m(p^*(\tilde{p}_m(\mathbf{e}), \bar{\mathbf{p}}_{\neg m}(\mathbf{e})) \text{ for all } \tilde{p}_m \neq \bar{p}_m. \quad (4.3)$$

A Nash equilibrium exists in the platform stage if Eq. 4.3 is satisfied for all entrepreneurs who have entered. One problem that could arise for party entrepreneurs who generate expectations about outcomes based on voting equilibria is that there could in principle exist multiple Nash equilibria in the voting stage. One could make further assumptions about equilibrium selection in such cases, but as will become clear later, this is not a problem in practice because the possibility of multiple Nash equilibria in voting never arises.

Next consider party entry. Let e_{jk}^m be a party formation strategy for a subgroup jk that can form P_m (because $j = m$ or $k = m$) and let $\mathbf{e}_{\neg m}$ be the vector describing which parties other than P_m have formed. Then the vector of party formation strategies is given by $(e_{jk}^m, \mathbf{e}_{\neg m})$, which will trigger the platforms and thus a policy outcome defined by $p^*(\mathbf{p}(e_{jk}^m, \mathbf{e}_{\neg m})$.

Subgroup *jk* will pay δ to enter if

$$u_{jk}^m(p^*(\mathbf{p}(e_{jk}^m = \mathbf{1}, \mathbf{e}_{\neg m}))) \geq u_{jk}(p^*(\mathbf{p}(e_{jk}^m = \mathbf{0}, \mathbf{e}_{\neg m}))). \qquad (4.4)$$

Each subgroup, then, must decide whether to pay the cost of entry given the entry strategies of other parties, and given the resulting platforms and voting outcomes from each vector of entry strategies. A Nash equilibrium exists in the initial platform stage if Eq. 4.4 is satisfied for all subgroup party formation decisions. That is, holding the party formation strategy of all other parties constant, members of each subgroup, for each party they could form, decide optimally about party formation, anticipating that the other party entrepreneurs choose their platforms optimally given party formation decisions and that voters choose optimally given the party system. I focus on pure strategy equilibria.

Analysis of the Plurality Rule Case

I begin by describing why there can only be two-party equilibria in the plurality rule case.

Lemma 1 *If a pure strategy equilibrium exists under plurality rule, there will be two (and only two) parties that form.*

Proof. *There can exist no one-party equilibria.* Suppose P_m is the only party to form. Then the rent-seeking incentives of P_m's entrepreneur require that P_m offer the smallest possible platform, say $p_m = \epsilon$. But given p_m approaches zero, it cannot have been an equilibrium for no other party to have entered. In particular, there is at least one potential party that represents a subgroup represented by P_m. Call this party $P_{m'}$ and this subgroup *jk*. Then if a voter from *jk* forms $P_{m'}$, it can offer a larger platform, either winning or forcing $p_m \geq p_{m'}$. Given δ is arbitrarily small, the entrepreneur for $P_{m'}$ prefers entering because it increases the policy payoff she receives. Thus, there can be no one-party equilibrium.

There cannot be more than two parties in any equilibrium. A potential entrepreneur will pay the cost of entry only if either (a) she is going to win, or (b) she is going to lose, but by entering obtains a better payoff from the platform of the winning party than she would if she did not enter. Suppose there are three or more parties that have formed. From the definition of voting strategies in Eq. 4.2 and the assumption about no ties in group size, there will be a unique winner for any vector of platforms. Let p_1 be the platform of the winning party, P_1. A potential entrepreneur for another party will pay the cost of entry only if the entrepreneur is represented by P_1 and if p_1 is larger if the potential entrepreneur enters. But given the rent-seeking incentives of entrepreneurs, the optimal platform by P_1 will be the smallest platform that wins, and this can be influenced by only one other platform, which means that it cannot be optimal for more than one other party to form. ■

Next, Lemma 2 shows that because the parties care about both rents and policy outcomes, the platforms of the two parties do not depend on the subgroup of the party's entrepreneurs. The rents from winning drive party entrepreneurs of winners to adopt the smallest possible proposal and the policy utility from platforms drives party entrepreneurs for losing parties to adopt the largest possible platform.

Lemma 2 *For any party, the optimal platform in a pure strategy equilibrium will be the same regardless of from which subgroup the entrepreneur is chosen.*

Proof. From Lemma 1, there can be only two parties. With two parties, one will always win because it represents a smaller majority. Thus, its entrepreneur, regardless of the subgroup it represents, has an incentive to offer the smallest winning platform. The losing party can form for only one reason: its entrepreneur is from a subgroup that is also represented by the winning party and thus it will receive a policy payoff based on the winner's platform. Any entrepreneur for this party has an incentive to offer the largest platform possible so as to force the largest possible platform by the winning party. This "largest" possible platform is constrained only by the size of the group the party represents, and so will be independent of the party entrepreneur's identity. ■

Because there are only two parties in any equilibrium, there must be one party that has a clear advantage because it represents a smaller majority. This fact makes it possible to clearly define the optimal party platforms in any equilibrium.

Lemma 3 *Consider a two-party system where P_m and $P_{m'}$ both form and $n_m < n_{m'}$. If there exists a pure strategy equilibrium, then it must be true that*
    (i) There exists one subgroup that is represented by both parties; and
    (ii) $p_m = p_{m'} = \frac{\pi}{n_{m'}}$ and P_m wins.

Proof. (i) If this were not true, then there would be one party representing the majority of one identity (either group or class) and another party representing the minority for this same identity. The party representing the majority party would win for any platforms by the two parties, and thus the net benefit for any entrepreneur for the minority party would be $-\delta$, implying it could not have been an equilibrium for this party to form.

(ii) In equilibrium, $p_m = p_{m'} = \frac{\pi}{n_{m'}}$ and P_m wins. For any $p_m \geq p_{m'}$, P_m will win. Since $n_m < n_{m'}$, P_m can always propose $p_m \geq p_{m'}$. Thus, there can be no equilibrium in which $p_m < p_{m'}$ (because P_m's entrepreneur would prefer to offer $p_m = p_{m'}$ and win), and there can be no equilibrium where $p_m > p_{m'}$ (because P_m's entrepreneur prefer the smallest winning platform possible so as to maximize her rents, r_m). Since $p_m = p_{m'}$ in any equilibrium, it must be true that $p_m = p_{m'} = \frac{\pi}{n_{m'}}$ because for any platform $p_m < \frac{\pi}{n_{m'}}$, the entrepreneur for $P_{m'}$ could offer a platform $p_{m'} > p_m$ and win. ∎

Lemma 3 indicates that if there exists a pure strategy equilibrium, it will be unique. There can be no pure strategy equilibrium in which the two parties do not promise the same amount to their constituents: if the losing party offers less than the winning party, the winning party's entrepreneur would have preferred to offer something smaller to extract more rents. It also cannot be an equilibrium for both parties to offer anything less than the maximum platform that could be offered by the party representing the larger group. If any party offers something less than this platform, the other party's entrepreneur would have preferred to have offered something more so it could win.

Why does the losing party pay the costs to form? Party entrepreneurs care both about rents and policy outcomes. The losing party's entrepreneur cares directly about the winning party's platform because the entrepreneur must belong to a group represented by the winning party. The benefit for the losing party's entrepreneur from entering, then, is that so doing affects the platform of the winner, which is why this party's entrepreneur proposes to distribute the entire platform to voters. If party entrepreneurs cared only about rents from winning, the entrepreneur for the losing party would never have an incentive to form. But rents are crucial as well. Because party entrepreneurs care about rents from winning, they want to offer the smallest winning platform possible. Thus, the losing party must form to force the winning party to pay as much as possible to the voters it represents.

Which two parties can form? Lemma 4 describes why the party of the rich and the party of the minority ethnic group can never form in a two-party equilibrium.

Lemma 4 *In any pure strategy equilibrium, no entrepreneur will form either P_R or P_B.*

Proof. I first show that P_R can never form. There are three possible two-party systems to consider where P_R forms, and none can be an equilibrium.

(1) P_R and P_{NR} form. This cannot be an equilibrium because P_{NR} would win for any p_R, yielding a negative net benefit for any entrepreneur forming P_R.

(2) P_R and P_A form: If only P_R and P_A have entered, it could not be an equilibrium for P_R not to have formed. Note that if $n_{ANR} > n_R$ then P_A would win for any p_A, making it nonoptimal for P_R to have formed. Thus, for P_R and P_A to be a possible equilibrium it would have to be true that $n_{ANR} < n_R$. Suppose this condition is satisfied and consider the payoff to an entrepreneur from forming P_{NR} given only P_R and P_A have formed. In any voting equilibrium, $v_{BR} = P_R$ and $v_{BNR} = P_{NR}$. It cannot be an equilibrium for $v_{ANR} = P_A$ because $n_{ANR} < n_R$, $v_{AR} = P_R$ and P_R wins (allowing the rich in A to share the pie with a smaller number of voters than would be the case if this subgroup supported P_A). Thus, if P_{NR} enters, it must be true that $v_{ANR} = v_{BNR} = P_{NR}$ and P_{NR} wins, yielding a higher utility to the entrepreneur for P_{NR} than would have been obtained from not forming. It therefore cannot be an equilibrium for P_{NR} not to form when only P_A and P_R have formed.

(3) P_R and P_B form: Consider the case in which the equilibrium voting outcome from this party system makes P_R the winner, which implies that the rich in B prefer P_R to P_B and $n_R > n_{BNR}$. If P_{NR} forms, then in any voting equilibrium, the rich in A support P_R and the nonrich in A support P_{NR}. If n_{ANR} is sufficiently large that the nonrich in A determine the voting outcome, then P_{NR} obviously has an incentive to form. So assume $n_{ANR} < min(n_R, n_B)$ and consider whether an entrepreneur has an incentive to form P_{NR}. As it must be true that $v_{ANR} = P_{NR}$ and $v_{AR} = P_R$, there are four possible voting equilibria to consider:

- $v_{BNR} = v_{BR} = P_B$. This is not an NE because the rich in B prefer P_R given $v_{ANR} = P_{NR}$ and $v_{BNR} = P_B$.
- $v_{BNR} = P_B$ and $v_{BR} = P_R$. This is not an NE because the outcome is P_R, which means the nonrich in B must prefer $v_{BNR} = P_{NR}$.

- $v_{BNR} = P_{NR}$ and $v_{BR} = P_B$. This is not an NE because the nonrich in B would prefer voting for P_B given that $v_{BR} = P_B$.
- $v_{BNR} = P_{NR}$ and $v_{BR} = P_R$. It is straightforward to verify that this satisfies Eq. 4.2 for all subgroups, and thus this would be the unique equilibrium if P_{NR} formed. Since P_{NR} would always win by entering, it cannot be an equilibrium for it to not enter when only P_R and P_B have formed and P_R is expected to win.

The logic is the same for why P_A must enter when only P_R and P_B have formed and P_B is expected to win.

The proof for why P_B can never form is analogous and is omitted. ∎

In any equilibrium only the parties representing majorities can form. Proposition 1 shows that there always exists a unique pure strategy equilibrium in which both of these parties form and offer the same platform, with the winning party being the one representing a smaller majority.

Proposition 1 *Under plurality rule with windfall revenues, there is a always a unique Nash equilibrium in pure strategies where*

- P_A and P_{NR} are the only two parties that form
- $p_A = p_{NR} = \frac{\pi}{n_{NR}}$ if $n_A < n_{NR}$
- $p_A = p_{NR} = \frac{\pi}{n_A}$ if $n_A > n_{NR}$

The equilibrium voting strategies given **p** are

- $v_{AR}(\mathbf{p}) = P_A$
- $v_{BR}(\mathbf{p}) = \emptyset$
- $v_{BNR}(\mathbf{p}) = P_{NR}$
- $v_{ANR} = P_A$ if $n_A < n_{NR}$ and
  $v_{ANR} = P_{NR}$ if $n_A > n_{NR}$

Proof. By Lemma 1, in any equilibrium, there must be two parties, and by Lemma 4, these parties cannot include P_R or P_B. By Lemma 3, if there is an equilibrium with P_{NR} and P_A, then $p_A = p_{NR} = \frac{\pi}{n_{NR}}$ if $n_A < n_{NR}$, and $p_A = p_{NR} = \frac{\pi}{n_A}$ if $n_{NR} < n_A$. Thus, if an equilibrium exists it must be unique and be the one described in the statement. It only remains to confirm that the voting strategies are optimal given the party system and that the party formation strategies are optimal for the entrepreneurs of P_A and P_{NR}.

Voting strategies. It is straightforward to confirm that the voting strategies satisfy Eq. 4.2: the nonrich in A are the only subgroup represented by more than one party, and they support the party representing the smaller electoral majority (and hence the party that yields the largest residual for the entrepreneur).

Party strategies are optimal for the entrepreneurs of P_A and P_{NR}. Consider the case in which $n_A < n_{NR}$.

(1) $p_{NR} = \frac{\pi}{n_{NR}}$ is optimal. By Lemma 3, $p_{NR} = \frac{\pi}{n_{NR}}$ if P_{NR} forms. It therefore remains to show that the entrepreneur prefers entering over not entering. By forming, the entrepreneur receives $\frac{\pi}{n_{NR}} - \delta$. Given the entry decisions by other parties, if P_{NR} does not form, the entrepreneur for P_A can offer $p_A = \epsilon$, yielding ϵ, which is worse than the payoff of forming given δ is arbitrarily small.

(2) $p_A = \frac{\pi}{n_{NR}}$ is optimal. Because P_A wins, the enterpreneur obviously prefers entering to not entering. Given $p_A = \frac{\pi}{n_{NR}}$, the entrepreneur for P_A prefers p_A to any platform less than p_A (because such a platform would lose). Similarly, since any $p_A \geq p_{NR}$ will win, the entrepreneur prefers p_A to anything larger (because this maximizes the residual).

The logic for the case where $n_{NR} > n_A$ is identical and is omitted. ■

Because P_A and P_{NR} must form in any two-party equilibrium, the nonrich in A are pivotal because they are represented by both parties. This means that the party representing the smaller majority has a clear advantage. The most that the party representing the larger majority can offer is to divide π equally among all members of this group. But an entrepreneur for a party representing the smaller majority group can always promise more because the party has fewer constituents who need to be paid if the party wins. Thus, if $n_A < n_{NR}$, an entrepreneur for P_A can offer more than the best platform that the entrepreneur for P_{NR} could offer. By contrast, if $n_{NR} < n_A$, an entrepreneur for P_{NR} can offer more than the best platform that the entrepreneur for P_A could offer. In either case, the winning party's entrepreneur reaps positive rents that increase as the size of the losing party's group grows larger. The losing party nevertheless has an incentive to form because so doing forces the winning party to offer a larger platform than would be necessary if the losing party did not form.

The Model under Proportional Representation

Under proportional representation (PR), the number of seats won by a party is proportional to the number of voters who support it. Elections might therefore produce no majority winner, resulting in coalition bargaining. This section explores the implications of PR for the emergence of ethnic- versus class-based electoral politics.

Interactions begin with party formation following the same structure as under plurality rule. Voters vote strategically so as to achieve the highest possible payoff given the voting strategies of others and the dynamics of coalition formation. As under plurality rule, indifferent voters select the party that produces the largest total residual.

If a party wins a majority, it implements its platform and the party leader keeps the residual. If no party wins a majority, then party platforms during the electoral stage become irrelevant and a coalition bargaining process begins. Each leader of a party that receives votes can make a coalition proposal, $c_{mm'} = x$, which states that P_m proposes a coalition with $P_{m'}$ to give x to each person represented by P_m and $P_{m'}$. Such proposals can win only if P_m and $P_{m'}$ represent a majority in the legislature and if $c_{mm'} = c_{m'm}$ (i.e., the two parties agree on the proposal). If P_R and P_B receive support from a majority, for example, and $c_{BR} = c_{RB} = x$, then P_B and P_R form a majority coalition and all individuals who are rich or in group B receive x. Under coalitions, party leaders share equally the residual that is not distributed to voters. Thus, leaders from different parties in the same coalition have identical interests – they want to offer the smallest amount possible to their voters so as to maximize their rents.

Without additional constraints, when no majority exists, party leaders in a coalition have opportunities to bargain in bad faith vis-à-vis their constituents. At the extreme, party leaders can keep π entirely for themselves. Such behavior would of course work only in the short term, as voters would punish party leaders who did not bargain faithfully on behalf of the groups they represent. It is therefore important to impose an additional constraint on party behavior, and I adopt the following "good faith" assumption: a party leader pays a large cost $\phi > 0$ if she accepts a coalition proposal that gives her party's constituents a lower payoff than these constituents would have received had they voted for any other party that has formed. Suppose, for example, that P_A forms and receives the support of the poor in A. If the rich in A support P_R in anticipation of a coalition with P_B, c_{BR} cannot give constituents less than the rich in A would have received from supporting P_A (the payoff of which is conditional on the voting strategies of other subgroups).

In equilibrium, party formation strategies must be optimal at the entry and platform stages, just as in the plurality case. Voters vote optimally given the party platforms and given expectations about coalition formation. And party entrepreneurs maximize their utility in the coalition bargaining stage by agreeing to coalition bargains that provide the highest possible utility, subject to the "good faith" constraint. Although there are up to four parties and a wide variety of coalitions, it is straightforward to show that there are only three possible equilibrium governance outcomes.

Lemma 5 *Under proportional representation, there exist only three possible equilibrium outcomes:*

  1. P_A *wins a majority; or*
  2. P_{NR} *wins a majority; or*
  3. *No party wins a majority and P_R and P_B form a majority coalition.*

Proof. By the same logic in the proof of Lemma 4, it can never be an equilibrium for P_R or P_B to win a majority. It therefore remains to show that the only possible equilibrium majority coalition includes only P_R and P_B. Any other coalition must include either P_A or P_{NR}. No equilibrium can result in a coalition of P_A with another party, P_k. Such a coalition could at most provide $\frac{\pi}{n_A+n_k}$ to individuals represented by P_A and P_k, which would yield no residual for the party entrepreneurs. But the entrepreneur for P_A could always offer a platform that all members of A prefer to this best possible outcome under the coalition, and that yields a positive residual for the entrepreneur. Thus it can never be an equilibrium for a party entrepreneur to adopt any p_A that leads the groups in A to split their vote in a way that results in a coalition of P_A with P_k. The logic for why there cannot be an equilibrium between P_{NR} and another party is identical: the entrepreneur for P_{NR} always prefers to offer a platform that wins a majority to offering a platform that results in a coalition. ∎

Lemma 5 makes it relatively straightforward to characterize equilibria under PR. Recall $\mathbf{p}^* = (p_A, p_{NR}, p_B, p_R)$ is the vector of equilibrium party platforms, and let $\mathbf{v}^*(\mathbf{p}^*) = (v_{ANR}, v_{AR}, v_{BNR}, v_{BR})$ be the equilibrium vector of voting strategies, and let $c_{mm'}^*$ be the equilibrium coalition agreement when no party wins a majority.

Proposition 2 *Under proportional representation,*

(1) If $n_A < n_{NR}$ and $n_{ANR} < n_B$ then P_A wins and

$$\mathbf{p}^* = (\tfrac{\pi}{n_{NR}}, \tfrac{\pi}{n_{NR}}, 0, 0)$$
$$\mathbf{v}^* = (P_A, P_A, P_{NR}, \emptyset)$$

(2) If $n_A < n_{NR}$ and $n_{ANR} > n_B$ then P_B and P_R form a majority coalition and

$$\mathbf{p}^* = (\tfrac{\pi}{n_A}, 0, p_B > 0, p_R > 0)$$
$$\mathbf{v}^* = (P_A,\ P_R,\ P_B, P_R\ or\ P_B)$$
$$c^*_{BR} = c^*_{RB} = \tfrac{\pi}{n_A}$$

(3) *If* $n_A > n_{NR}$ *and* $n_{ANR} < n_R$, *then* P_{NR} *wins and*

$$\mathbf{p}^* = (\tfrac{\pi}{n_A},\ \tfrac{\pi}{n_A},\ 0,\ 0)$$
$$\mathbf{v}^* = (P_{NR},\ P_A,\ P_{NR}, \emptyset)$$

(4) *If* $n_A > n_{NR}$ *and* $n_{ANR} > n_R$ *then* P_B *and* P_R *form a majority coalition and*

$$\mathbf{p}^* = (0,\ \tfrac{\pi}{n_{NR}}, p_B > 0, p_R > 0)$$
$$\mathbf{v}^* = (P_{NR},\ P_R,\ P_B, P_R\ or\ P_B)$$
$$c^*_{BR} = c^*_{RB} = \tfrac{\pi}{n_{NR}}$$

Proof. (1) $n_A < n_{NR}$ and $n_{ANR} < n_B$: Following the same logic found under plurality rule, the specific platforms of P_{NR} and P_A are optimal given that P_B and P_R do not form, and the voting strategies are optimal given the party system. It therefore remains to show that P_B and P_R cannot enter. Since $n_{ANR} < n_B$ implies $n_A < n_R + n_{BNR}$, there cannot exist an equilibrium in which a coalition of P_R and P_B is the winner (because the entrepreneur for P_A can always ensure that the rich in A prefer P_A to this coalition). And since $n_A < n_{NR}$, an entrepreneur for P_A can always ensure that the poor in A prefer P_A to P_{NR} (and the entrepreneur has an incentive to do so in order to obtain the residual). Thus, there cannot exist an equilibrium in which any members of B receive a payoff from the winning party, and P_B therefore cannot form (because the expected payoff of doing so is negative). Given P_B will never form, P_R can never be a credible coalition partner (because the rich in A will never prefer a coalition between P_A and P_R to a majority victory by P_A), and thus the optimal platform for P_A is independent of p_R, making the expected payoff of forming P_R negative.

(2) $n_A < n_{NR}$ and $n_{ANR} > n_B$: Given the party system, the voting strategies are optimal. Since $P_{NR} = 0$, in any voting equilibrium, $v_{ANR} = P_A$ and $v_{BNR} = P_B$. The rich in B receive a payoff only if the election results in a $P_R + P_B$ coalition, and thus the voters in this subgroup are indifferent between supporting these two parties. Thus, the rich in A are pivotal, and given the anticipated payoff from a coalition is the same as the payoff from a P_A majority (i.e., $p_A = c_{BR}$), the rich in A vote for the party that yields the largest total residual, which is P_R given $n_{ANR} > n_B$. Thus, it remains to show that party formation strategies are optimal.

By Lemma 5, there cannot be an equilibrium in which only P_R and P_B form (because if this occurred, one of these parties would win a majority). There also cannot be an equilibrium in which P_R and P_B do not form because by forming they win with certainty (because $n_{ANR} > n_B$ ensures that no party can offer a platform that defeats the coalition) and reap a positive residual for their entrepreneurs. Thus, in any equilibrium P_R and P_B and at least one other party must form.

For $P_R + P_B$ coalition to prevail and satisfy the "good faith" assumption, it must be true that $c_{BR} \geq p_A$ (because given $v_{ANR} = P_A$, P_A will win if the rich in A change their vote to support P_A). Thus, the optimal platform for P_A is $\frac{\pi}{n_A}$ (because this maximizes the policy payoff for the rich in A). Since P_A adopts $p_A = \frac{\pi}{n_A}$, the optimal coalition agreement is also $\frac{\pi}{n_A}$ (because this maximizes the rents and giving any less to supporters would make v_{NR} nonoptimal).

(3) $n_A > n_{NR}$ and $n_{ANR} < n_B$: The structure of the proof is identical to that of (1) and is omitted.

(4) $n_A > n_{NR}$ and $n_{ANR} > n_B$: The structure of the proof is identical to that of (2) and is omitted. ∎

The Model When Government Revenues Come from Taxes on the Rich

Assume that only the rich pay taxes, and that the rich receive utility from consumption, C and leisure, $\mathcal{L}$. They can supply labor, L, at a fixed wage, w (which is set equal to 1), and they have a fixed stock of capital, K. There is a proportional tax rate, t, on labor income. If P_{NR} wins, the rich receive nothing from the government; they only pay taxes. I will not make an assumption about how revenues are shared among the rich and nonrich if P_A wins, but rather assume the (tax-free) transfer to the rich in group A will be λ_{AR}. The budget constraint on consumption is $C = (1-t)L + K + \lambda_{AR}$, where $\lambda_{AR} = 0$ if P_{NR} wins. The rich in B always receive 0 under group or class politics, so $\lambda_{AR} = 0$ for the rich in B. The time constraint is $T = \mathcal{L} + L = 1$. Let α be the weight that the rich give to consumption, and for simplicity assume that α is the same for the rich in both groups. Then the preferences over consumption and leisure are given by $U(C, \mathcal{L}) = \alpha \, ln \, C + (1 - \alpha) \, ln \, \mathcal{L}$, which (substituting the budget and time constraints) can be written as $U(C, \mathcal{L}) = \alpha \, ln \, ((1-t)L + K + \lambda_{AR}) + (1 - \alpha) \, ln \, (1 - L)$.

Let $L_C^*(t)$ be the equilibrium labor output as a function of t if class politics prevails because P_{NR} wins, and let $L_E^*(t)$ be the equilibrium labor output if ethnic politics prevails because P_A wins. I focus on parameter values that produce an interior solution. It is straightforward to show that if we fix the tax rate, labor output is higher under class politics than under ethnic politics.

Lemma 6 $L_C^*(t) > L_E^*(t) \ \forall t.$

Proof. Note that $U(C, \mathcal{L})$ is concave in t for both ethnic and class-based politics. Solving the first-order conditions when $\lambda_{AR} = 0$ yields $L_C^*(t) = \frac{K(\alpha-1)+\alpha(1-t)}{1-t}$, which is decreasing in t. And for ethnic politics (when $\lambda_{AR} > 0$), $L_E^*(t) = \frac{(K+\lambda_{AR})(\alpha-1)+\alpha(1-t)}{1-t}$, which is also decreasing in t. $L_C^*(t) > L_E^*(t)$ whenever $\lambda_{AR} > 0$, which is always true by the definition of ethnic politics. ∎

Let t_C^* be the equilibrium tax rate under class politics (i.e., the tax rate set by P_{NR} if it wins) and let $\pi_C^*(t_C^*)$ be total government revenues when the rich are making optimal labor decisions in response to t_C^*. Similarly define t_E^* as the equilibrium tax rate under ethnic politics and $\pi_E^*(t_E^*)$ as the resulting government revenues. Even though the entrepreneurs for P_A and P_{NR} have the same incentives – to set t^* to maximize revenues so as to maximize rents – Lemma 7 shows that total government revenues are always greater in an equilibrium when P_{NR} wins than when P_A wins.

Lemma 7 $\pi_C^*(t_C^*) > \pi_E^*(t_E^*).$

Proof. If class politics prevails, the rich in both groups respond identically (because no rich receive transfers) and thus total government revenue is given by

$$\pi_C^*(t_C^*) = t_C^* * L_C^*(t_C^*) * n_R$$
$$= \left[t_C^* * L_C^*(t_C^*) * n_{AR} \right] + \left[t_C^* * L_C^*(t_C^*) * n_{BR} \right].$$

Under ethnic politics, the rich in A respond differently to t_E^* than do the rich in B. The rich in B receive no transfers, and thus their optimal labor output is given by $L_C^*(t_E^*)$. The rich in A do receive transfers, and thus their optimal labor output is given by $L_E^*(t_E^*)$. Total revenues are therefore

$$\pi_E^*(t_E^*) = \left[t_E^* * L_E^*(t_E^*) * n_{AR} \right] + \left[t_E^* * L_C^*(t_E^*) * n_{BR} \right].$$

Consider two possible cases. In the first, $t_E^* = t_C^*$. This implies that the revenues received from labor output by the rich in B will be the same under ethnic and class politics, and thus $\pi_C^*(t_C^*) > \pi_E^*(t_E^* = t_C^*)$ if the rich in A produce more revenues under class politics than under ethnic politics, which is true if $t_C^* * L_C^*(t_C^*) > t_C^* * L_E^*(t_E^* = t_C^*)*$, or if $L_C^*(t_C^*) > L_E^*(t_C^*)$, which is true by Lemma 6.

In the second case, $t_E^* \neq t_C^*$. Given t_C^* is revenue maximizing when the rich receive no transfers, we know that there are more revenues generated by the rich in B under class politics than under ethnic politics (i.e., $t_E^* * L_C^*(t_E^*) < t_C^* * L_C^*(t_C^*)$ for any $t_E^* \neq t_C^*$). Consider the rich in A. By Lemma 6, for any $t_E^* \neq t_C^*$ it must be true that $t_E^* * L_E^*(t_E^*) < t_E^* * L_C^*(t_E^*)$. In addition, given t_C^* is revenue maximizing under class politics, it must also be true that $t_E^* * L_C^*(t_E^*) < t_C^* * L_C^*(t_C^*)$. By transitivity, $t_E^* * L_E^*(t_E^*) < t_C^* * L_C^*(t_C^*)$, and the rich in A thus produce less in equilibrium when ethnic politics prevails. Because both the rich in A and the rich in B produce less under ethnic politics, $e\pi_C^*(t_C^*) > \pi_E^*(t_E^*)$. ∎

We can now describe the conditions under which ethnic or class politics prevails in the model in which government revenues are endogenously determined by taxes.

Proposition 3 *In any pure-strategy equilibrium under plurality rule where revenues come from income taxes on the rich, P_A can win only if $n_{NR} > \frac{\pi_C^*(t_C^*)}{\pi_E^*(t_E^*)} n_A$, which implies that the conditions for class politics are easier to satisfy when government revenues are obtained from taxes on the rich than when they are obtained from exogenous windfalls.*

Proof. In Proposition 1, where revenues are from windfalls, the nonrich in A are pivotal and ethnic politics prevails if $n_{NR} > n_A$. With taxes on the rich, the maximum that an entrepreneur for P_A could offer is $\frac{\pi_E^*(t_E^*)}{n_A}$ and the maximum that an entpreneur for P_{NR} could offer is $\frac{\pi_C^*(t_C^*)}{n_{NR}}$. Thus, an entrepreneur for A could win only if $n_{NR} > \frac{\pi_C^*(t_C^*)}{\pi_E^*(t_E^*)} n_A$. From Lemma 7, $\pi_C^*(t_C^*) > \pi_E^*(t_E^*)$, which implies that it is more difficult for the entrepreneur for P_A to win when revenues derive from taxes on the rich. ∎

5

Inequality, Ethnic Divisions, and the Democratic Process

Chapter 4 described how ethnic and class identities could be integrated into a distributive theory of elections, where parties form and compete in response to social structure. The central insight from the chapter concerned the interaction of the number of nonrich (n_{NR}) and the number in the majority group (n_A). As the party representing the smaller of these two groups has an advantage, whether a class-based or ethnic party wins should be influenced by the relative sizes of these two groups.

This chapter uses the theoretical model to develop substantive expectations about electoral competition and policy outcomes, but I first take up the question of whether it makes sense to treat the number of nonrich as exogenous in the first place. Why can't the winning party simply use policy to determine the number of "nonrich" voters following an election (e.g., by setting an income-based threshold for receiving benefits)? The answer to this question provides part of the answer to a second question posed in this chapter, which concerns measuring the number of nonrich. I argue that the Gini coefficient is an appropriate substantive measure because it emerges analytically from the parameters in the model and because it is related to the types of policies that a class-based party could be expected to implement if elected.

If the Gini is a reasonable proxy for the number of nonrich, what is a reasonable proxy for n_A, the size of the majority group? I argue that "ethnic polarization" (EP) is the most appropriate measure of ethnic diversity, with ethnic polarization decreasing as n_A increases. Ethnic polarization is preferable to the main alternative, ethnolinguistic fractionalization (ELF), because it more clearly taps the degree to which the size of a majority ethnic coalition departs from a bare majority.

With the Gini coefficient of inequality and ethnic polarization as measures of the central parameters in the model, it is possible to state the main substantive elements of the argument in terms of ethnic diversity and inequality. The interaction of these two variables should be related to the nature of electoral competition, and in particular the importance of income and ethnic identity in voting. And the variables should also be related to the extent to which government policy should redress inequality.

5.1 WHY CAN'T THE GOVERNMENT SIMPLY DETERMINE n_{NR}?

The assumption in the theoretical model that there are only two incomes is made for analytic convenience to convey intuitions, and so doing follows a modeling strategy that is widely used in the political economy literature. But an alternative approach, one that is widely used in standard "tax-and-transfer" models, is to assume that there is a continuous distribution of incomes, and that "n_{NR}" – the set of individuals who receive redistributive benefits – is determined by the winning party, which uses policy to determine which individual incomes will be eligible to receive government benefits.

Governments must decide both how to collect and distribute revenues. The standard tax-and-transfer model collapses these two decisions into one. A common assumption, for example, is that governments set only the tax rate, and that revenues must be shared equally among all voters. This modeling strategy is very tractable: the assumption of equal shares in distribution converts two dimensions – revenue and spending policy – into one, and thus leads to standard median voter results (on the tax dimension). As the median income is less than the mean, the preferred tax rate for the median voter increases – and the amount of redistribution that occurs increases – as inequality increases (i.e., the distance between the median and mean income increases). Viewed this way, the intensity of "class politics" – and the redistributive consequences of democracy – are achieved exclusively through tax rates at the revenue collection stage.

The median voter result just described relies on the useful simplifying assumption that parties cannot target specific voters. Such targeting is nonetheless the bread and butter of actual electoral politics. Parties argue about who will get what, and their policies vary in the distributive consequences not simply because of the way they tax, but also because of the way they spend. Indeed, in developing countries, taxes on individual incomes often represent a relatively small proportion of total government revenues, with much of the pie coming from natural resources, other commodities, foreign aid, sales from state-owned industries, or tariffs on international trade. In such cases, the distributive consequences of spending are particularly central in electoral competition, making it useful to explore models that allow credible commitments on the spending side.

In the "class-only" tax-and-transfer models, if parties could target any voter they wished, we would be back to the problems of pure distributive models discussed in conjunction with Figure 3.1 in Chapter 3. Assume, for example, that voters are arrayed from poorest to richest along a single income dimension, that there is an exogenous pie to be distributed, and that parties compete by stating the *highest point* in the income distribution that will be eligible for redistributive benefits. This assumption imposes a redistributive mandate on party competition – for example, it precludes distribution to a rich person at the expense of a nonrich one – and it has been made in models such as that of Iversen and Soskice (2006). Under this assumption, a party representing the nonrich could target the median income in society (and everyone below), and would defeat a party targeting any voter with a higher income (and everyone below). In such a framework, n_{NR}, as conceptualized in the identity politics model developed here, would be endogenously determined by government policy and would always include "50%+1" individuals. If this approach to "class politics" were embedded in a model of identity politics like the one described earlier, "class politics" would alway win because the winning party could use "income" to carve out the smallest majority. One could not of course use a marker like ethnic identity in the same way because it is not a continuous metric like income.

It is worth highlighting a couple of limitations inherent to developing a "class-only" theory in this way. First, such a model would predict that only class politics will prevail, that democratic competition always results in policies that reduce inequality, and that voting behavior will divide sharply along income lines. Each of these implications is suspect empirically. Second, the "redistributive consequences" of democracy in such a model are assumed ex ante, through the assumption that politicians target voters with income below an upper threshold. But why assume that politicians must target the nonrich? If politicians can set a precise upper bound on who receives benefits, why not assume they can also set a precise lower bound? A plausible variant of the tax-and-transfer model just described might have parties set an interval in the income distribution,

$[\underline{x}, \bar{x}]$, where $\underline{x}$ is the lower bound on incomes that receive distributive benefits and $\bar{x}$ is the upper bound. A minimal majority could be described with many $[\underline{x}, \bar{x}]$. Parties, for example, could target the 50%+1 richest individuals just as easily as the 50%+1 nonrichest individuals. And they could target any 50%+1 interval in between the nonrichest majority and the richest majority, making it unclear how to think about what would happen in such a framework.

Third, ignoring these issues, suppose there is something about democratic politics that encourages parties to target the median voter and everyone below. For this strategy to produce bare winning majorities, parties must be able to target benefits to voters very accurately: the individual with the median income and everyone with a lower income than the median receive benefits, but everyone with an income even one penny higher does not. This is a strong assumption, and we can imagine problems that voters might have with viewing such promises as credible. Even within this framework, however, we can imagine that n_{NR} could represent the expected size of a class coalition when governments try to target benefits to everyone at or below the median income. I return to this interpretation below when I describe the link between n_{NR} and the Gini.

In sum, the assumption of only two incomes is obviously a strong one, and some may prefer instead to assume there exists a continuous income distribution and that government policy establishes which voter incomes receive distributive benefits. But such an approach raise its own set of questions and leads to the uncomfortable conclusion that ethnic politics can never defeat class politics. The hope is that by making the "two-incomes" assumption, even though it has its own limitations, it might be possible to gain insights that help us make progress on the empirical front.

5.2 THE GINI COEFFICIENT OF INEQUALITY AND THE NUMBER OF NONRICH

Intuitively it makes sense to think about n_{NR} as a measure of inequality. If there are a fixed number of individuals in society, if a rich person becomes nonrich, that is, if n_R goes down by 1 and n_{NR} goes up by 1, inequality increases. Thus, n_{NR} is positively related to inequality, and the arguments about n_{NR} are arguments about inequality. But what type of inequality?

Inequality can be measured in different ways. Prominent recent research, for example, focuses on how income shares of the very richest individuals has been growing (e.g., Piketty 2014). Others focus on differences between the rich and nonrich, say the income of the individual at the 90th percentile and the individual at the 10th percentile in the income distribution. Such measures, however, do not capture the idea of n_{NR} in the model. Rather, if n_{NR} is related to a measure of inequality, the measure of inequality should be linked to variation in the size of a coalition that would share in government distribution if such distribution were based on income. In this section, I argue that there are two ways to think about how n_{NR} is related to the Gini coefficient, perhaps the most well-known measure of inequality.

The first approach simply involves showing that n_{NR} as used in the model is related mathematically to the Gini. The Gini coefficient, which ranges from 0 (perfect equality) to 1 (maximal inequality, where one person controls all the income), can be depicted by the Lorenz curve. The x-axis of the Lorenz curve depicts the different percentiles in the income distribution, with individuals arrayed from poorest to richest. The y-axis depicts the proportion of income held by all individuals below each percentile. If the two numbers are equal – that is, if the individuals below the 30th percentile in the income distribution have 30 percent of income, the individuals below the 50th percentile in the income distribution have 50 percent of income, the individuals below the 90th percentile have 90 percent of the income, and so on for each possible percentile, then the Lorenz curve is a 45-degree line representing perfect equality.

Incomes are of course never perfectly equal, so the Gini coefficient is derived from comparing a given income distribution with this 45-degree line representing perfect equality. Two examples when incomes are continuous are found in the top panel of Figure 5.1 . The figure depicts two Lorenz curves, one solid, one dashed, as well as the 45-degree line. For the solid curve, the individuals below the 50th percentile have roughly 25 percent of the income in society (as marked by the solid circle). Similarly, the individuals below the 80th percentile have 60 percent of the income (as marked by the open circle). For the dashed curve, the individuals below the 50th percentile have roughly 8 percent of the income (as marked by the solid square) and the individuals below the 80th percentile have just under 30 percent of income (as marked by the open circle). The areas marked A (the area between the curve and the 45-degree line) and B (the area southeast of the curve) in the figure can be used to calculate the Gini coefficient, which is given by $G = \frac{A}{A+B}$. As inequality increases, the Lorenz curve will bend to the southeast – the area in A will increase and the area in B will decrease. At the extreme of inequality, where one person controls all of the income in society, the

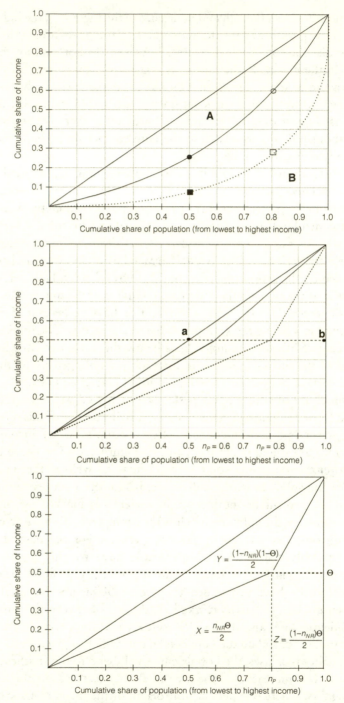

FIGURE 5.1. The number of nonrich voters and the Gini.

area A will comprise all of the area under the 45-degree line and $G = 1$. At the other extreme of perfect equality, the Lorenz curve will follow the 45-degree line, and the area B will comprise all of the area under the 45-degree line (with the area A equal to 0). For continuous distributions of income, where the Lorenz curve is given by $L(x)$, the Gini coefficient is

$$G = 1 - 2 \int_0^1 L(x)\, dx. \tag{5.1}$$

Now consider the Lorenz curve when there are only two incomes, rich and nonrich. To link variation in n_{NR} to variation in the Gini, we need to make an assumption about the incomes of the rich and nonrich, and to make valid comparisons across different n_{NR}, we want to hold the total income in society fixed (so that we are changing only the distribution of individuals across incomes, not the wealth of society). To this end, it is useful to assume that nonrich and rich each control a specific proportion of income in society. Suppose, for example, that the proportion of total income control by the nonrich control is Θ (and that the rich control $1 - \Theta$). Since the population has measure 1 (see appendix in Chapter 4), for the nonrich to have lower incomes than the rich, we need $\Theta < n_{NR}$.

Consider the middle panel in Figure 5.1, where $\Theta = 0.5$. Perfect equality would imply $n_{NR} = 0.5$, which I rule out by assuming there are more nonrich than rich. Because the nonrich control half the income and the incomes are identical among members of the rich and nonrich groups, the Lorenz curve is composed of two line segments: a straight line from $(0, 0)$ to $(n_{NR}, 0.5)$, and a straight line continuing from $(n_{NR}, 0.5)$ to $(1, 1)$. If $n_{NR} = 0.6$, so that 60 percent of the population is nonrich, then the Lorenz curve is depicted by the solid line going from $(0, 0)$ to $(0.6, 0.5)$ and continuing to $(1, 1)$. The dashed line depicts the case where $n_{NR} = 0.8$, which occurs where 80 percent of the population is sharing 50 percent of the income. Obviously the Gini is greater in the second case than in the first. In general, as n_{NR} goes from 0.5 to 1, the point of inflection in the Lorenz curve will go from point **a** to point **b** in the figure.

It is straightforward to show that the formula for the Gini can be derived directly from n_{NR}. Returning to the top panel, the Gini is given by $G = \frac{A}{A+B}$, and $A + B = \frac{1}{2}$, so $G = 1 - 2B$. Now consider the bottom panel, where where X, Y, and Z represent three components of B that are straightforward to calculate. Simple algebra shows that

$$G = \Theta(2n_{NR} - 1).$$

Thus, all else equal, as n_{NR} goes up, the Gini increases. It is worth observing that although n_{NR} maps directly to the Gini, like any measure of inequality, the Gini collapses two types of information about the income distribution into a single number. One is the number of individual at different income levels (n_{NR}, for example) and the other is the actual income of individuals at different income levels (Θ, for example). The Gini could therefore vary without changes in n_{NR} if only the income of the richest person changed. There are important methodological debates about which particular types of inequality measures are most appropriate for particular research questions (e.g., De Maio 2007), but there is no measure that does not have trade-offs given the incorporation of both types of information. Thus, although this noise inherent to the Gini is unfortunate, it nonetheless captures the key parameter in the model as well as we can hope to do.

n_{NR} *and the Gini in a Median Voter Framework.* The central intuition of the model concerns how the ability of parties to make credible distributive proposals is constrained by the size of the groups they represent. But what if instead of assuming two income groups, we assumed n_{NR} is endogenously determined by the efforts of a class-based "party of the nonrich" to target the median voter. Can this framework be consistent with the "group size" framework here? It can if a class-based party cannot target perfectly those individuals with incomes at or below the median income.

Let $\bar{x}_{50}$ be income of the voter with the median income. Suppose a class party cannot precisely target the median income, but rather distributes the pie to voters who have an income $I \leq \bar{x}_{50} + \epsilon$, where $\epsilon > 0$ is some "insurance policy" that the class party uses to ensure it has majority support. If the median voter has an income of 100, for example, we might imagine that a class-based party cannot perfectly target those with incomes exactly 100 or less, but rather would ensure a majority by offering benefits to those with an income that is somewhere near 100 (or less), say at 105. Then for any ϵ, the proportion of the population that receives government benefits will increase as there are a greater proportion of voters near the median income. That is, if a relatively large proportion of the population that is richer than the median are very close to the median income, then the credible commitments of class parties will be to a relatively large number of voters.

Consider Figure 5.2, a histogram describing the distribution of household incomes in Brazil and Bulgaria. In Brazil, more than 12 percent of the population is included in the median income bin, and roughly

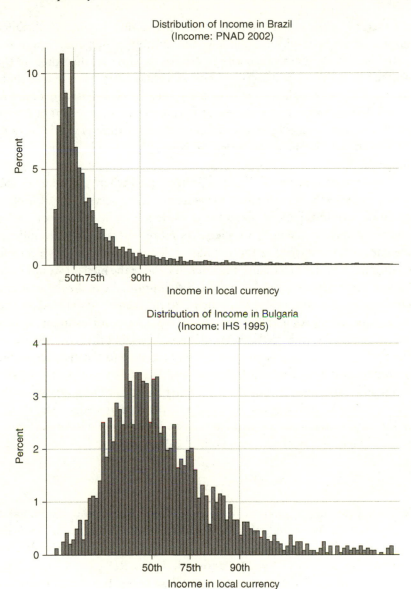

FIGURE 5.2. Income distributions in Brazil and Bulgaria.

17 percent of the population are in the three income bins (out of 100) adjacent to the median. And incomes are quite compressed just above the median. One can see this compression by noting how close the income of the individual at the 75th percentile is to the median, compared to, say,

the income of the individual at the 90th percentile. To put this distance in perspective, consider the income distribution in Bulgaria, where the individual at the 75th percentile is almost as close to the voter at the 90th as to the voter at the 50th. Thus, if a class party were to distribute to $\bar{x}_{50} + \epsilon$, more individuals would receive the class-based benefits in Brazil than in Bulgaria. It is therefore reasonable to assume that in Brazil, credible commitments by parties to class-based coalitions would have to be spread over larger proportions of voters than would be the case in Bulgaria.

From the perspective of a median voter model where class parties can target imperfectly, a reasonable measure of the expected size of a class coalition would therefore take into consideration the density of voters above the median income in society. As more voters cluster around the median, a party targeting the median will represent a larger electoral coalition. One way to measure such density above the median would be to choose some percentile in the income distribution above the median and compare the income at this percentile to (a) the income of the median and (b) the income at some richer percentile. Figure 5.2, for example, marks the income at the 50th, 75th, and 90th percentiles. In Brazil, the income at the 75th percentile is closer to the median (relative to the distance to the 90th percentile) than it is in Bulgaria, and as already noted, the density of incomes just above the median is higher in Brazil. Formally we could choose some $\bar{x}_n \in (\bar{x}_{50}, \bar{x}_{n'}]$ and then calculate the relative distance, $RD_{x_n}^{x_{n'}}$, to the median and to the richer person at $\bar{x}_{n'}$. For example, as in the figure, we could let for $n = 75$ and $n' = 90$ and calculate

$$RD_{75}^{90} = \frac{\bar{x}_{90} - \bar{x}_{75}}{\bar{x}_{75} - \bar{x}_{50}}.$$

When we do this calculation for Brazil, $RD_{75}^{90} = 2.22$ and for Bulgaria $RD_{75}^{90} = 1.28$. We could of course choose some other point between the 50th and 90th percentile. If we focus on the 60th percentile, for example, in Brazil $RD_{60}^{90} = 11.9$ and in Bulgaria $RD_{75}^{90} = 7.2$. Thus, if a class party targeted the median voter (and all voters below this point) by offering $\bar{x}_{50} + \epsilon$, the class party would distribute to more voters in Brazil than in Bulgaria because there are many more voters near the median in Brazil.

From a "median voter" perspective, then, a reasonable proxy for n_{NR} would be a variable like RD_{75}^{90} that measures the extent to which incomes are concentrated or dispersed in the region of the income distribution above the median. Unfortunately, calculating such a measure requires very detailed information about the income distribution, which is not widely available. But data on Gini coefficients are widely available, and the Gini will capture much of the same information that is captured by, for example, RD_{75}^{90}. Recall from the discussion of the Lorenz curve in the preceding text that the Gini will increase as the proportion of income held by individuals at the nth percentile decreases. Similarly, $RD_{x_n}^{x_{n'}}$ will increase as the income of the person at $\bar{x}_n$ moves closer to the median income. So an increase in $RD_{x_n}^{x_{n'}}$ must correlate with an increase in the Gini.

We can see that this is true empirically. In the Brazil distribution depicted earlier, the Gini is 0.58 whereas it is 0.27 in Bulgaria. In addition, I have identified high-quality fine-grained household income or expenditure surveys from 23 countries that are very diverse in their levels of inequality (with Gini ranging from 0.25 to 0.62). Using these surveys to calculate RD_{75}^{90} yields a correlation of RD_{75}^{90} and Gini of 0.81. The choice of $n = 75$ and $n' = 90$ is of course somewhat arbitrary, so I have also calculated RD_{60}^{90} and the correlation with the Gini is 0.76. Thus, if one prefers to impose a "median voter" framework on class politics, the Gini is a reasonable proxy for the expected size of a class coalitions because it provides crucial information about how concentrated the income distribution is in the region just above the median, which should affect the types of policies that class-based parties can credibly promise.

5.3 THE NUMBER IN THE MAJORITY GROUP, n_A

The theoretical framework assumes there are only two ethnic groups, a simplifying assumption that makes it easier to convey the logic of how the size of an ethnic electoral majority shapes party politics and the salience of particular identities. The real world, of course, does not have societies that neatly divide into two groups, and it is important to consider how to translate n_A into a measure the maps nicely to the logic of the model. This first requires that we identify ethnic groups.

For the purposes here, where we wish to understand when ethnic identity will become salient in electoral competition, it is important not to allow their political salience determine the identification of groups. Instead, we wish to identify individual markers that are difficult to change, and that in principle could be used as a basis for inclusion and exclusion. To this end, I rely on Fearon's (2003) definition of groups. Fearon (2003) nicely describes many of the problems inherent to defining a list of ethnic groups, including the impossibility of implementing a purely primordialist perspective (where there is an effort to base definitions more or less on biological factors), the perils of defining groups post hoc based on their emergence in contexts of research interest, and the fact that there are multiple identities (e.g., language and race), some of which are nested, with groups having subgroups. Fearon argues that ideally we would define groups based on the perspective of individuals within a country regarding which groups are socially relevant, a conceptual approach that itself could be plagued by disagreements within a society.

What makes the Fearon definition of groups particularly attractive in the research here is that he is quite cognizant of the importance of defining groups in a way that does not depend on their political relevance. His approach is driven by a conceptualization of a "prototypical" ethnic group. There are seven features of a prototypical group, which are, quoting from Fearon (2003):

1. "Membership in the group is reckoned primarily by descent by both members and non-members."
2. "Members are conscious of group membership and view it as normatively and psychologically important to them."
3. "Members share some distinguishing cultural features, such as common language, religion, and customs."
4. "These cultural features are held to be valuable by a large majority of members of the group."
5. "The group has a homeland, or at least 'remembers' one."
6. "The group has a shared and collectively represented history as a group. Further, this history is not wholly manufactured, but has some basis in fact."
7. "The group is potentially "stand alone" in a conceptual sense – that is, it is not a caste or caste-like group (e.g., European nobility or commoners)." (Fearon 2003, p. 201)

Fearon's conceptualization clearly leads to definitions of groups that allow group identity to serve as a basis for inclusion or exclusion (primarily because of the role of "descent" and the importance of "distinguishing cultural feature," and also because of the role of a homeland). And it is flexible in the sense that it makes it possible to define groups based on a range of characteristics, including religion, ethnicity, language, tribe, and race. And equally important is what is not on the list, which is the political salience of groups themselves. As Fearon nicely summarizes, any list of groups in a country should be based on "the idea that members and non-members recognize the distinction [on which group identity is based] and anticipate that significant actions are or *could be* conditioned on it" (p. 198, emphasis mine). For both conceptual and empirical purposes, then, the criteria used by Fearon are attractive for the purposes here.

The theoretical framework requires that we take information about the distribution of group identities and link it to the size of an ethnic-based coalition. We therefore need to aggregate information about group size. There are two measures that are widely used in this regard. The most well-known is fractionalization, or ELF (for "ethno-linguistic fractionalization"). ELF measures the probability that two randomly chosen individuals will not belong to the same group, and it increases as the number of groups proliferate or as the groups become more equal in size. It is written as

$$\text{ELF} = 1 - \sum_{i=1}^{G} s_i^2, \tag{5.2}$$

where s_i is the proportion of individuals who belong to group i and there are G groups.

The second approach, *ethnic polarization* ("EP"), was originally developed to study civil conflict, and is based on the idea that conflict is most likely when there are two groups of equal size. If there is a group that has a small majority and a group that has a large minority, the potential for conflict should be much greater than if there is a dominant group or a proliferation of groups (see Reynal-Querol 2002 and Montalvo and Reynal-Querol 2005 for a discussion). EP is written as

$$EP = 1 - \sum_{i=1}^{G} \left(\frac{1/2 - s_i}{1/2} \right)^2 s_i. \tag{5.3}$$

As Montalvo and Reynal-Querol (2005) demonstrate, ELF and EP are highly correlated when ELF is relatively low (below around 0.25). But in mid-ranges of ELF, there is no correlation between ELF and EP, and at high ELF, the two measures are negatively correlated. Thus, the choice between them is not trivial.

An appropriate measure for testing the argument should take a higher value as the size of a winning majority gets smaller, and in some respects, both EP and ELF could work. For example, if there were a majority and a minority group, then both measures would increase as the majority group gets smaller. Similarly, if there were a majority group and a fixed number of equal sized minority groups, then both measures would increase as the majority group got smaller. But suppose you had one country where a majority group had 51 percent of the population and a minority group had 49 percent. This would yield an ELF of close to 0.5 and and EP of close to 1. Now compare this to a situation in which the groups proliferated, say now there are five equal-sized groups. Now ELF rises to 0.8 and EP drops to 0.64. But according to the theory, an ethnic coalition would be more attractive in the first case. In general, there is no theoretical reason to believe that as groups proliferate, voters should expect an ethnic majority to grow smaller, as happens with the ELF measure.

This observation also raises an issue regarding bargaining across groups that is outside the theoretical argument presented earlier. Suppose there were many groups, say 100, each of roughly equal size. This would make it possible to fashion a small ethnic majority, but there would be many small majorities, creating the problem that arrises with atomistic voters. In addition, the proliferation of groups will introduce bargaining costs across groups. Suppose we had one case in which there was a majority group with 51 percent of the vote and two equal size minority groups. This would yield an ELF of 0.62 and an EP of 0.87. Compare this with the case where the majority group of 51 percent was split into three groups of 17 percent each, making it possible for the three groups to form an electoral coalition representing 51 percent. Should we expect this change to make ethnic politics more attractive to the individuals in the majority or less attractive? It seems that voters should have more confidence about what they would receive under ethnic politics if they are in a single group of 51 percent than if they are part of a coalition of three groups that together represent 51 percent, because the first situation avoids any problems that are likely to exist in having the different groups bargain with each other (which may be enhanced by past disputes between groups or by cultural differences) and in having groups commit to excluding other groups from the coalition. Thus, if the measure of ethnic diversity captures how attractive are ethnic politics, we would want the measure to take a higher value in the first case than in the second. This is true for the EP measure (which goes from 0.99 to 0.63 as one moves from the first case to the second) but is not true for an ELF measure, which increases with the proliferation of groups (and goes from 0.50 to 0.87 as one moves from the first case to the second). This example also highlights why it is more attractive to use the polarization measure than a measure that simply measures the size of the smallest possible ethnic coalition. Such a simple count, for example, would privilege a majority of three groups of 17 percent each over a majority of one group at 53 percent, but in the first case we would have to worry about ignoring the bargaining costs across groups. It is appropriate and useful, then, to focus on a measure of ethnic polarization as a proxy for the attractiveness of ethnic politics in elections.

5.4 INEQUALITY, ETHNIC DIVERSITY, AND IDENTITY POLITICS

I can now link the intuitions about group size in the theoretical model to empirically testable arguments. The theoretical framework suggests that the relationship between the number of nonrich (n_{NR}) and the number in the majority ethnic group (n_A) shapes which types of "identity" will prevail in electoral behavior and how government resources will be distributed. Since the Gini coefficient is a reasonable proxy for n_{NR} and ethnic polarization is a reasonable (albeit negatively related) proxy for n_A, we can state the expectation from the argument in terms of these measures of economic inequality and ethnic polarization.

In general, as *inequality increases* (n_{NR} increases), it is more difficult for class parties to win, and as *ethnic polarization increases* (n_A decreases) it is easier for ethnic parties to win. Importantly, however, the model also emphasizes the relative levels of inequality and ethnic polarization. Class politics can most easily emerge at low levels of inequality, but how low inequality must go depends on the size of the alternative ethnic coalition, and thus on ethnic polarization. Similarly, ethnic politics can most easily emerge when ethnic polarization is high, but how high ethnic polarization must be depends on the size of class coalitions, and thus on inequality. The model therefore encourage us to consider their interaction. In the empirical chapters that follow, I discuss the types of results from models with interactions that would be consistent (or not) with the theoretical argument.

Expectations Regarding Voting Behavior. When ethnic politics prevails in equilibrium, the rich split their vote (with the rich in one group supporting a different party than the rich in the other group) and the nonrich split their vote. By contrast, when class politics has an advantage, the rich vote together and the nonrich vote together. Thus, the relationship between income and voting behavior should be a function of whether class or ethnic politics prevails, which is a function of the interaction of ethnic polarization and inequality. As inequality increases relative to ethnic polarization, ethnic politics should be stronger, and there should be a weaker relationship between income and the vote.

It is worth noting that standard tax-and-transfer models should lead to quite different predictions. If we assume that income must determine distributive benefits, then the effect of inequality on voting behavior should be independent of the level of ethnic polarization. And inequality should strengthen the relationship between income and the vote: as the rich become relatively richer, there is more to be gained by the lower half of the income distribution from banding together and forcing rich-to-poor redistribution, and more by the rich to protect from such redistribution.

The model presented in the preceding text is based on the assumption that ethnic identity is particularly useful attribute for credible commitments to voters when the conditions for class politics are relatively weak. This leads to a second expectation from the model concerning voting. When the conditions for class politics are weak, voters should sort themselves more clearly by ethnic identity, and the ethnic bases of support for parties should be stronger. I can therefore test the micro-level voting implications of the model in two ways, one concerning the relationship between income and the vote (a measure of class politics) and one concerning the ethnic bases of support for parties (a measure of ethnic politics). Both should be related to the conditions for class politics, and thus to the interaction of ethnic polarization and inequality.

Expectations Concerning Redistribution. The second empirical implication of the theory explored in the text that follows concerns the impact of government policy on inequality. In the model, when ethnic politics prevails, some nonrich voters (those in the losing ethnic group) receive no distributive benefits and some rich voters (those in the winning group) receive distributive benefits. By contrast, when class politics prevails, all the nonrich receive distributive benefits and rich voters receive nothing. Thus, the redistributive effect of government policy should depend on the conditions for ethnic and class politics, and thus on the interaction of inequality and ethnic polarization.

It is useful to juxtapose the impact of ethnic diversity on redistribution in this model compared to that in previous research, which has also emphasized that ethnic diversity can diminish redistribution. The argument here differs in two respect from these existing arguments. The first concerns the mechanism. As note in Chapter 2, existing research often emphasizes intergroup antipathies: nonrich essentially shoot themselves in the foot economically by supporting parties that oppose redistribution, and they do this to avoid helping people from groups they do not like. Because ethnic differences create the antipathies, redistribution should be less in diverse societies (e.g., Gilens 1999; Alesina and Glaser 2003). As in these existing studies, redistribution in the argument here will often be lower when ethnic politics prevails than when class politics prevail, but the logic is quite different. In the model here, voters act purely out of economic self-interest, not because they are distracted by some second dimension, such as group-based antipathy. Ethnic politics can nonetheless prevail because some poorer voters do better by supporting parties that distribute government resources based on ethnic rather than class identity. Thus, ethnic politics is one that divides some nonrich voters against other nonrich voters precisely because this helps these voters do better economically. Second, from the intergroup antipathies framework, economic inequality plays no role in determining when ethnic diversity can lead to the election of parties that oppose class-based parties. Here, inequality plays a central mediating role. If ethnic polarization is sufficiently high, anti-redistributive politics should be more likely when inequality is high.

Expectations Concerning Democratization. The theoretical model presented in this book does not explicitly examine democratization by autocratic elites, or incentives and capacity of citizens to mobilize for democracy. But the theoretical model has clear implications for the redistributive consequences of democracy, and these implications could be incorporated into existing frameworks for thinking about strategic democratization. A central premise in these theories is that autocratic elites are rich, and thus will lose economically under democracy. A question one must therefore ask is, "What will be the cost of democracy for the rich?" Existing models invoke a class-based tax-and-transfer framework where under democracy, more inequality leads to more redistribution. Thus, the cost to the rich of democratizing increases as inequality increases. Boix (2003) uses this intuition to suggest that more inequality should lead to less democratization. Acemoglu and Robinson (2005) emphasize that there are several channels by which inequality influences expected patterns of democratization: by affecting the incentives of elites to democratize (as inequality increases, elites have more to lose from the redistribution that occurs under democracy); by affecting the capacity of elites to repress mass (repression capacity increases with inequality); by affecting incentives of citizens to revolt against elites (more inequality increases incentives); and by the capacity of citizens to revolt (more inequality decreases capacity). Their model leads to the expectation of an inverted-U relationship between democracy and democratic transitions, with most democratization occurring at intermediate levels of inequality. At low levels of inequality, there are few incentives for social mobilization against democracy, and at high levels elites have a high repression capacity and considerable incentives to repress, while citizens have a low capacity to revolt. At intermediate levels, masses have incentives and capacity to press for democracy.

The theoretical model in this book would emphasize a different relationship between inequality and the cost of democracy. First, it would suggest that the effect of inequality should depend on the level of ethnic polarization. Second, when ethnic polarization is sufficiently large, inequality should discourage class-based politics. Because class-based politics is more redistributive than ethnic politics, the redistributive cost to democracy should be *smallest* when inequality is *highest*.

5.5 SUMMARY

This chapter has argued that n_{NR} – the number of nonrich in the model – can be measured using the Gini coefficient of inequality, which emerges directly from the model parameters, and which also captures the types of offers that class-based parties can credibly offer to voters if policy can only imperfectly target the median income. I have also argued that n_A – the size of the majority group – is best measured using ethnic polarization. When ethnic polarization is high, n_A is small. Thus, these two measures can be used to test implications of the model concerning voting behavior and redistribution.

PART II

EMPIRICAL EVIDENCE FOR THE ARGUMENT

Part II includes four chapters focusing on the empirical implications of the theoretical argument developed in Part I. Chapter 6 discusses the issue of identifying causal effects. My empirical evidence does not allow me to estimate causal effects of anything at all, which leaves open a host of questions about what we should believe following the presentation of such evidence. I point out that a focus on identification issues can create unhelpful biases in how we do social science research. More importantly, I argue for a particular way to integrate theory with empirical research, one that can help us update our beliefs about causality even when we do not have direct empirical evidence of causal effects.

Chapters 7 to 9 present the empirical evidence. The theoretical argument suggests that the relationship between income and the vote should be strongest when the conditions for class politics related to inequality and ethnic polarization are strongest. Chapter 7 explores this theoretical implications by estimating individual-level models of vote choice across a range of countries. The argument also suggests that we should see stronger ethnic bases of support when the conditions for class politics are weak. This is the focus of Chapter 8.

After exploring patterns related to voting behavior in Chapters 7 and 8, Chapter 9 turns to macropolitical outcomes. The main focus of the chapter is on whether patterns of redistribution are consistent with the theory, where redistribution is highest when the conditions for class politics are strongest. In addition, I explore indirect implications of the model for understanding transitions to democracy.

6

Theory and Causal Identification

A central emphasis in recent empirical social science research is that we should be skeptical of what we can learn from traditional regression-type approaches to analyzing observational data. This presents an obvious problem for me, as I hope the reader will take my evidence seriously, but I will be employing the sort of cross-national regressions that are often viewed as particularly unconvincing. The purpose of this chapter is to address this skepticism in two ways. First, I argue that the research tools that have been developed to address the shortcomings of traditional methods are much better suited for addressing some types of empirical questions than others. As a consequence, when we emphasize the use of these tools we bias our research agendas against exploring particular types of research questions. By thinking about the types of questions for which the methods are least well suited to study, it becomes clear why it would be essentially impossible to apply these methods to the questions central to this book. Thus, to test the theory I employ traditional methods.

But the fact that I must rely on the traditional methods does not obviate the concerns about them. My second response is to argue that we can learn the most from traditional methods if we carefully integrate theory and empirical work. Specifically, by developing theories that imply a range of related but conceptually distinct empirical relationships and by examining evidence for the range of these relationships, we can increase our confidence in the theory, even when evidence for specific relationships implied by the theory has the flaws of traditional approaches. And if we can increase our confidence in the theory, we should increase our confidence in the causal processes implied by the theory. A tighter integration of theory – as narrowly conceived here – and empirical evidence can therefore help us make progress on the types of questions that research methods focusing on causal identification are least well equipped to address. This is the approach I follow, and in this chapter, I develop these two responses in turn, beginning with the argument about biased agendas in research motivated by causal identification.

6.1 THE BIAS OF IDENTIFICATION-DRIVEN RESEARCH AGAINST STUDIES LIKE THE ONE IN THIS BOOK

The central problem with traditional regression-based approaches to observational data is biased parameter estimates. The most troublesome sources of bias are usually measurement error, unclear or reciprocal directions of causation, and omitted control variables. Concern about bias has led scholars to develop and emphasize new empirical approaches that involve some sort of "randomization." The randomization is often real, as occurs in lab, field, and survey experiments. The "randomization" can also involve using observational data in ways that aim to mimic actual randomization, such as exploiting natural experiments, using instrumental variables, or examining regression discontinuities. Since the goal driving these alternative approaches is empirical causal identification, I will call these methods "identification driven research" (or "IDR").[1]

The power of IDR typically stems from two characteristics. The first is a focus on particular cases. Experiments, for example, are a form of case study in which random assignment of a treatment variable occurs in a specific, well-defined context. Regression discontinuity approaches, or, relatedly, approaches that rely on natural experiments, have the same flavor, exploiting a narrow and well-defined context to make inferences about causality. In general, the extent to which IDR convincingly addresses questions of causality is strongly correlated with the specificity of the case being studied. The second characteristic of IDR is a focus on "treatment variables" that can be reasonably viewed as exogenous and randomly assigned. In the context of experimental research, this means that in practice, IDR typically involves treatments of individuals, and estimating the effect of individual response to treatments is the central concern.

---

[1] I will ignore the use of instrumental variables in what follows. It is extremely difficult using instrumental variables (IVs) to meet the standards for casual identification that are at the heart of IDR (e.g., Deaton 2010), particularly when we need to instrument for highly endogenous macrovariables such as income, inequality, and ethnic identity across a wide range of contexts, as would be necessary in this book.

These two characteristics lead to clear limitations – or biases – in the types of questions for which IDR can offer convincing answers, and thus in the types of questions explored in such research. It is useful to think about these biases from the perspective of the issues that motivate the research in this book. The first bias is against studying questions where there is strong reason to believe that the effects of a variable of interest might vary with the broad social, political, or institutional context. A well-executed IDR can estimate an average treatment effect from the specific case, and with careful forethought can identify how the treatment differentially affects subjects with different characteristics within that case. But given that narrow cases provide the most power in estimating causal effects, it is often a practical challenge to draw inferences from cases if we believe that context affects the size of the treatment. Thus, though it can be possible to design studies that estimate heterogeneous treatment effects, in practice the IDR approaches are often best suited to informing our empirical understanding when we believe that estimated treatment effects are relatively homogeneous across cases.

Consider the example from the theory in this book regarding the link between income and voting behavior, which is the focus of the next chapter. The model suggests that the strength of the income–vote relationship should be related to the social context, and in particular to the levels of inequality and ethnic diversity. The empirical strategy, described in the next chapter, uses a traditional approach to observational data: in broad strokes, using surveys from a range of countries, I regress a measure of vote choice on a measure of income, examining whether the estimated coefficient on income varies with the social context.

These empirical tests are unconvincing from standard perspectives on causal identification. Even setting aside measurement issues with surveys, income is endogenous and correlates with many things we cannot observe. Thus, we can conclude little about the causal effect of income on vote choice using this traditional approach. Moreover, inequality and ethnic diversity are endogenous and correlate with things we cannot observe. Thus, we cannot conclude anything about the causal effects of inequality and ethnic diversity on the causal effect of income on vote choice.

Randomizing the relevant x's might be one response by IDR, but that would be an extraordinary challenge here. Given that income is believed to have a different effect in different contexts, one could not draw inferences about the argument by randomizing income in one setting. Instead, one would need to randomize three variables: income at the individual level, inequality at the system level, and ethnic diversity at the system level (which in turn would require randomizing ethnicity at the individual level). An alternative might be to exploit observational data in a way that permits causal identification. Perhaps there are uncorrelated real-world shocks to individual income, inequality, and ethnic identity that could be used to this end, though I haven't been able to figure out what those would be. Given the nature of the problems with doing convincing IDR on the empirical question here, IDR is unlikely to engage this sort of empirical question. This is an example of how the motivation to identify causal effects can bias us against engaging research questions where there is reason to believe the "treatment" of interest varies with the context.

The second bias is against studying questions where the central explanatory variables are broad features of the social, political, or institutional context. Examples of such socially determined macrovariables include inequality, formal political institutions such as electoral laws or federalism, ethnic divisions (when we take a constructivist perspective on identity), economic development, levels of violence in a community, and levels of redistribution or public goods provision, to name but a few. The challenge of focusing on such explanatory variables from the perspective of IDR is that they are so obviously endogenous. Consider the argument in this book that inequality affects redistribution. Is there a convincing way to think about the average treatment effect of inequality if inequality results from a web of reciprocal relationships, our understanding of which is is limited at best? Even if we could develop a study in which for the specific context it was plausible to view the level of inequality as if randomly assigned, what would we really learn? The challenge is that when "exogenous" causal variables in IDR are endogenous in the real world, it makes interpretation of estimated causal effects quite difficult.

To see the problem, consider an analogy from medicine. A treatment that is "exogenous" in the real world might be a particular drug that a doctor administers for a given disease, or a particular surgical procedure that is selected to address a specific injury. Such treatments are more or less imposed on subjects, even if doctors discuss options with patients. This exogeneity makes the interpretation of evidence from a randomized controlled trial less complicated than is the case when the treatment is endogenous. An endogenous treatment in IDR is one in which the treatment itself is the result of some social and/or individual dynamic in the real world. A good example in medicine is exercise. In the real world, whether an individual undertakes exercise is determined by a variety of factors, some of which we understand, some of which we do not. Among those who choose *not* to exercise, it is not easy to discern why. Some might be true couch potatoes (they absolutely do not want to exercise and therefore do not if given the choice) and others might be frustrated eager beavers (they believe they would like to exercise but life keeps getting in the way). Whether non-exercisers are one or the other type might be genetic, and it might be influenced by their social context – the nature of their job, their family obligations, their colleagues at work, friends, partners, or the nature of the community in which they live. An identification-driven study might respond to this problem by randomizing exercise. One could do so in principle – cudgeling both couch potatoes and frustrated eager beavers in a treatment group into an appropriate level of sweat – and estimate a treatment effect. But if exercise in the real world is endogenous and we don't know a person's type, how could we interpret the estimated causal effect of exercise? Would "forced exercise" have the same effect on couch potatoes as on frustrated eager beavers? Would it have the same effect on individuals where social circles encourage exercise as it would on individuals where social circles discourage exercise? Would exercise that is forced on individuals have the same effect as exercise that is chosen voluntarily?

To interpret the estimated causal effect of a variable that, although plausibly exogenous in a specific IDR, is in fact endogenous in the real world, we need to have a clear understanding of the sources of the endogeneity and how they matter. If the propensity to exercise is social, then imposing it on individuals in communities that sneer at exercise may have the opposite effect as imposing it on communities that sneer at couch potatoes. Returning to the argument in this book, even ignoring the problem of finding a case that resembles randomly assigned economic inequality, given that inequality is part of a complex web of reciprocal relationships, it would be difficult to interpret the meaning of such a study. For this reason, research motivated by identifying causal effects would be unlikely to engage the arguments that are central here, where the concept of causality is murky to begin with.

A third bias, one perhaps less strong than the first two, is against testing arguments about strategic equilibrium behavior. This bias is related to the previous one in that "treatments" in strategic equilibrium arguments are highly endogenous. In the argument in this book, party entrepreneurs respond optimally to each other and to voters, as do voters to each other and to party entrepreneurs. The optimal responses are conditioned by the social context. How would one think about causality or random assignment in this context? Would we want to randomly assign behavior of one actor and see if the other responds as the theory predicts? Would we be confident in any inferences that we draw from such an exercise if in fact we view behavior as mutually reinforcing? Equilibrium arguments obviously produce testable implications that are sometimes tested using the toolkit of IDR, particularly in the lab. But it is probably much more common in political science for IDR research on individual behavior to have a center of gravity rooted more in social psychology, where issues of strategic behavior are not central and where it is reasonable to view treatments as exogenous.

In sum, the methods developed to address issues of causal identification – methods typically involving either direct randomization or the use of observational data in a way that can approximate randomization – are often most convincing when they focus on specific cases, on treatments that can be expected to have similar effects across different kinds of cases, and on explanatory variables that can be reasonably viewed as exogenous in the real world. These methods are most useful for describing causal effects within the cases, but typically struggle to offer convincing evidence about questions where the broader social context plays an important role, either in directly affecting outcomes we care about or in conditioning the effects of other variables we might care about. The methods also tend to be applied to questions where strategic equilibrium behavior is not central, as a good deal is endogenous and mutually reinforcing in such models.

Thus, IDR would be very unlikely to engage the questions central to this research. Hopelessly endogenous variables – particularly inequality but also ethnic diversity – play a central role in the argument. The model suggests that the effects of individual attributes such as income and ethnicity on voting should vary with the broader social context. And the theoretical perspective relies heavily on the notion of strategic equilibrium behavior by parties and voters. Given the problems with establishing causal relationships in an argument of this sort, from the perspective of IDR, it might be better if I simply acknowledged the issues and turn to writing a conclusion that invites the reader to judge the theory on its intuitive appeal.

These biases that IDR creates for our research agendas are not a good thing for social science. Social scientists should not – and thankfully often do not – give up on studying questions where socially determined macrovariables play a leading role, either directly or by influencing the effects of other variables. Such macrovariables, and the thorny webs of reciprocal causation in which they are embedded, are tremendously important to study, both their causes and their consequences. One should hope that IDR figures out better ways to study them, rather than marginalizing them from research agendas, but many of the challenges described here are quite difficult, making it important to think of ways outside the IDR toolkit for making progress.

In the meantime, it is useful to ask whether the cost of any bias to research agendas is worth paying, which requires that we consider the actual gains reaped from a laser focus on identification problems. There is obviously no clear-cut answer to this question, but I am perhaps a bit more skeptical than some because of a bias of my own, which is that the broader macro context in which social behavior unfolds has a large impact on that behavior. Put somewhat differently, my biases cause me to worry about external validity more than most engaging in IDR. Being poor or religious in one country will affect voting behavior differently than being poor or religious in another. The way inequality influences political competition often depends on other factors. The effect of ethnic diversity on redistribution depends on the level of inequality. The effect of development programs will work differently in some communities than in others. To the extent that IDR is most successful at estimating unbiased treatment effects in specific cases, it can be unclear what we learn from specific IDR studies without an extremely expensive and difficult proliferation of IDR.[2]

6.2 THEORY AND CAUSAL INFERENCE

If IDR is unlikely to engage successfully the central empirical questions in this book, what is the way forward? After all, the problems associated with traditional regression-based approaches are no less real when IDR challenges increase. In what follows, I sketch a strategy that invokes a connection between theory and empirics, one that may allow us to learn about causality even if our empirical approach risks bias.

The word "theory" can be used in different ways, and is often used to refer to a causal logic, or mechanism, linking x and y. Testing theories can therefore imply testing mechanisms. In the theory developed here, if the outcome is the level of redistribution, the theoretical mechanism

---

[2] And when research programs lead to the proliferation of cases on the same question, it can be very difficult to draw inferences, as Fearon, Humphreys, and Weinstein (2015) note in their study of community-driven development programs. Furthermore, it is not always clear that we should expect that adding cases will improve the inferences we make (Ioannidis 2005).

might be voting behavior, which determines the electoral outcomes that in turn determine redistributive outcomes. Viewed this way, the tests of voting behavior that follow are "tests of the mechanism," while the tests of redistribution are tests of the outcome if the mechanism is operating.

But this is not the way I want to think about the role of theory. Instead of an argument describing the reasons for a specific causal relationship, we could instead use "theory" to refer to a unified and integrated framework for thinking about different types of empirical relationships and their connections with each other. In physics, superstring theory endeavors to explain *all* fundamental forces in nature, which means that the theory offers a breathtaking range of testable implications (including implications that are not easy to test). Theory has also been central to studies of global warming, where IDR on the effects of human activity is impossible, but where theory-driven models yield a wide range of expectations about patterns we should observe in the world if human activity is contributing to global warming. Social phenomena are much messier than, say, the laws of gravitational or other scientific forces, and it would be strangely optimistic to imagine we could develop something like a general theory of social behavior. The examples of string theory and global warming are nonetheless useful because they remind us that the most useful theories do not provide intuitions about a single empirical relationship, but rather provide intuitions about a range of phenomena and the connections between them.

For this reason, it is not always clear how much we gain when we write down a formal model or other theoretical argument to explain a specific empirical relationship between two variables. An example from this book can be taken from Chapter 4. The chapter explores the model of elections under the assumption of majoritarian and proportional electoral laws, and it shows that we should expect more political parties under proportional representation. If I offered causally identified evidence that the numbers of parties are in fact larger under proportional representation and then held that up as evidence for the theory, one should be skeptical about what we've learned about the theory because there is a wide range of alternative theories linking the electoral law and the number of parties. Similarly, the model in Chapter 4 suggests that when government revenues come from windfalls rather than taxes, there will be an economic cost to the economy. Again, evidence of a relationship between revenues sources and economic development would provide limited support for the theory because there are numerous alternative explanations for this "resource curse." In general, then, although empirical evidence of a specific relationship implied by a theory can be helpful, particularly when the posited relationship has not been previously understood or considered, such evidence typically provides only limited support for the applicability of a specific theory or explanation.

But if we think about a theory as an internally coherent argument for describing why we should expect to observe a range of *different types* of empirical relationships, then testing a theory involves moving beyond considering a specific empirical relationship in isolation from other empirical relationships. Instead, it requires examining a range of relationships implied by the theory. Before elaborating on this idea, it is important to underscore that I am not trying to focus on the importance of using different types of evidence to learn about the causal relationship between some x and some y. King, Keohane, and Verba (1994), for example, emphasize the importance of "multiple observable implications," which implies looking for different ways to measure x and y when doing qualitative research. And Humphreys and Jacobs (2015) describe how qualitative and quantitative data can be combined to improve causal inference about the relationship between x and y. Although both works are valuable contributions to how we can bring different types of evidence to bear on an empirical question about causality, their primary concern is not with theory as I am using the term here.

Suppose that a theory has one empirical implication, $x \to y$, or that empirical research focused exclusively on such a single implication from a theory that has several. As noted previously, if we could provide evidence for this implication, the degree to which we update our beliefs about the theory's plausibility should be modest. If we improved the quality of the tests to increase our confidence regarding the causal relationship between x and y or in the robustness of this relationship, this would improve our confidence regarding how x and y are related, but would not add significantly to our confidence in the theory, or to our understanding of why x and y are related.

Now suppose that a theory has two distinct empirical implications. If we can present evidence for both implications, then the degree to which we can update our beliefs about the plausibility of the theory itself should increase over the case when we find evidence for only one implication. This is particularly true when it is hard to imagine alternative theories that generate the expectation that we should observe both empirical implications. Returning to the example above from this book: isolated evidence that the number of parties is higher under PR would not be convincing evidence for the theory, nor would isolated evidence that windfall revenues should have a negative economic consequences. But the fact that the theory provides intuitions about why both relationships should hold could begin to give us confidence in the theory, particularly if it is difficult to imagine alternative theories suggesting that both relationships should exist in the data. More generally, the richer a theory – that is, the wider the range of substantively distinct empirical implications it implies – the lower the ex ante beliefs we might have about jointly observing this range of implications, and thus the greater our confidence in the theory itself if we observe the range of empirical implications.

This discussion has implications for how we think about what constitutes the most useful sorts of theories. It is easier to draw inferences from data about the plausibility of a theory that says $x_1 \rightarrow y_1$ and $x_1 \rightarrow y_2$ than it is to draw inferences about a theory that says only that $x_1 \rightarrow y_1$. An even better theory, by this logic, might imply that $x_1 \rightarrow y_1, x_1 \rightarrow y_2$ and $x_1 \rightarrow y_3$ because the more relationships implied by a particular theory, the harder it might be to imagine an alternative theory consistent with each of the relationships. For this reason, it is crucial that y_1, y_2, and y_3 be conceptually distinct, not alternative measures of the same underlying concept. From this perspective, we might care not only about how many relationships are implied by a theory, but also what types of relationships the theory implies. We might call the three relationships above *partially overlapping* in that each has a conceptually distinct variable to be explained (y_1, y_2, and y_3), but each invokes the same causal variable (x_1) to explain these distinct variables. When a theory implies overlapping relationships, it might be easier to imagine alternative theories consistent with the relationships than if the theory implies nonoverlapping hypotheses, where both the x's and the y's differ, such as when $x_1 \rightarrow y_1$ and that $x_2 \rightarrow y_2$.

The central point, then, is that theories, as conceptualized here, are more than explanations of singular empirical relationships, and that empirical support for theories therefore requires *constellations of evidence about different types of relationships*. To the extent that such evidence exists, and to the extent that it is difficult to develop alternative explanations for the *constellations* themselves, we can have greater confidence in a theory. Because theories not only explain particular relationships but also help us to see connections in the social world that we might not know to look for in the absence of theories, theory building should be an important component of our research tool box.

The approach in this book adopts this theory-centric perspective on empirical research. The theory has a variety of empirical implications regarding social structure – that is, regarding inequality, ethnic polarization, and their interaction. Social structure should be related to the degree to which an individual's income is related to her voting behavior. It should be related to the circumstances under which parties have strong ethnic bases of support. It should be related to our expectations about redistribution within democracies. And it should be related to the conditions under which we should expect transitions from autocracy to democracy. These are overlapping relationships in the sense that they involve the same explanatory variables, although I have not seen alternative theories that emphasize the interaction of inequality and ethnic diversity, or the connection of social structure to each of these types of outcomes. In addition, the theory suggests a nonoverlapping relationship that I test empirically, which is that the level of ethnic voting itself is related to redistribution. And it has the nonoverlapping relationships mentioned previously – about electoral laws and windfall revenues – that I do not test. If one accepts the value of this theory-centric approach, then even if I cannot provide causal evidence for any particular relationship implied by the theory, and even if there are alternative arguments that are consistent with particular empirical relationships implied by the theory here, if there is evidence for the constellation of theoretical implications, we should increase our confidence in the theoretical framework.

If we think about theories as integrated arguments about diverse but related social relationships, some of which are causal, then theory might be useful not simply for understanding and interpreting the social world, but also for making causal inferences about it. This might be particularly important when we care about relationships that are difficult to test using the methods of IDR. The basic idea is quite simple: if we provide evidence that increases our belief in a theory, then it should increase our belief in the particular causal relationships implied by the theory, even if we cannot apply standard IDR techniques to the particular causal relationships.

Return to the link between income and voting behavior implied by the theory here, and discussed in the previous section. Although we cannot use the traditional cross-national regressions to say something about the causal relationship between income and voting behavior, the theory can be helpful. The key is not to study the income–vote relationship in isolation, but rather to study it as part of a broader empirical investigation of a theory. If we can provide evidence for the constellation of relationships implied by the theory, we should increase our confidence that there exists a causal impact of the macro context on the causal impact of income on the vote, even if we cannot test these causal relationships directly.

This argument informally invokes a Bayesian framework for learning from evidence, as was recently adopted, for example, in the Humphreys and Jacobs (2015) study of how we can learn from combining qualitative and quantitative information. A Bayesian approach begins by acknowledging that when we try to learn about an empirical relationship in social science, we start with a set of beliefs about this relationship. The Bayesian framework provides a way to think about how we should change our beliefs when confronted with new evidence. Because we cannot help but impose our own predilections on our prior beliefs and on the extent to which particular types of evidence cause us to update these beliefs, a Bayesian framework helps us to understand how different types of empirical evidence should affect our beliefs given our predilections.

In most empirical social science, a Bayesian approach is invoked to think about relationships between two variables. The wrinkle here is to add the role of "theory," conceptualized narrowly as a framework that produces and integrates insights about multiple types of empirical relationships. That is, "theory" in the discussion here is a framework for thinking about why we should expect a constellation of empirical relationships. Testing a theory therefore requires evidence about the constellation, and our confidence that the theory is helpful increases as we accumulate evidence for the different relationships implied by the theory.

A tighter integration of theory and empirical research as described here could help diminish concern about bias in traditional approaches when IDR is difficult or impossible. If we develop a hypothesis for a singular relationship that for whatever reason cannot be evaluated using the toolkit from IDR, it is very difficult to draw causal conclusions by focusing on this singular relationship. But if we provide evidence regarding a constellation of relationships that are consistent with a theory, then the risk of bias should have less impact on how we update our beliefs about the theory than in the case of evaluating a singular relationship. Suppose, for example, that the theory predicts $x_1 \rightarrow y_1$ and $x_2 \rightarrow y_2$. The theory implies that both relationships hold in the data, but a potential bias in a separate study of each relationship does not automatically imply a bias in their joint probability. That is, to the extent that the same underlying bias does not lead to "false positives" on each of the theory's implications, evidence for the constellation of empirical implications should increase our confidence in the theory and the causal relationships it implies, even if we lack reliable causal estimates of the specific relationships.

This idea of a tighter link between theory, narrowly conceived, and data is of course only a partial one. Certain issues are ignored, such as how we evaluate a theory when the evidence does not support *all* the theory's posited relationships. And even if the approach is embraced as useful, it is partial in the sense that it cannot help us obtain unbiased estimates of any causal relationships. But we need to think hard about how to make empirical progress on these sorts of problems, and theory can help to this end.

6.3 CONCLUSION

I have argued that identification-driven research naturally biases us against studying particular types of research questions where causal identification is most challenging, even if such questions are of central substantive importance. There are reasons for concern about such bias, given the importance of the questions that are most likely to be neglected. But this is not to say that when we study questions for which existing IDR methods are of limited use, we can ignore the problem of causal identification. Instead, we need to continue developing our methodological tool kits with an eye toward these questions. Theory can play a helpful role in this regard. If we attempt to develop theories that are internally coherent arguments that describe why we should observe constellations of empirical relationships, we not only focus on the "explanation" part of our jobs, but also provide a way to update our beliefs about causal relationships, even if we are unable to undertake identification-driven research using existing methods. This is the path that I am attempting to follow in this book. In the chapters ahead, although I am unable to provide estimates of causal effects, I hope I can help readers think about the plausibility of the theory by providing evidence about a range of patterns in the data.

7

Income and Voting Behavior

The theoretical argument provides intuitions about how economic inequality and ethnic diversity interact to influence electoral politics. This chapter focuses on one micro-level empirical implication of the argument for electoral behavior, which is whether the relationship between income and vote choice differs with a country's level of inequality and ethnic polarization. When class politics is prevalent, voters should be more likely to sort themselves by income, with poorer individuals supporting more left-wing parties that favor economic redistribution and richer individuals supporting more right-wing parties that oppose such redistribution. Thus, when the conditions for class politics that are related to economic inequality and ethnic diversity are strong, income should play a stronger role in vote choice. Similarly, if the conditions for class politics lead to an emphasis on redistribution in electoral competition and electoral behavior, attitudes toward such redistribution should have the strongest relationship with individual income when the conditions for class politics are strongest. The empirical results provide consistent support for the theoretical argument. When the conditions for class politics are strong, there is a stronger relationship between income and voting behavior.

The chapter is organized as follows. The next section describes the data, and then Section 7.2 presents the analysis of the relationship between an individual's income and his or her voting behavior, as well as an analysis of the relationship between income and attitudes toward inequality. Finally, Section 7.3 explores these same types of relationships, but dividing up the data into countries that have recently democratized and countries that have a longer history with democracy.

7.1 THE DATA

Testing the micro-level implications of the argument about income and vote choice requires individual-level data on income and voting behavior across a large number of democratic countries that vary in their levels of inequality and ethnic diversity. In addition, it will be important to place parties on a left-right redistributive scale. To this end, I use the World Values Survey (WVS), which measures income, respondents' preferred party, attitudes toward redistribution, and a number of important control variables.

The WVS includes a large number of countries, many of which have conducted surveys at multiple points in time. For the purposes here, a number of requirements place limits on which countries are included. First, a survey must contain a measure of income, which for the WVS asks the respondents their household income ("all wages, salaries, pensions, and other incomes that come in...") and reports the response roughly in deciles. Measures of income from surveys suffer measurement error, and in addition many respondents simply refuse to answer the question. This is a particular concern here if the measurement error in particular countries is correlated with inequality or ethnic polarization, something that is difficult to know. One response to this issue is to test the theory in ways that do not require measures of individual income, which is the approach in Chapters 8 and 9. In addition, I estimate all "income-based" models in two ways. The first uses the income variable as reported by WVS, thus dropping all missing observations. These are the results I present in what follows. The second uses imputed incomes for missing data. I do not report these results, but they are qualitatively identical to those results when missing income are dropped.[1]

A second requirement for including a WVS survey is driven by the substantive focus on inequality and redistribution, as well as our need to place political parties on a redistribution scale (see later). This requires that we include only surveys with the following question:

Now I'd like you to tell me your views on various issues. How would you place your views on this scale? 1 means you agree completely with the statement on the left; 10 means you agree completely with the statement on the right; and if your views fall somewhere in between, you can choose any number in between:

---

[1] For the imputation, for each survey I use Stata's "impute" command with right-hand-side variables for sex, age, marital status, whether the respondent lives at home, education level, whether the respondent lives with parents, whether the respondent is the chief wage earner, subjective social class, region, size of town, and type of living dwelling.

"Incomes should be made more equal vs We need larger income differences as incentives."

Finally, given the theory concerns electoral politics, I include only countries that are sufficiently democratic, which I define as having a Polity2 score of 6 or higher, a standard cut-off in the literature. Given these various constraints, I am left with fifty-three surveys from thirty-three countries.[2]

How representative are the WVS countries when compared with a broader set of democracies? Table 7.1 provides descriptive statistics on central macrovariables, as well as information about the regional distribution of countries.[3] The table compares the countries in the WVS sample with all countries for which data on the main macrovariables are available from the same time period, and using the same Polity2 cutoff of 6 or greater. With respect to inequality, economic development, the level of democracy, and electoral law, the WVS sample is very similar to the broader sample of countries. The WVS countries do have a slightly higher average level of ethnic diversity than does the population of countries, using both EP and ELF. With respect to regional distribution, the WVS has a higher proportion from central Europe and a lower proportion from Africa and Latin America, although the WVS is reasonably representative from a regional perspective. Thus, there are no particularly unsettling aspects of the distribution of countries available for use from the WVS.

The two central macrovariables in the analysis that follows are inequality and ethnic polarization, *EP*. To measure ethnic polarization, *EP*, I utilize the data provided by Fearon (2003). It is important to note that the Fearon measures, like other data on ethnic diversity, do not vary over time. This is unlikely a significant issue given that the ethnic composition of countries generally changes slowly.

Data measuring the Gini coefficient are taken from Frederick Solt's SWIID data on gross Gini (before taxes and transfers) (see Solt 2009). Solt's data set draws on a large number of surveys[4] in an effort to create comparable measures of the Gini across a wide range of countries over

---

[2] The countries include Australia, Bangladesh, Brazil, Bulgaria, Canada, Cyprus, Estonia, Finland, Georgia, Germany, Ghana, Guatemala, India, Indonesia, Israel, Latvia, Lithuania, Macedonia, Mali, Moldova, New Zealand, Peru, Romania, Slovakia, South Africa, Spain, Sweden, Taiwan, Turkey, Ukraine, USA, Uruguay, and Venezuela.

[3] I use the regional categories from Haber and Menaldo (2011). "Neo-Europe" includes western Europe, as well as the advanced democracies such as the United States, Canada, New Zealand, and Australia that are former European colonies.

[4] The most relevant ones are the WIID and the Luxembourg Income Studies (LIS), with others including the World Bank's Povcalnet, the Socio-Economic Database for Latin

TABLE 7.1. *The WVS sample of countries*

Macrovariable	All countries	Included WVS countries
Gini	44.4	43.7
EP	0.53	0.60
ELF	0.40	0.46
GDP/capita	13,386	13,526
Polity2	8.5	8.6
Proportion PR	0.76	0.70

Region	All countries (%)	Included WVS countries (%)
	Regional distribution of countries	
Central Europe	22	32
Latin America	25	15
Middle East	0.5	0
Africa	15	8
NeoEurope	27	32
East Asia	7	4
South Asia	4	9

Note: The table compares the fifty-three surveys from thirty-three WVS countries with the ninety-eight countries for which the macrodata are available for the 1995–2008 period covered by the WVS sample. The data include all countries with Polity2 scores of 6 or greater (and there are ninety-eight countries that had a polity2 score of at least 6 in some year during this time period). The top half of the table provides means of the macrovariable, and the bottom half of the table provides the percentage of country-years from each region.

time. To this end, Solt exploits comparisons with the LIS data, which is widely regarded as the best available survey for calculating income inequality. By comparing Ginis from non-LIS surveys with Ginis from LIS surveys (where such comparisons are possible), Solt obtained information that can be used to impute Ginis. This results in a data set that covers a very wide range of countries and a reasonably long time period, which is a central reason for using the data set. The other important reason for the purposes here is that the SWIID data contains the only broad, cross-national data set with information about market Gini (before taxes and transfers) and net Gini (after taxes and transfers). It therefore can

America, Branko Milanovic's World Income Distribution data, and the International Labour Organization's Household Income and Expenditure Statistics, as well as data from other national statistical offices.

be used to measure redistribution, which is particularly important in Chapter 9.

Any broad cross-national data set on inequality will have measurement error, and the SWIID may be particularly susceptible to this error because of the fact that country-year observations are imputed. In response to this issue, I adopt a number of strategies. One is to estimate the models on different subsets of countries, which likely vary in their measures of inequality. "Neo-European" countries, for example, likely have more accurate measures of inequality than others. Second, where possible, I test the robustness of the empirical results to alternative measures of inequality. To this end, I rely on the Estimated Household Income Inequality (EHII) data set from the University of Texas Inequality Project (http://utip.gov.utexas.edu/). Like SWIID, this data set adjusts the Ginis using information from outside particular surveys, but it does not impute missing data (which means it has considerably less coverage than SWIID).[5] The correlation of the SWIID Gini and the EHII Gini is 0.513 and the average difference between the two measures is 0.026. Although there are differences in the approach to estimating the Ginis between the two sources, Galbraith et al. (2015, p. 2) state that the "SWIID appears to be largely consistent with EHII so far as we have observed on a case-by-case basis." Third, when redistribution is the dependent variable (see Chapter 8) we can utilize a measure of redistribution that is not taken from the SWIID.

7.2 INCOME AND VOTING BEHAVIOR

What is the relationship between income and the vote, and how does this relationship vary with the level of inequality? Theories of elections and redistribution that focus only on class would lead us to expect that inequality should strengthen the relationship between income and the vote: as the rich become relatively richer, there is more to be gained by the nonrich from banding together and supporting parties that advocate rich-to-poor redistribution, and more to be gained by the rich from avoiding such redistribution. The theory developed in the preceding text suggests the opposite: greater inequality is associated with a larger number of nonrich individuals with whom the pie must be shared, encouraging the use of markers other than income for targeting the

---

[5] See Galbraith et al. (2014 and 2015) for a discussion of the data set and a comparison to other inequality data sets.

distribution of government benefits. The theory also suggests that the effect of inequality on the effect of income on the vote may vary with the level of ethnic polarization. In the text that follows, we consider this triple interaction, but we begin by asking the simpler question of whether the estimated relationship between income and the vote is weakest when inequality is highest, controlling for the level of ethnic polarization.

To this end, it is necessary to have a measure of the location of political parties on a left–right redistributive scale that is comparable across the countries in the WVS data set. I use the mean of the party supporters on the redistribution question described in the previous section as the dependent variable in these regressions. This vote variable should clearly tap the location of parties in the redistributive space: if a party is supported, for example, by voters who take a left-wing position on redistribution, we should expect the party to be more left-wing on this issue than if a party is supported by voters who take a right-wing position on this issue.

Figure 7.1 plots the coefficients on *income* from regressions using the fifty-three WVS surveys across different levels of inequality. The dependent variable is the ideological location of the party supported by the respondent, and the right-hand-side variables include *age*, *gender* and *education level*, in addition to *income*. The larger the coefficient, the stronger the relationship between income and the vote, with richer individuals supporting more right-wing parties.

The graph shows a great deal of variation in the size of the estimated coefficients, even at specific levels of inequality. It also reveals that South Africa (ZAF) is a considerable outlier, with a very high level of inequality and a very strong relationship between income and the vote. In fact, the direction of the correlation between the *Income* coefficient and inequality changes direction if South Africa is excluded. One can see this in the graph of the linear relationship between the *Income* coefficients and *Gini*. When South Africa is included (the dashed line), this relationship is slightly positive, whereas when South Africa is excluded (the solid line), the relationship is slightly negative. South Africa is obviously a unique case – with a very strong correlation between income and race, a history of apartheid, and the dominance of one party, the African National Congress (ANC), in elections – and the results for this country in Figure 7.1 do not fit the argument developed here well at all. It is perhaps interesting to ask whether South Africa might be moving in recent years to a closer fit with the theory, with a weakening of the ANC, a stronger role for identity categories other than black and white, and traditional

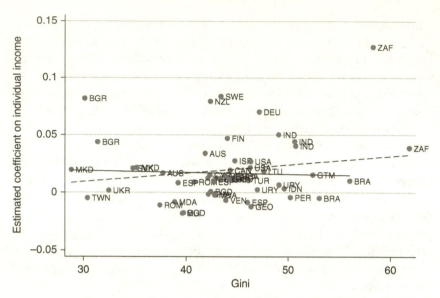

FIGURE 7.1. Scatterplot of the income–vote relationship at different levels of inequality.

Note: Regression coefficients for *Income* from models where the DV is the ideological position of the party supported and right-hand-side variables also include age, education, and gender. The solid regression line plots the slope of the coefficient when South Africa (ZFA) is excluded and the dashed line plots this line when this country is included.

ethnic politics becoming more central. In any event, in what follows in this section, I will account for South Africa's uniqueness by including an indicator variable for this country, as well as an interaction of this indicator variable with *income*. Similar results are obtained by simply excluding South Africa, but including the country helps remind us that the relationship between *income* and the vote can be very strong in ethnically diverse societies when inequality is high if income and ethnic identity are highly correlated, as they are in South Africa. I return to the issue of how income and ethnic identity are related in the concluding chapter of the book.

The tests here include a large number of individual-level surveys nested within different macro contexts, and our main goal is to understand how estimates of the coefficient for one individual-level attribute – income – vary with elements of this context, and in particular with GINI and EP. To this end, I estimate random effects models, allowing for random intercepts (and thus for baselines in the strength of the income–vote relationship that vary across country and time). The variables of central substantive interest are *Income*, *Inequality*, and *EP*. The models also include a South Africa dummy variable and its interaction with *Income*. Individual-level controls include *Age*, *Education* (the respondents' level of education, ranging from 1 [less than primary] to 8 [university degree or higher]) and gender (an indicator variable, *Female*). In addition, there are a number of country-level controls. *Polity2* is a measure of the level of democracy in a country; *Population* is the log of population, as reported by the World Development Indicators; *GDP* is the log of GDP per capita in constant dollars (also from the WDI); and *PR* is an indicator that takes the value 1 in countries that use proportional representation. Note the theoretical model provides intuitions about how individual income should be related to vote choice under different levels of inequality. It does not provide expectations about how the macro level variables themselves, including *Gini* and *EP*, should be related to individual voting behavior. These macrovariables simply tell us whether on average voters support parties that are more to the left or right. For time-varying right-hand-side variables, I use lagged values (by one year) to ensure that voting behavior is not causing outcomes, like *Gini*, that are right-hand-side variables.

It is reasonable to be wary of making cross-national comparisons using attitudinal survey data. There might be differences across countries in question wording, in cultural understandings of inequality itself, and in underlying social conditions, including underlying levels of inequality or government efforts to redress it. Like any attempt to measure party positions across countries on the same scale, these differences likely introduce certain biases in the measures of party positions, making it more difficult to draw inferences from cross-national comparisons. It is possible, however, to alleviate this concern to a certain degree by including a variable on the right-hand side that measures the mean of the ideology variable (*Ctry. Ideol.*). Thus, the left–right position of a respondent's preferred party is relative to the center of gravity of the left-positions in the respondent's country.

Table 7.2 presents results from the random-effects regressions, with *p*-values given in parentheses.[6] The first model includes the control variables and the core variables of interest: *income* and *Gini*, but not their interaction. The results indicate a precisely estimated positive relationship between *income* and right-wing voting, with richer individuals voting for

---

[6] I estimate the random-effects models using Stata's "mixed" command.

TABLE 7.2. Income and party choice

	1	2	3	4	5	6	7
Income	0.0204***	0.0572***	0.0570***	0.0533***	0.0366***	0.0543***	0.0389***
	(0.0000)	(0.0000)	(0.0000)	(0.0000)	(0.0008)	(0.0000)	(0.0002)
Gini(SWIID)	−0.0030*	0.0007	0.0007		−0.0005	0.0006	−0.0011
	(0.0942)	(0.7474)	(0.7316)		(0.8329)	(0.7702)	(0.6319)
Income*Gini (SWIID)		−0.0008***	−0.0008***		−0.0005*	−0.0008***	−0.0004
		(0.0002)	(0.0002)		(0.0632)	(0.0002)	(0.1235)
Gini (EHII)				0.0011			
				(0.7603)			
Income*Gini (EHII)				−0.0008***			
				(0.0058)			
EP	0.0462	0.0414	0.0351	0.0560	0.0161	0.0333	0.0205
	(0.3389)	(0.3914)	(0.5071)	(0.4701)	(0.7773)	(0.5302)	(0.6988)
Population (log)	0.0057	0.0055	0.0051	0.0021	0.0062	0.0049	0.0041
	(0.3636)	(0.3843)	(0.4292)	(0.7871)	(0.3420)	(0.4486)	(0.5324)
GDP (log)	0.0051	0.0044	0.0065	0.0275	0.0131	0.0032	0.0080
	(0.6469)	(0.6948)	(0.6265)	(0.1367)	(0.3732)	(0.8366)	(0.5697)
Polity2	−0.0020	−0.0009	−0.0005	−0.0090	−0.0002	−0.0014	−0.0012
	(0.8296)	(0.9272)	(0.9623)	(0.4308)	(0.9831)	(0.8893)	(0.8990)
PR	0.0237	0.0230	0.0236	0.0356	0.0208	0.0270	0.0259
	(0.2809)	(0.2960)	(0.2851)	(0.2619)	(0.3537)	(0.2539)	(0.2535)
Crry. Ideol.	1.0113***	1.0117***	1.0121***	0.9982***	1.0160***	1.0112***	1.0102***
	(0.0000)	(0.0000)	(0.0000)	(0.0000)	(0.0000)	(0.0000)	(0.0000)
Female	−0.0154***	−0.0154***	−0.0154***	−0.0110*	−0.0153***	−0.0153***	−0.0154***
	(0.0034)	(0.0034)	(0.0034)	(0.0795)	(0.0036)	(0.0036)	(0.0033)
Education	0.0161***	0.0163***	0.0163***	0.0206***	0.0164***	0.0164***	0.0164***
	(0.0000)	(0.0000)	(0.0000)	(0.0000)	(0.0000)	(0.0000)	(0.0000)

	(1)	(2)	(3)	(4)	(5)	(6)	(7)
Age	0.0010***	0.0010***	0.0010***	0.0007***	0.0011***	0.0010***	0.0010***
	(0.0000)	(0.0000)	(0.0000)	(0.0007)	(0.0000)	(0.0000)	(0.0000)
Income*S.Africa	0.0802***	0.0944***	0.0943***	0.0815***	0.0911***	0.0963***	0.0843***
	(0.0000)	(0.0000)	(0.0000)	(0.0000)	(0.0000)	(0.0000)	(0.0000)
S. Africa	−0.3006***	−0.3601***	−0.3645***	−0.3547***	−0.3593***	−0.3710***	−0.3318***
	(0.0000)	(0.0000)	(0.0000)	(0.0000)	(0.0000)	(0.0000)	(0.0000)
Redistribution			−0.0306	−0.2030	−0.0666	−0.0408	−0.0667
			(0.7695)	(0.1593)	(0.5573)	(0.7078)	(0.5810)
Cen.Eur.					−0.0379		
					(0.2274)		
Income*Cen.Eur.					0.0127***		
					(0.0000)		
NeoEurope						−0.0126	
						(0.7495)	
Income*NeoEur						0.0052**	
						(0.0302)	
Latin Am.							0.0760**
							(0.0406)
Income*LatinAm.							−0.0208***
							(0.0000)
Constant	−0.5301***	−0.5303***	−0.5303***	−0.5154***	−0.5305***	−0.5303***	−0.5305***
	(0.0000)	(0.0000)	(0.0000)	(0.0000)	(0.0000)	(0.0000)	(0.0000)
No. Ctry Surveys	53	53	53	39	53	53	53
N	50,979	50,979	50,979	36,538	50,979	50,979	50,979

Note: The dependent variable is the ideological location (on the redistribution scale) of the party supported. Time-varying right-hand-side variables are lagged one year. Results are from random effects models (with varying intercepts), with p-values in parentheses. * $p < .10$, ** $p < .05$, *** $p < .01$.

more right-wing parties on the redistribution dimension. The coefficient for *Income* in South Africa is also extremely large and precisely estimated, indicating (as we would expect based on Figure 7.1) that the relationship between *Income* and the vote is much stronger in South Africa than in other countries. The results also reveal a negative relationship between inequality and right-wing voting, although the coefficient for this (and other macrovariables) is not of particular substantive relevance. Instead, our interest lies in the interaction of Income and Gini: Does the estimated effect of income diminish as inequality increases?

Model 2 adds this interaction. The coefficient on *Income* remains positive, precisely estimated, and is substantially larger. The coefficient on *Gini* is now very imprecisely measured, and the coefficient on the interaction is negative and precisely estimated, suggesting that when we control for *EP* (and other variables) the relationship between income and right-wing voting is weakest in countries that have the highest levels of inequality. I interpret these results substantively in the text that follows.

We might worry that countries that have a weak relationship between income and the vote are countries that allow inequality to grow. I return to this issue in the text that follows, but it is important to bear in mind that the regressions here use market inequality (before taxes and transfers) to reduce concerns that the measure of inequality taps government efforts to reduce inequality. But because market inequality can also be influenced by government policy, as an additional robustness check, model 3 adds a variable that measures the redistributive effects of government policy, *Redistribution* (see Solt 2009). Let $Gini_M$ be the Gini coefficient before taxes and transfers and $Gini_N$ be the Gini coefficient after taxes and transfers. Then *Redistribution* is defined as follows:

$$Redistribution = \frac{Gini_M - Gini_N}{Gini_N}.$$

Redistribution is therefore a measure of the proportion of market inequality that is removed via taxes and transfers. The variable, like the measure of Gini and other right-hand-side variables, is lagged one year. The coefficient for *Redistribution* is negative – suggesting that voting is more left-wing on average in countries with more redistribution – but it is estimated with substantial error ($p = .77$). But the main results for *Income*, *Gini* and their interaction are unaffected by the inclusion of this variable.

To gauge the substantive effect of inequality on the relationship between income and voting, consider the top panel in Figure 7.2, which

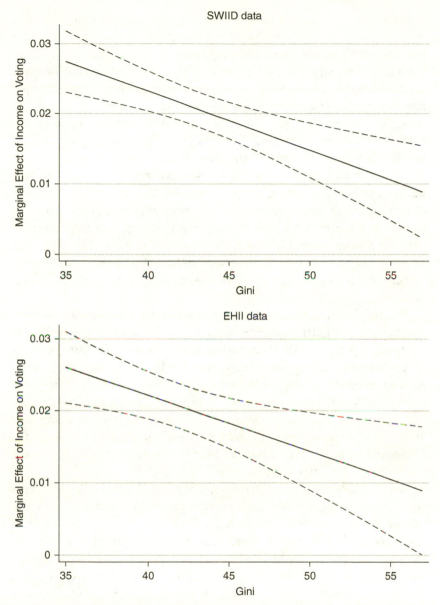

FIGURE 7.2. The relationship between income and the vote at different levels of inequality.
Note: Results from model 3 in Table 7.2.

describes the coefficient on *income* (and its 95 percent confidence interval) at different levels of *Gini* (based on model 3). For a country at the low end of *Gini*, the estimated coefficient is approximately 0.03. By contrast, for a country at the high end of *Gini*, the estimated coefficient is approximately 0.01. Thus, in the most unequal countries, the estimated effect of income is approximately one-third less than in the more equal countries. To put this effect in perspective, it is useful to consider the coefficients of other individual level variables. The effect of going from poorest to richest individual in the most equal country is roughly 0.3 on the 10-point party-system scale (because income ranges from 1 to 10), but is under 0.1 in the most unequal countries. By comparison, the effect of going from the least educated to the most educated is around 0.13, the difference between a man and woman is 0.015, and the difference between a twenty-year-old and a sixty-year-old is 0.04. The mediating effect of inequality on the income–vote relationship is thus quite strong when evaluated in comparison with the effects of other individual-level attributes.

To test robustness to alternative measures of the Gini, model 4 presents results using the EHII measure of Gini. Using the EHII results in the loss of about 25 percent of the data, and there are thirty-nine country-surveys rather than fifty-three. Nonetheless, the results are remarkably similar to those in model 3. The coefficient on *income* is positive and precisely estimated, the coefficient on *Gini* is positive but very small and measured with substantial error. And the coefficient on the interaction is negative and precisely estimated. The bottom panel in Figure 7.2 plots the estimated coefficient for *Income* at different levels of inequality and the results are very similar to those in the top panel.

Next consider regional differences. The majority of the WVS surveys come from three regions: central Europe, Latin America, and the advanced democracies of NeoEurope. Each of these regions has quite distinctive experiences with democracy, and we might also worry that income or inequality might be measured with more error in some regions than in others. It is therefore useful to explore whether the results from model 3 are driven by voting dynamics in a particular region. To gauge this possibility, I have created three regional dummy variables, as well as the interaction of these variables with income. I then estimate model 3 three additional times, each time including one of these pairs of variables (the regional dummy and its interaction with *income*). The results are in models 5 to 7 of Table 7.2. Model 5 includes a dummy variable for central Europe and its interaction with *income*. The coefficient for income of 0.037 describes how income is related to the vote in countries outside central Europe. The coefficient on the interaction of *income* with central Europe is 0.013 and is precisely estimated, suggesting the income-vote relationship is stronger in the central European countries than in the non-central European countries. Model 6 is similar, but instead isolates NeoEurope (and its interaction with *income*) and model 7 isolates Latin America (and its interaction with *income*). The income–vote relationship is slightly stronger in the NeoEurope countries than in the non-NeoEurope countries, and slightly weaker in the Latin American countries. But the estimated coefficient for *income* is positive in all these models, and the interaction with *Gini* has a negative coefficient. Figure 7.3 plots the coefficient for income across the range of *Gini* for each of the three models. In each, the estimated relationship between income and the vote is strongest when inequality is lowest. Thus, the results in model 3 are largely robust to excluding the surveys from any of these three major regions.

In sum, the data show that controlling for ethnic polarization, the relationship between income and the vote differs with the overall level of inequality in society. At low levels of inequality, there is a relatively strong relationship, with richer people supporting more right-wing parties and poorer people supporting more left-wing ones on the redistribution dimension. At high levels of inequality, this relationship between income and the vote weakens, with substantial similarities in the voting behavior of rich and poor.

Attitudes Toward Inequality

If the conditions for class politics are strong, we might expect individual orientations toward inequality and government redistribution to be related to income. Individuals on the lower half of the income distribution should prefer rich-to-poor redistribution and individuals at the top of the income distribution should oppose such redistribution. By contrast, if the conditions for class politics are weaker, then voters with similar incomes will often be divided against each other (when they are from different ethnic groups), and policies that transcend ethnic groups in order to redress general inequality should be deemphasized. We might therefore expect that when the conditions for class politics are weak, voter attitudes toward redistribution will be less clearly tied to income.

We can look for these patterns in the data by examining how attitudes toward inequality are related to income across different types of societies.

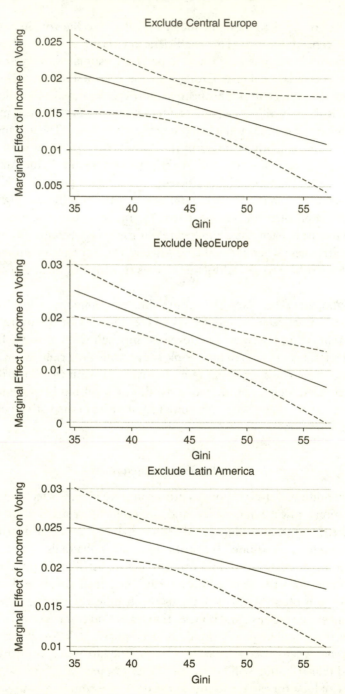

FIGURE 7.3. The relationship between income and the vote after removing regional effects.

Note: Results from models 5 to 7 in Table 7.2.

The relationship between income and redistributive attitudes should be relatively strong when inequality is low – because low inequality encourages class politics – and this relationship should weaken as inequality increases. The results are in Table 7.3. Model 8 reestimates model 3, but using the ideological position of the respondent rather than the respondent's vote choice as the dependent variable. We see that *income* has a positive and precisely estimated coefficient, indicating that richer individuals are more likely to oppose government efforts to address inequality than are poorer ones. The coefficient on *Gini* is also positive and relatively precisely estimated, and the interaction of *Gini* and *Income* has a negative coefficient, suggesting that the difference between the attitudes of a rich person on the inequality issue and the attitudes of a poor person are strongest in the most *equal* societies.

The top left panel in Figure 7.4 describes the estimated marginal effect of *Income* on attitudes at different levels of *Gini*, along with the 95% confidence interval. In countries where inequality is lowest, the estimated coefficient on *Income* is approximately 0.11. In countries where inequality is highest, the estimated coefficient for *Income* is about 0.08. Thus, the difference between the richest and poorest person in an equal society is approximate 1.1 points on the 10-point scale, and the difference is 0.8 points in the most unequal country. By comparison, the estimated effect of being a woman is roughly −0.11. The change in the estimated coefficient for *income* as *Gini* changes, then, although modest, is not trivial.

Model 9 reestimates model 8 using the EHII inequality data. The results are remarkable similar to those in model 8, even though there are substantially fewer country-surveys. The top right panel in Figure 7.4 plots the marginal effect of *Gini* using EHII, confirming the similarity in the results from models 8 and 9.

The theoretical framework is specifically about class versus ethnic distribution, and thus makes rather clear predictions about attitudes toward inequality and the government's role in redistribution. It does not, by contrast, make predictions about other types of attitudes. It is therefore useful to explore the *Income–Gini* interaction in a model that uses attitudes unrelated to class politics. This "placebo" test should find no effect of this income–inequality interaction on attitudes unrelated to inequality, and if we find such null effects, we can have more confidence that the findings in the previous models are not simply capturing some unmeasured systematic variation in attitudes across countries that is unrelated to the theory.

TABLE 7.3. *Income and attitudes toward inequality*

	8	9	10	11
Income	0.1438***	0.1416***	−0.0159	−0.0002
	(0.0003)	(0.0045)	(0.5935)	(0.9707)
Gini (SWIID)	0.0100*		−0.0018	0.0001
	(0.0803)		(0.6214)	(0.8622)
Gini (SWIID) *Income	−0.0011		0.0004	−0.0000
	(0.2407)		(0.5504)	(0.9950)
Gini (EHII)		0.0188**		
		(0.0271)		
Income (EHII)*Gini		−0.0009		
		(0.4337)		
Polity2	0.0129	−0.0081	−0.0042	0.0003
	(0.5576)	(0.7281)	(0.7033)	(0.8681)
GDP (log)	−0.0639**	0.0023	0.0081	−0.0024
	(0.0359)	(0.9512)	(0.5906)	(0.3908)
Population (log)	0.0155	0.0189	0.0008	−0.0001
	(0.2954)	(0.2350)	(0.9092)	(0.9296)
PR	0.0542	0.0972	0.0189	−0.0008
	(0.2749)	(0.1227)	(0.4160)	(0.8464)
Redistribution	−0.0200	0.1949	−0.0354	0.0110
	(0.9344)	(0.5197)	(0.7772)	(0.6255)
EP	0.0758	0.0838	−0.0304	0.0059
	(0.5289)	(0.5970)	(0.6296)	(0.5779)
Female	−0.1059***	−0.0800***	0.0176	0.0038
	(0.0000)	(0.0025)	(0.3160)	(0.2439)
Education	0.1129***	0.1058***	−0.0056	0.0003
	(0.0000)	(0.0000)	(0.1856)	(0.6690)
Age	−0.0005	−0.0009	−0.0004	0.0001
	(0.5193)	(0.3132)	(0.4358)	(0.1742)
Income (S. Africa)	0.1222***	0.1039***	−0.0239	0.0021
	(0.0000)	(0.0000)	(0.1561)	(0.4954)
S. Africa	−0.5598***	−0.4172***	0.1189	−0.0093
	(0.0002)	(0.0004)	(0.1642)	(0.5464)
Inequality attitudes (ctry. mean)	0.9954***	0.9503***		
	(0.0000)	(0.0000)		
Life Satis. (ctry. mean)			0.9991***	
			(0.0000)	
Trust (ctry. mean)				0.9987***
				(0.0000)
Constant	1.0351***	1.0499***	0.8103***	−0.8901***
	(0.0000)	(0.0000)	(0.0000)	(0.0000)
No. of country-surveys	53	39	53	53
N	65,462	47,351	66,563	65,639

Note: The dependent variable is individual attitudes toward inequality (models 8 and 9), individual life satisfaction (model 10) and trust in others (model 11). Time-varying right-hand side variables are lagged one year. Results are from random effects models (with varying intercepts), with *p*-values in parentheses. * $p < .10$, ** $p < .05$, *** $p < .01$.

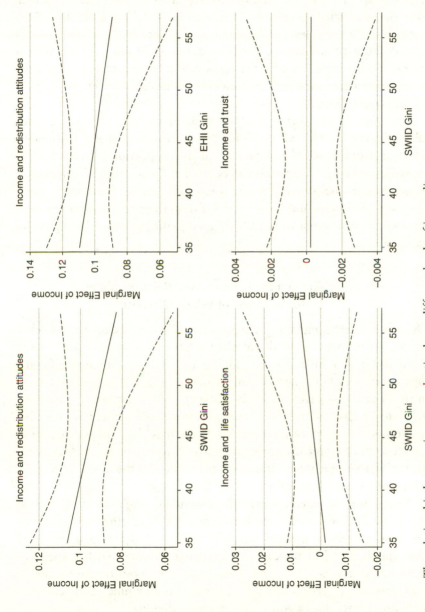

FIGURE 7.4. The relationship between income and attitudes at different levels of inequality. Note: Results from models in Table 7.3.

To this end, models 10 and 11 present estimates using two widely studied attitudes: general satisfaction with life (model 10) and generalized trust (model 11). The satisfaction variable ranges from 1 (least satisfied) to 10 (most satisfied). Model 10 is the same as model 3 except it includes a control for the mean level of satisfaction in society (rather than the mean attitudes toward inequality). The coefficients on *Income*, *Gini*, and their interaction are all essentially 0, and as can been seen in Figure 7.4: the plot of the income variable's coefficient is essentially a flat line at 0 across all the range of Gini.

The trust dummy variable is coded so that it takes the value 0 for "People cannot be trusted" and 1 for "People can be trusted." I estimate a linear probability model and control for the proportion of individuals in the society who say that people can be trusted. Again, the estimated effect of *income* in model 11 is essentially 0 across the range of inequality. Thus, the predicted interaction on the redistribution dimension does not exist in these two tests using attitudes unrelated to inequality as the dependent variable.

Inequality and the Income–Vote Relationship at Different Levels of Ethnic Diversity

The theoretical model suggests that the effect of inequality on class voting should depend on the level of ethnic diversity. Moving from a particular level of inequality to a higher level of inequality may influence the importance of income to voting behavior, or it may not, depending on the level of ethnic diversity. In the language of the model, a move from $n_{NR} = 60$ to $n_{NR} = 70$ would trigger less class-based voting if $n_A = 65$ but would not if $n_A = 55$ or $n_A = 80$. While the models in Table 7.2 control for the level of ethnic diversity, an approach to testing more directly the mediating role of ethnic polarization is to consider the interaction of *EP* with *Gini–income* interaction.

To test for the interaction at the individual level, we need to look at a triple interaction (income with inequality with ethnic polarization) across two levels (individual and country), which demands a great deal from the data and in any case is a challenge to interpret. It is therefore more straightforward to consider the argument about the interaction in the Chapter 8, where the dependent variable is an ethnic voting score for a country rather than a vote choice for an individual.

One possibility for estimating the interaction is to examine whether the interaction of ethnic diversity and inequality is related to variation in the income coefficients depicted in Figure 7.1. We might expect that if we regress these income coefficients on inequality, ethnic polarization, and their interactions, the net effect of inequality would be negative (more inequality would lead to a weaker relationship between income and the vote) and would become less negative as ethnic polarization increases (because ethnic politics would crowd out any effect of inequality). A similar pattern should hold for ethnic polarization. When I estimate these models with appropriate controls (not reported), there is only one variable that has a coefficient that is remotely significant, and that is the mean ideology score on the inequality question – the coefficient on income decreases as average ideology in a country on the issue of inequality becomes more right-wing. The coefficients for inequality, ethnic polarization, and their interaction are all estimated with huge error (with p-values greater than .48 for each of these variables, and often much larger). This may be due to the functional form that the model imposes on the interaction.

An alternative and easily interpretable way to explore this mediating role of ethnic diversity is to estimate models on two sets of data: those with high *EP* and those with low *EP*. We do not obtain a clear prediction from theory about how this interaction should manifest itself. One possibility is that the income–vote relationship becomes weaker with increases in inequality only in countries with sufficiently high ethnic diversity. When *EP* is too low, ethnic politics is difficult to establish at any level of inequality. Another possibility is that the income–vote relationship becomes weaker with increases in inequality only when *EP* is below a certain threshold. When *EP* is sufficiently large, it may be too difficult for class politics to prevail except at extreme levels of inequality.

Though both types of findings would be consistent with the theory, two types of results would not be consistent. First, there should be some range of EP – either sufficiently high or sufficiently low – in which higher inequality is related to a weaker income–vote relationship. Thus, if we do not find that the income–vote relationship becomes weaker as inequality increases in either the high or low EP countries, this test involving the triple interaction does not support the argument. Second, in high-EP countries, where ethnic politics is most feasible, income–vote relationship should never become stronger as inequality increases. If it did, this would imply that inequality encourages class politics, even when ethnic diversity is sufficiently high to allow ethnic politics.

Table 7.4 presents results when we classify countries by their ethnic polarization scores. Models 1 to 3 include the countries where ethnic

TABLE 7.4. The income-vote relationship at different levels of ethnic polarization

	1	2	3	4	5	6	7	8
Income	0.0705***	0.0730***	0.0731***	0.0204	0.0193	0.0198	0.1051***	0.0520***
	(0.0000)	(0.0000)	(0.0000)	(0.1369)	(0.1588)	(0.1490)	(0.0000)	(0.0012)
Gini (SWIID)	0.0013	0.0006	0.0006	−0.0018	−0.0018	−0.0002		
	(0.6366)	(0.8268)	(0.8258)	(0.5234)	(0.5225)	(0.9582)		
Income*Gini (SWIID)	−0.0010***	−0.0011***	−0.0011***	−0.0002	−0.0002	−0.0002		
	(0.0013)	(0.0007)	(0.0007)	(0.5485)	(0.6070)	(0.5811)		
Gini (EHII)							0.0058	−0.0005
							(0.3245)	(0.9306)
Income*Gini (EHII)							−0.0016***	−0.0010**
							(0.0001)	(0.0120)
Polity2	−0.0023	−0.0043	−0.0042	−0.0050	0.0024	0.0018	−0.0365*	−0.0102
	(0.8635)	(0.7313)	(0.7455)	(0.6991)	(0.8511)	(0.8867)	(0.0823)	(0.4915)
PR	0.0370	0.0217	0.0211	0.0212	0.0124	0.0230	0.0836	0.0412
	(0.1919)	(0.4115)	(0.4671)	(0.5119)	(0.6889)	(0.4823)	(0.5378)	(0.2362)
GDP (log)	−0.0225	−0.0469***	−0.0467***	0.0178	0.0374	0.0348	−0.0724*	0.0793**
	(0.1208)	(0.0042)	(0.0054)	(0.4362)	(0.1202)	(0.1452)	(0.0522)	(0.0313)
Population (log)	−0.0024	−0.0028	−0.0027	0.0075	−0.0004	0.0001	−0.0121	−0.0072
	(0.8074)	(0.7505)	(0.7685)	(0.4799)	(0.9730)	(0.9963)	(0.5874)	(0.5515)
Ctry Ideol.	1.0092***	1.0040***	1.0041***	1.0090***	1.0162***	1.0138***	0.9768***	1.0279***
	(0.0000)	(0.0000)	(0.0000)	(0.0000)	(0.0000)	(0.0000)	(0.0000)	(0.0000)
Female	−0.0059	−0.0059	−0.0058	−0.0260***	−0.0258***	−0.0258***	0.0084	−0.0271***
	(0.4407)	(0.4473)	(0.4475)	(0.0001)	(0.0001)	(0.0001)	(0.4344)	(0.0001)

Education	0.0193***	0.0192***	0.0192***	0.0131***	0.0130***	0.0131***	0.0297***	0.0115***
	(0.0000)	(0.0000)	(0.0000)	(0.0000)	(0.0000)	(0.0000)	(0.0000)	(0.0000)
Age	0.0023***	0.0023***	0.0023***	-0.0004**	-0.0004**	-0.0004**	0.0021***	-0.0003
	(0.0000)	(0.0000)	(0.0000)	(0.0440)	(0.0477)	(0.0459)	(0.0000)	(0.1955)
Income (S. Africa)	0.0902***	0.0913***	0.0913***				0.0653***	
	(0.0000)	(0.0000)	(0.0000)				(0.0000)	
S. Africa	-0.3363***	-0.2905***	-0.2899***				-0.2751***	
	(0.0000)	(0.0000)	(0.0000)				(0.0000)	
Redistribution		0.2786***	0.2811**		-0.2904*	-0.3115**	0.1468	-0.4798**
		(0.0100)	(0.0195)		(0.0649)	(0.0473)	(0.3703)	(0.0142)
EP			0.0057			-0.1756	-0.2553	0.0844
			(0.9619)			(0.3784)	(0.1760)	(0.7968)
Constant	-0.4336***	-0.4336***	-0.4336***	-0.6970***	-0.6970***	-0.6970***	-0.3610***	-0.7132***
	(0.0000)	(0.0000)	(0.0000)	(0.0000)	(0.0000)	(0.0000)	(0.0000)	(0.0000)
N	28,896	28,896	28,896	22,083	22,083	22,083	17,130	19,408
Countries included	Low EP	Low EP	Low EP	High EP	High EP	High Ep	Low EP	High EP

Note: The dependent variable is the ideological location (on the redistribution scale) of the party supported. Time-varying right-hand-side variables are lagged one year. Results are from random effects models (with varying intercepts), with *p*-values in parentheses.
* *p* < .10, ** *p* < .05, *** *p* < .01.

polarization is below the median in the data set. The first model is the same as model 2 in Table 7.2, but it excludes *EP* (because the data are limited to the lower EP countries). Model 2 is the same as model 3 in Table 7.2, though it excludes *EP*. Model 3 is the same as model 2 but it adds the *EP* variable to the right-hand side. In all three models, the coefficient for *Income* is positive and precisely estimated, the coefficient for *Gini* is positive (but not precisely estimated), and the coefficient for their interaction is negative and precisely estimated. The results are quite stable across the three models. Models 4 to 6 have the same structure as models 1 to 3, but include only the countries with high ethnic polarization. In these countries, the coefficient for income is positive, the coefficient for Gini is negative, and the coefficient for their interaction is positive, but none of these coefficients is precisely estimated. Models 7 and 8 reestimate models 3 and 6, but using the EHII data on the Gini. The results for model 7 are very similar to those in model 3, with a positive and significant coefficient on *Income* and a negative and significant coefficient on the interaction of *Income* and *Gini*. Both coefficients are somewhat larger in absolute magnitude than found in model 3. In model 8, both coefficients are significant, unlike in model 4, but they are much smaller in magnitude than in model 7.

Figure 7.5 graphically depicts the substantive results for the income coefficients in Table 7.4. The top two panels show the results for the *income* coefficient using SWIID and the bottom two panels using EHII. Consider the top two panels. In the countries with low EP (top left), when inequality is low, which invites class politics, there is a very strong relationship between income and the vote, with an estimated coefficient on income around 0.035. But in countries with high inequality, the relationship between income and the vote is much weaker, declining to about one-third the level in high-Gini countries than in low-Gini countries. In this set of countries and elections, then, where ethnic polarization is relatively low, greater inequality diminishes the income–vote relationship. Next consider countries where *EP* is high, making class politics more difficult at any level of inequality. Here the income–vote relationship is both weak and unrelated to the level of inequality. The coefficient on *income* is always below 0.015, and though it declines slightly with inequality, this decline is not remotely significant. Next consider the bottom two panels. Again, we find that in the low-EP countries (left panel), there is a very strong income–vote relationship in countries with low inequality, and that this relationship diminishes as inequality increases. In the high-EP countries, the relationship between

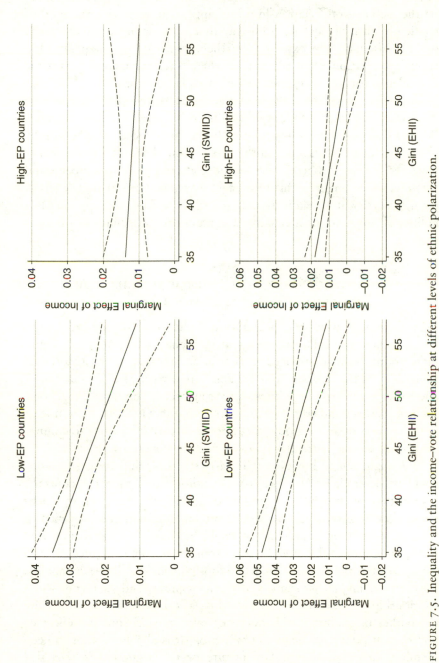

FIGURE 7.5. Inequality and the income–vote relationship at different levels of ethnic polarization.

Note: The top two figures (using the SWIID Gini) are based on models 3 and 6 in Table 7.4, and the bottom two figures (using EHII Gini) are based on models 7 and 8 in that table.

income and the vote is weak at all levels of inequality, though it declines slightly as inequality increases. Thus, the estimated effect of inequality on the income–vote relationship does appear to vary with the level of ethnic polarization, but not in a way that is the same across the range of EP. This may help explain why the coefficients on inequality and ethnic polarization, from regressions where the income coefficient is the dependent variable, are estimated with such large error.

Using both measures of the Gini, the degree to which the income–vote relations varies with inequality depends on the level of ethnic diversity. When *EP* is low, there is a strong relationship between income and the vote when inequality is low, but this relationship diminishes as inequality increases. When *EP* is high, there is little relationship between income and the vote, which might be due to the fact that at sufficiently high levels of ethnic diversity, it is relatively easy for ethnic politics to supplant class politics at any level of inequality. I explore this possibility in the next chapter.

7.3 ENDOGENEITY AND ELECTORAL BEHAVIOR IN OLD AND NEW DEMOCRACIES

In the theoretical argument, inequality and ethnic diversity are exogenous, and together they influence the strategic behavior of party elites and mass voting behavior. Indeed, a central assumption of the theoretical framework is that income and ethnicity are attractive electoral tools – and we see them arise in politics – precisely because both are exogenous. Because incomes and ethnic identity are very difficult to change – at least in the context of an election – they provide a way for parties to commit credibly to serving particular types of electoral coalitions.

One might worry, however, that party strategies and voting behavior could be determining the level of inequality rather than the contrary. It's not exactly clear how to think about this without a clear argument about how reverse causation would produce the patterns identified in the data here. One basic concern might be that for reasons unrelated to the dynamics of the model, voters sometimes vote their income, and when they do, the parties that win adopt policies that lower inequality. We therefore find an association between inequality and the income–vote relationship. As noted previously, this is a motivation for focusing on market inequality, which does not take into account the effect of government policy on inequality reduction. It is also important to keep in mind, however, that a key feature of the argument is that this relationship between inequality and the income–vote relationship should be conditioned by ethnic diversity, a pattern we also see in the data. Thus, the degree to which one might be concerned about reverse causation should be influenced by the plausibility of arguments one can imagine about these interactions, not just about the possibility that when voters vote their income, inequality goes down.

But one can also turn to the model itself for a completely different type of response to this concern. By treating party system formation as equilibrium choices, the model describes the following strategic dynamic: inequality and ethnic diversity interact to influence voting behavior and party strategies, a winner emerges, and then government distribution occurs, changing the income distribution. Consider what might happen if we allowed this dynamic to play out repeatedly over time. If there are conditions encouraging class politics, then electoral politics should encourage redistribution from rich to poor, producing the maximal possible effect on inequality reduction, and thus further reinforcing the conditions for class politics. If nonrich voters looked ahead, considering not just how their behavior today affect their outcome today (an assumption about voting behavior that some might find dubious), then nonrich voters would be even more attracted to class politics than they are in the static model. And if social conditions encourage ethnic politics, government policy should benefit some voters who are rich and hurt other individuals who are poor, doing less to reduce inequality, and perhaps even making it worse. This in turn should reinforce the conditions for ethnic politics. Thus, if we think through the implications of the model for how this might play out over time, we should expect both class politics and ethnic politics to reinforce each other, producing the patterns we see in the data even though there is an equilibrium relationship between income and the vote that implies the absence of a clear "direction of causation."

There are two additional sorts of analysis that can shed further light on questions of reverse causation. First, suppose that there is a moment where the social conditions central to the model influence identity politics and party competition, but that once party systems and identities are established, they change slowly, and in fact may be reinforced. If this is true, then we might expect the interaction of past inequality – more distant "past" than than the one-year lag used earlier – with ethnic diversity to affect the importance of class and ethnicity in electoral politics. Examining "more distant past" inequality will obviously further address any concerns that voting behavior shapes inequality. Second, we can consider electoral behavior in the early days of democracy, where voting behavior can have little effect on inequality because voters have been given little chance to express their preferences. In such conditions, where there has been recent regime change, it is even less plausible that current voting outcomes reflect electoral dynamics and their policy outcomes from the past.

We therefore can learn from estimating empirical models such as those examined previously, but focusing on two groups of countries. The first is "new democracies," where there is little past effect of electoral politics on policy outcomes. The second is "more established democracies," where we can examine the relationship between voting behavior and inequality in the more distant past. To examine elections in the early period of a democracy after a transition, I examine countries that were not democratic ten years prior to the year in which the relevant survey was conducted using a Polity2 cutoff of 6. This results in sixteen countries (sixteen surveys) satisfying the conditions for "new" democracy twenty-six countries (thirty-eight surveys) satisfying the conditions for "old" democracy. This is not a very large number of surveys in either category, and it would of course be difficult to divide these two groups further (e.g., by electoral law or the level of ethnic diversity). But we can at least examine whether the estimated effected of income declines as inequality increases. In the next chapter, data permit us to examine the interaction implied by the model directly.

Models 1 and 2 include surveys in countries that satisfy the definition of established democracies, and the measure of income inequality is *Gini*, lagged ten years. Column 1 includes the full set of controls, and model 2 includes only the controls that are precisely estimated in column 1. In both columns, the coefficient on *Income* is positive and precisely estimated, and in both columns the interaction of *income* and lagged *Gini* is negative and precisely estimated. Thus, in established democracies, countries with higher past inequality have a weaker link between income and the vote. Models 3 and 4 include surveys from countries that satisfy the definition of new democracies, and the measure of inequality is lagged 1 year. Column 3 includes the full set of controls and column 4 includes only those controls that are reasonably precisely estimated. The results are similar to those in the established democracies. Figure 7.6 graphs the estimated coefficient for *income* at different levels of *Gini* and the

TABLE 7.5. *Random effects models of vote choice in old and new democracies*

	1	2	3	4
Income	0.0495***	0.0495***	0.0724***	0.0740***
	(0.0000)	(0.0000)	(0.0000)	(0.0000)
Gini (lag 10)	0.3323*	0.3174*		
	(0.0695)	(0.0775)		
Income*Gini (lag10)	−0.0614***	−0.0615***		
	(0.0033)	(0.0032)		
Gini (lag 1)			0.2695	0.3525
			(0.3121)	(0.2147)
Income*Gini (lag 1)			−0.1434***	−0.1458***
			(0.0000)	(0.0000)
Ethnic Polarization	0.0576	0.0513	−0.1067	−0.0733
	(0.2412)	(0.2708)	(0.1053)	(0.3144)
CtryPolity2 (lag)	−0.0044		0.0186**	
	(0.6768)		(0.0336)	
Population	0.0057	0.0015	−0.0057	0.0037
	(0.4348)	(0.8028)	(0.5338)	(0.6812)
GDP(lag)	0.0000		0.0000*	0.0000
	(0.3706)		(0.0975)	(0.1784)
Redistribution (lag10)	0.0259			
	(0.8126)			
Redistribution (lag 1)			−0.3138***	−0.2400**
			(0.0042)	(0.0424)
PR	0.0294		−0.0299	
	(0.2397)		(0.3049)	
Ideol.	1.0145***	1.0124***	0.9879***	0.9841***
	(0.0000)	(0.0000)	(0.0000)	(0.0000)
Female	−0.0167***	−0.0165**	−0.0124	−0.0124
	(0.0098)	(0.0109)	(0.1386)	(0.1380)
Education	0.0129***	0.0130***	0.0260***	0.0255***
	(0.0000)	(0.0000)	(0.0000)	(0.0000)
Age	0.0018***	0.0018***	−0.0023***	−0.0023***
	(0.0000)	(0.0000)	(0.0000)	(0.0000)
Income (S. Africa)	0.0365***	0.0364***	0.1566***	0.1567***
	(0.0000)	(0.0000)	(0.0000)	(0.0000)
S. Africa	−0.2267***	−0.2267***	−0.6000***	−0.5921***
	(0.0009)	(0.0011)	(0.0000)	(0.0000)
Constant	−0.5934***	−0.4978***	−0.0356	−0.1093
	(0.0027)	(0.0001)	(0.8282)	(0.5090)
Old or new democracy?	Old	Old	New	New
N	36,548	36,548	16,040	16,040

Note: The dependent variable is the ideological location (on the redistribution scale) of the party supported. Columns 1 and 2 are old democracies (and inequality lagged ten years) and columns 3 and 4 are new democracies (where inequality is lagged one year). Results are from random effects models (with varying intercepts), with p-values in parentheses. * $p < .10$, ** $p < .05$, *** $p < .01$.

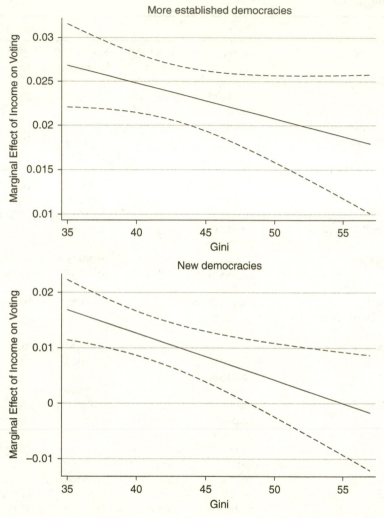

FIGURE 7.6. Gini and the income–vote relationship in older and newer democracies.

relationship is quite similar in the two sets of countries, and in both cases consistent with the theory.

7.4 CONCLUSION

The patterns in the data are consistent with the theoretical argument about the mediating role of inequality in electoral politics. When inequality is high, the conditions for class politics should be weak, and the data reveal a weaker association between income and the vote. The theory also suggests that this mediating role of inequality in the income–vote relationship should depend on the degree of ethnic divisions, a pattern we also find in the individual-level data when we segregate the data by levels of ethnic polarization. Thus, the patterns in the data are consistent with one implication of the theory, which concerns the role of income in voting behavior. In Chapter 8, we consider the empirical patterns related to ethnic voting.

8

Inequality, Ethnic Diversity, and the Ethnification of Party Systems

Chapter 7 presented evidence that when the conditions for class politics in the theoretical model are weak, so is the relationship between income and voting behavior. The theoretical argument also suggests, however, that when the conditions for class politics are weaker, the conditions for ethnic politics should be stronger. This chapter takes up this second implication of the argument. When the conditions for class politics are weak – and thus the conditions for ethnic politics are strong – is there evidence of a stronger role of ethnicity in voting? To address this question, I examine how the ethnic bases of support for political parties vary with the conditions for class and ethnic politics.

8.1 MEASURING ETHNIC VOTING BEHAVIOR

We can think of the ethnic basis of support for a given party as a function of the degree to which the ethnic composition of the party's supporters differs from the ethnic composition of support for other parties. Suppose there are two parties and two groups. If 70 percent of Party A's support comes from the Green group and 30 percent comes from the Blue group, is this party "ethnified"? We cannot answer this without knowing the support for Party B. If 70 percent of Party B's support also comes from the Green group and 30 percent comes from the Blue group, then both parties simply reflect the distribution of groups in society, and it would be odd to say either is particularly ethnified. But if 30 percent of Party B's support comes from the Green group and 70 percent comes from the Blue group, then both parties are relatively ethnified, and they would be even more ethnified if they each received 90 percent from their primary support group and 10 percent from the other group.

To test the theoretical argument about inequality, we need to use a measure of party-system ethnification that captures this basic idea of what it means for any given party to be "ethnified." The goal of the test is to determine if such a measure is related to the interaction of income inequality and ethnic polarization. We expect, for example, that when ethnic diversity permits a small winning coalition, it will be likely that inequality should have little effect on party system ethnification because there should be a strong incentive for ethnic politics at almost any level of inequality. As societies become less diverse in the sense that forming small ethnic majorities becomes more difficult, inequality should become more salient to party system ethnification, with greater inequality tipping politics in the direction of ethnic rather than class coalitions. Thus, the effect of inequality on ethnic voting should be positive but should decline as the ethnic polarization of society increases, disappearing when society is sufficiently polarized that its difficult for class politics to prevail at any level of inequality.

To measure the extent to which patterns of party support are "ethnified," I focus primarily on the "Party Voting Polarization" (*PVP*) measure from Huber (2012). To construct *PVP*, one first compares the ethnic basis of support for each party with the ethnic basis of support for each other party to measure the extent to which any two parties differ in their ethnic bases of support. This measure of difference takes the value 0 if the ethnic basis of support is identical for the two parties (e.g., if both parties get 80 percent of their support from group 1 and 20 percent from group 2), and it takes its maximum value 1 if one party receives all its support from one group and the other party receives all its support from a different group. Formally, $\tilde{r}_{ij}$ is the distance in the electoral bases of support for parties *i* and *j*, which is defined as

$$\tilde{r}_{ij} = \sqrt{\frac{1}{2} \sum_{g=1}^{G} (P_g^i - P_g^j)^2}, \qquad (8.1)$$

where P_g^i and P_g^j are the proportion of supporters of parties *i* and *j* who come from group *g*, and there are *G* groups. To create a measure of how "ethnified" the party system is, one aggregates the measures of distance, invoking the polarization perspective to weight the party distances by party size, so that

$$PVP = 4\sum_{i=1}^{N}\sum_{j=1}^{N}p_i p_j^2 \tilde{r}_{ij}. \tag{8.2}$$

PVP, then, is a measure of the role that ethnic identity plays in describing the bases of support for parties. Because it invokes the polarization perspective in aggregating the differences between pairs of parties, it takes its maximum value when there are two parties, each of equal size and each with its own basis of ethnic support.[1] The expectation from the model is that the degree to which voters will sort themselves at election time based on ethnicity will depend on inequality and EP. We should expect to find that *PVP* increases with *Gini* and *EP*, but that there should be an interaction between these two right-hand-side variables, with the association between *Gini* and *PVP* being largest at low levels of *EP*, and with this association diminishing as *EP* grows large. Similarly, the association between *EP* and *PVP* should be positive but should diminish as *Gini* grows large.

Using *PVP* to test the theory has a couple of advantages. First, calculating this variable does not require that we have a comparable survey question on inequality, making it possible to use more data. Using the Polity2 cut-off of countries with a score of 6 or higher, the Huber (2012) data has fifty-one surveys from thirty-two countries, and the surveys come from the Comparative Study of Electoral Systems (CSES, twenty-one surveys), the Afrobarometer (thirteen surveys), and the WVS (seventeen surveys). Since that paper was published, I have added forty-four surveys from thirty-two countries using the WVS. Combining these two data sets results in ninety-five surveys from forty-six countries.[2] The ethnic identity of respondents is based on the Fearon (2003) categories, as discussed in Chapter 5.

Second, tests of the ethnification of party systems at the country level, unlike the individual-level survey regressions, make it straightforward to test the interaction between *EP* and *Gini* that is predicted by the theory. In addition, in the individual-level tests, the focus was on how inequality mediates the income–vote relationship, and the interpretation of the other right-hand-side variables was unrelated to the theory. Here, the other right-hand-side variables have a straightforward interpretation.

---

[1] See discussion in Huber (2012).
[2] The actual number of observations in each regressions varies slightly with the nature of the set of control variables, due to missing values on some controls.

PVP ranges from 0.003 to 0.40 and has a mean of .12 with a standard deviation of .09. Figure 8.1 plots *PVP* against *Gini* (left panel) and against Ethnic Polarization (right panel), along with the regression line. The graphs show that ethnic voting is increasing on average with inequality and ethnic diversity. But the level of variation in ethnic voting at all levels of inequality and (except in the very homogeneous countries) all levels of ethnic diversity is striking. These figures of course do not control for any other variables, but they suggest that if one looked only at the direction of these effects, there would be little relationship with *PVP*.

8.2 GINI, EP, AND PARTY SYSTEM ETHNIFICATION

This section presents results using all data I have available on ethnic voting in democratic systems. I estimate ordinary least squares (OLS) models using *PVP* as the dependent variable, with robust standard errors clustered at the country level. The control variables considered here include

- *PR*, an indicator variable that takes the value 1 if the electoral law is proportional representation.
- *Afrobarometer, CSES*, indicator variables for surveys used (with WVS the omitted category), to capture possible differences due to question wording (see Huber 2012).
- *gdp*, the lagged value (by one year) of the log of real GDP per capita.
- *pop*, the log of the population in millions, lagged one year.
- *Groups-Parties ratio*, the number of groups divided by the number of parties, a ratio that can directly affect the value of *PVP*, as discussed in Huber (2012).
- Decentralization, an indicator variable that takes the value 1 if there exist subnational regions that have autonomous taxing capacity. The data are taken from the "auton" variable in the Data Base of Political Institutions, Beck et al. (2001).
- *Polity2*. The lagged value of Polity 2.
- *Nat. Resources.* the log of the value per capita of natural resources such as oil and diamonds, taken from Haber and Menaldo (2011).

Model 1 in Table 8.1 includes *Gini* and *EP* (but not their interaction) and the full set of controls. *EP* has the expected positive coefficient but is not very precisely estimated, and the coefficient for *Gini* has the wrong (negative) sign and is very imprecisely estimated. The only control variables that are at least somewhat precisely estimated are *CSES* and

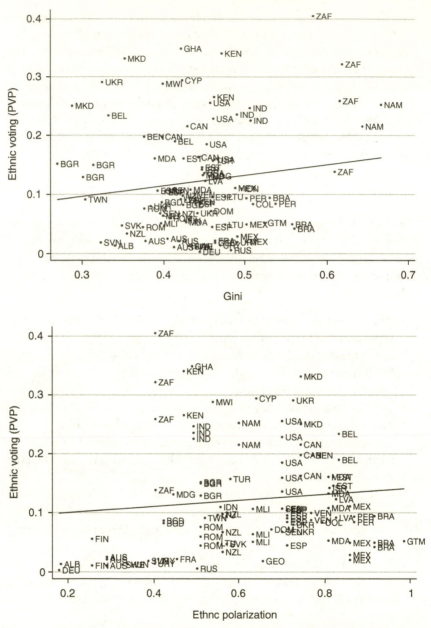

FIGURE 8.1. PVP at different levels of inequality and ethnic polarization.

TABLE 8.1. *Inequality, ethnic diversity, and the ethnic bases of parties*

	1	2	3	4	5	6	7
Gini (SWIID)	−0.0468	0.0998	2.3352***	2.3562***		4.4415**	2.1801***
	(0.8414)	(0.7099)	(0.0004)	(0.0000)		(0.0245)	(0.0007)
EP	0.0933	0.0704	1.8814***	1.8524***	1.6513***	3.0224**	1.8010***
	(0.2857)	(0.3938)	(0.0000)	(0.0000)	(0.0002)	(0.0306)	(0.0000)
Gini (SWIID)*EP			−3.9309***	−3.8996***		−6.8100**	−3.7989***
			(0.0000)	(0.0000)		(0.0440)	(0.0000)
Gini (EHII)					2.3970***		
					(0.0026)		
Gini (EHII) *EP					−3.8322***		
					(0.0005)		
Polity2	0.0052		0.0010				
	(0.4369)		(0.8599)				
Parties-Groups Ratio	−0.0030		−0.0046*	−0.0034		−0.0168**	−0.0005
	(0.2877)		(0.0935)	(0.1789)		(0.0360)	(0.8673)
Afrobarometer	0.0394		−0.0062				
	(0.4025)		(0.9022)				
CSES	−0.0268*	−0.0417**	−0.0131		−0.0320**		
	(0.0957)	(0.0302)	(0.2765)		(0.0437)		
Redistribution	−0.1309		−0.0648				
	(0.3041)		(0.5291)				
Decentralization	0.0061		−0.0230	−0.0370**		0.0114	−0.0440***
	(0.7811)		(0.1766)	(0.0418)		(0.7688)	(0.0079)

(continued)

TABLE 8.1 continued

	1	2	3	4	5	6	7
PR	−0.0505	−0.0544*	−0.0590**	−0.0562**			
	(0.1346)	(0.0938)	(0.0138)	(0.0319)			
Natural Resources	−0.0036		−0.0031				
	(0.5077)		(0.5050)				
GDP	0.0004		−0.0031				
	(0.9538)		(0.6495)				
Population	−0.0022		0.0007				
	(0.8133)		(0.9262)				
Constant	0.1371	0.0828	−0.8976***	−0.9355***	−0.8956***	−1.7785**	−0.9178***
	(0.4326)	(0.4428)	(0.0010)	(0.0001)	(0.0025)	(0.0239)	(0.0007)
R^2	0.242	0.138	0.468	0.412	0.248	0.458	0.452
N	91	99	91	99	66	29	70

Note: The DV is PVP. The p-values in parentheses are based on robust standard errors clustered by country. * $p < .10$, ** $p < .05$, *** $p < .01$.

PR. Given the large number of control variables in model 1 with no clear relationship to *PVP*, model 2 reestimates the model, excluding those control variables that do not have a coefficient estimate with a *p*-value of .20 or less. In this model, *Gini* and *EP* both have positive coefficients, but neither coefficient is estimated with precision.

The theoretical model emphasizes that the *interaction* of ethnic diversity and inequality should influence the behavior of individuals and parties. Including an interaction therefore makes it possible to examine whether the estimated coefficient for *Gini* (or *EP*) changes with the level of *EP* (or *Gini*). In general, the level of inequality needed to facilitate ethnic politics should decrease as ethnic diversity increases. If ethnic diversity is relatively high, for example, then the amount of inequality necessary to accommodate ethnic politics might be very modest, making it possible for ethnic politics to prevail at even low levels of inequality. But at lower levels of ethnic polarization, the level of inequality would become more salient to the level of ethnic politics. This would imply that the estimated effect of inequality would be largest when ethnic diversity was lowest, and would fade to zero as ethnic diversity became sufficiently large. Alternatively, the "cut-point" might work so that it is impossible for ethnicity to emerge as salient in elections at sufficiently low levels of ethnic diversity, but that above this threshold, the level of inequality becomes relevant. In this case, the model suggests that once above the threshold, the marginal effect of inequality should decline as ethnic diversity increases. The model obviously does not tell us where the threshold is – and this might be a function of which specific countries are included in the data set. But it does tell us that the effect of each variable should be positive, and should diminish as the other variable becomes larger. Thus, *Gini* and *EP* should have positive coefficients and *Gini**EP should have a negative coefficient.

The results for the model with the interaction and all controls are presented in column 3. *Gini* and *EP* both have positive coefficients and *Gini**EP has a negative coefficient. All three coefficients are very precisely estimated. In the text that follows I interpret these coefficients graphically.

I focus on *PVP* because it is linked to the polarization perspective, and is thus linked directly to a central independent variable, Ethnic Polarization. Huber (2012), however, also offers three other measures of ethnic voting behavior: Group Voting Fractionalization, Group Voting Polarization, and Party Voting Fractionalization. Although *PVP* captures most directly the strategic dynamic of the model presented earlier, where the value of ethnic politics is strongest when the size of the ethnic majority is smallest, it is useful to consider if the results are robust when other measures of ethnic voting are used. I therefore reestimated model 3 with each of these three dependent variables and the results (not reported here) are qualitatively very similar to those in model 3. This is not surprising because these variables are correlated with each other.

Model 4 presents the results from a more parsimonious model, where the variables with imprecisely measured coefficients in model 3 are removed. With fewer controls, there are now ninety-nine surveys from forty-eight countries, but even with the different set of control variables and the different set of countries, the results for the three variables of interest are remarkably stable. Finally, model 5 presents the results using the parsimonious model with the EHII measure of the Gini. Using the EHII data results in a loss of about one-third of the observations and there are only thirty-four countries (compared to forty-eight in model 4). When estimating model 3 with the full set of controls using the EHII Gini, the only control variable that is significant at the 0.20 level is the indicator variable for the *CSES* surveys, and thus it is the only control included in model 5. The results are quite similar to those of 4: both *Gini* and *EP* have coefficients that are positive and precisely estimated, though in model 5 the size of the *EP* coefficient is larger than that of *Gini* (in contrast to model 4). And the coefficient on the interaction is negative and precisely estimated.

Figure 8.2 provides a graphical depiction of the results. The panels on top are from model 4 (using SWIID) and the panels on the bottom are from model 5 (using EHII). Consider the top right panel, which depicts the estimated coefficient for *Gini* (and the 95% confidence interval) at different values of *EP* (ranging from the 10th percentile of EP to the 90th percentile). At low levels of *EP*, the estimated coefficient for inequality is large and positive, implying that in countries where the level of ethnic diversity is not too large, there is a strong relationship between inequality and party system ethnification, with parties more likely to have a stronger ethnic basis of support when inequality is high. The estimated coefficient of *Gini* declines as *EP* increases, suggesting that in societies with high ethnic diversity, inequality has a less clear relationship with the ethnification of parties. This is consistent with the findings on the income–vote relationship given earlier, where *Gini* had a strong estimated effect at lower levels of ethnic polarization, but much less so at higher levels of ethnic polarization. At very high levels of ethnic polarization, the estimated coefficient for *Gini* actually becomes negative, suggesting – in contrast to the argument from the model – that more inequality leads to less ethnification. The bottom left panel present the same graph from

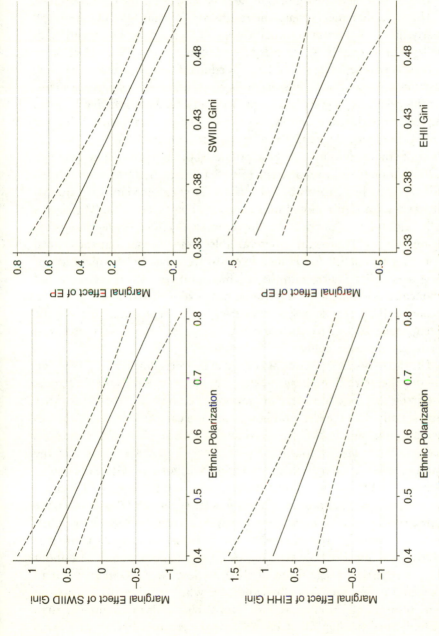

FIGURE 8.2. The estimated coefficients for Gini (or EP) at different levels of EP (or Gini).
Note: Results from model 4 (top panels) and model 5 (bottom panels) in Table 8.1.

model 5. Again, the results are very similar using the EHII data, although they are somewhat more consistent with the theory in that the range of EP over which there are significant negative values for the Gini is smaller.

The top right panel presents the results for *EP* using SWIID. The graph clearly shows that estimated coefficient of EP changes considerably with the level of inequality. When inequality is low, the ethnification of party systems is very sensitive to the level of ethnic diversity, with more ethnic diversity associated with higher levels of ethnification of party systems. But this relationship goes to zero as inequality becomes sufficiently large. The bottom right panel shows that the results are very similar using the EHII Gini. Thus, the results are consistent with the argument that the effect of ethnic diversity on ethnic politics should depend on inequality.

In addition to those reported in Table 8.1, I estimated two other models (not reported here) to probe robustness. First, to account for regional differences, I added regional indicator variables to model 4. The results indicate that Latin American has lower levels of ethnic voting than other regions, controlling for the other variables in the model. But the central results for inequality and ethnic diversity are robust to the inclusion of these regional variables, with the coefficient on *Gini* always positive and significant, declining as *EP* increases, but never negative and significant. Second, as Figure 8.1 shows, South Africa is a bit of an outlier in its ethnic voting score, so I added an indicator for South Africa and the central results again remain robust.

The theoretical framework presented in the preceding text suggests two additional empirical implications that we can explore with the *PVP* data. The first is that the effect of the interaction of *Gini* and *EP* should not vary substantially with the electoral law. Is this the case? Model 6 reestimates model 4, but only in the twelve countries with single-member districts. The results are largely consistent with those in model 4. If we plot the marginal effect of *Gini* as we did in Figure 8.2 (not shown), it is of course declining in *EP*, and it is positive over most of the range of *EP*, with a maximum value of almost 1. When *EP* is large enough (about 0.65), the coefficient becomes negative, but is never statistically significant when negative. Similarly, the marginal effect of *EP* is declining in *Gini*. It is positive over most of the range of *Gini*, has a maximum value of about 0.65, is statistically significant at the 0.05 level when *Gini* is less than 0.43, and is never statistically significant when it is negative. Thus, in some respects, the results are more consistent with the argument than we find when pooling the data (because the estimated effect of *Gini* is never statistically significant and negative). Model 7 presents the same analysis with the thirty-seven PR countries. The results are very similar to those in model 4, and when we plot the coefficients as in Figure 8.2, the qualitative results are almost identical. Thus, there is evidence that the results are similar in PR and SMD systems.

Second, the theoretical argument suggests that class politics can emerge more easily when government revenues are from taxes than when they are from exogenous sources, like resources. While we do not have precise data on the proportion of government revenues from natural resources, we do have data on the total natural resources per capita. The results for this variable would support the theory if PVP increases as natural resources increase. We find instead that Natural Resources has a negative coefficient, though it is not precisely estimated. I return to the role of natural resources in Chapter 9.

8.3 OLD AND NEW DEMOCRACIES

As in Chapter 7, we can also examine ethnic voting in new democracies (countries that were not democratic ten years prior to the year in which the relevant survey was conducted using a Polity2 cutoff of 6).[3] Model 1 in Table 8.2 presents the results using the same set of variables included in model 3 of Table 8.1. With a relatively small number of countries, there are quite limited degrees of freedom in this "kitchen sink" model, so model 2 excludes those control variables that are measured with considerable error in model 1. The results are very similar to model 3 in Table 8.1. The ethnification of party systems increases with inequality, but this estimated relationship decreases as ethnic polarization increases. The top panel in Figure 8.3 plots the marginal effect of *Gini* at different levels of EP, and it is important to note the similarity with Figure 8.2, where all countries are used. Indeed, the results are in some sense more consistent with the argument when we focus on the new democracies in that the estimated effect of *Gini* is never negative and significant. The results in model 2 also show that the estimated effect of ethnic diversity on party system ethnification is positive but decreasing as inequality increases.

[3] This results in twenty-two countries from thirty-five surveys in the baseline model where all controls are included: Bangladesh (1 WVS), Bulgaria (1 WVS), Estonia (2 WVS), Georgia (1 WVS), Guatemala (1WVS), Indonesia (1 WVS), Kenya (2 Afrobarometer), Latvia (1 CSES and 1 WVS), Lithuania (1 CSES and 1 WVS), Mexico (3 CSES and 1 WVS), Moldova (3 WVS), Peru (1 WVS), Romania (1 CSES and 2 WVS), Russia (1 CSES), Senegal (2 Afrobarometer), Slovak Republic (1 WVS), Slovenia (1 CSES), South Africa (1 WVS), Taiwan (1 WVS), and Ukraine (1 WVS and 1 CSES).

TABLE 8.2. *The ethnification of party systems in older and newer democracies*

	1	2	3	4
EP	1.2506***	1.4582***	1.2581***	1.3948***
	(0.0045)	(0.0047)	(0.0024)	(0.0000)
Gini (lagged1)	2.4884***	2.5859***		
	(0.0003)	(0.0006)		
Gini (lagged1)*EP	−3.3253***	−3.6673***		
	(0.0006)	(0.0012)		
Gini (lagged10)			1.4123**	1.8500***
			(0.0470)	(0.0000)
Gini (lagged10)*EP			−2.5514***	−2.8484***
			(0.0096)	(0.0000)
Polity2	0.0005		−0.0139	
	(0.9581)		(0.3180)	
Parties-Groups Ratio	−0.0035		0.0041	
	(0.2767)		(0.6619)	
Afrobarometer	−0.0336		0.0337	
	(0.6572)		(0.6641)	
CSES	−0.0056		−0.0058	
	(0.8227)		(0.7621)	
Redistribution (lagged1)	−0.4267***	−0.3529**		
	(0.0045)	(0.0104)		
Redistribution (lagged10)			−0.0027	
			(0.9821)	
Decentralization	−0.0469	−0.0803***	−0.0015	
	(0.1661)	(0.0083)	(0.9623)	
PR	−0.0791	−0.0830*	−0.0381	
	(0.1363)	(0.0672)	(0.2127)	
Natural Resources	0.0034		−0.0008	
	(0.6276)		(0.9003)	
GDP	−0.0175	−0.0076	−0.0018	
	(0.1333)	(0.5460)	(0.8804)	
Population	−0.0337***	−0.0212**	0.0082	
	(0.0011)	(0.0457)	(0.3967)	
Constant	−0.2197	−0.5082	−0.5066*	−0.7712***
	(0.5225)	(0.1908)	(0.0958)	(0.0000)
Type of democracy	New	New	Established	Established
N	32	35	55	59
R^2	.80	.70	.44	.33

Note: The DV is PVP. The p-values in parentheses are based on robust standard errors clustered by country. * $p < .10$, ** $p < .05$, *** $p < .01$.

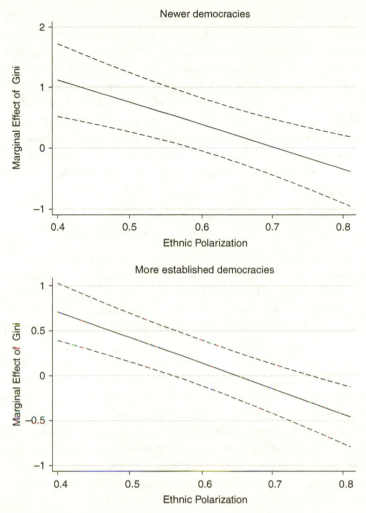

FIGURE 8.3. The estimated coefficients for Gini at different levels of EP in new and old democracies.

Note: Results from model 2 (top panel) and model 4 (bottom panel) in Table 8.2.

Thus, in new democracies, we find evidence consistent with the argument that inequality and ethnic diversity interact to influence the degree to which voters sort themselves by ethnicity when they vote.

Next consider the more established democracies: Are levels of inequality and ethnic diversity from the past associated with current levels of party system ethnification? I consider countries that have been continuously democratic for more than ten years (using the Polity2 cutoff of 6), which includes thirty-two country-surveys.[4] The measure of inequality is the Gini coefficient ten years prior to the survey, and Redistribution is also lagged ten years. Model 3 includes all the control variables and model 4 includes only those with coefficients that are reasonably precisely estimated in model 3 (which excludes all control variables). We can see that coefficients for *Gini*, *EP* and their interaction are in the expected direction and precisely estimated. The bottom panel in Figure 8.3 plots the estimated effect of Gini at different EP. Again, the patterns are consistent with the argument in established democracies when we measure inequality ten years in the past.

8.4 CONCLUSION

The empirical analysis in this and the previous chapter suggest there is a relationship between the conditions for class politics and the strength of the income–vote relationship, on one hand, and the strength of ethnic voting, on the other. These results are robust to different ways of measuring key variables, different subsets of the data, and different model specifications. And the results are inconsistent with arguments that democracies will respond to inequality by advantaging class-based parties that emphasize redistribution. Instead, we find that conditional on the presence of ethnic diversity, more inequality is associated with less income-based voting and more ethnic-based voting.

The empirical patterns from these chapters are significant in several respects. First, to the extent they support the theoretical model, they suggest that inequality itself may make it more difficult to redress inequality through the democratic process. When inequality is high, advocating rich-to-poor redistribution seems a weak tool for attracting votes and forming electoral coalitions. The theory suggests this is true because when inequality is high, class coalitions are large, making them less valuable to the members of such coalitions than would be smaller

---

4 The countries are Australia (2 CSES and 2 WVS), Bangladesh (1 WVS), Belgium (1 WVS and 1 CSES), Brazil (2 WVS and 1 CSES), Bulgaria (1 CSES and 1 WVS), Canada (2 WVS and 1 CSES), Colombia (1 WVS), Cyprus (1 WVS), Finland (1 WVS), France (1 CSES), Germany (1 WVS), Hungary (1 CSES), India (3 WVS), Israel (1 WVS), Macedonia (1 WVS), Madagascar (1 Afrobarometer), Mali (2 Afrobarometer and 1 WVS), Moldova (1 WVS), Namibia (2 Afrobarometer), New Zealand (2 CSES and 1 WVS), South Africa (2 Afrobarometer and 1 WVS), Spain (3 CSES and 2 WVS), Sweden (1 WVS) , Turkey (1 WVS), Ukraine (1 WVS), United States (2 CSES and 3 WVS), Uruguay (2 WVS), and Venezuela (3 WVS).

winning coalitions based on something other than class identity. This opens the door to ethnic politics. But electoral coalitions based on ethnicity should do less to address inequality than electoral coalitions based on class because ethnically based coalitions will favor some rich individuals who would be excluded from class coalitions (i.e., the rich in the winning ethnic groups) and will exclude some nonrich individuals who would be included in class coalitions (i.e., those in the losing ethnic groups). Thus, the evidence presented here is consistent with a theoretical framework suggesting that democracy will do the least to redress inequality precisely when inequality is highest.

Second, the analysis suggests a different pathway than has been emphasized in the literature regarding how ethnic diversity influences electoral behavior and redistributive outcomes. Previous research often argues that ethnic diversity leads some poorer individuals to vote against their economic interests by opposing redistributive policies from which they would benefit, and that they do this to prevent benefits from going to groups that they do not like or believe to be undeserving. Thus, there is a sort of group-based enmity that leads to opposition to redistributive policies in diverse societies. The analysis here suggests quite a different theoretical mechanism: poorer voters do not oppose redistribution out of enmity, but rather because it benefits them economically to support group- rather than class-based distribution. An important distinction between these two perspectives is that the group-enmity perspective should operate independent of the level of economic inequality in society, whereas the perspective based on economic self-interest suggests an interaction of ethnic diversity with economic inequality. The empirical analysis above provides evidence for the importance of this interaction, suggesting that the link between ethnic diversity, voting, and redistribution across societies may not be based as much on group enmity as traditionally argued.

Finally, the analysis emphasizes the value of linking the study of class politics and the study of ethnic politics. Although there is a strong tradition in social science of studying ethnic electoral politics, and also a strong tradition of studying class politics, these two research programs typically unfold in isolation from each other. The analysis here suggests there is much to be gained by integrating the two, as the emergence of ethnic (or class) politics should depend on factors related to class (or ethnic politics). This in turn means that the effects of ethnic (or class) politics should depend on these conditions that lead to their emergence in the first place.

9

Social Structure, Redistribution, and Democratic Transitions

The theoretical argument suggests that when the conditions for ethnic politics are met, some rich – those in the winning group – benefit from government distribution, and some poor – those in the losing group – are excluded from government redistribution. By contrast, when the conditions for class politics are met, all of the nonrich receive distributive benefits, while the rich all receive none. Thus, the extent to which electoral politics encourage government actions that reduce inequality should depend on the conditions that encourage ethnic and class politics, and thus on inequality, ethnic polarization, and their interaction.

Chapter 8 noted that the interaction between inequality and ethnic polarization could manifest itself in different ways that are consistent with the theoretical model. In the analysis of ethnic voting, which included a quite broad range of countries, I found that when ethnic diversity was low, there was a strong effect of inequality on ethnification of party systems. As ethnic diversity increased, the estimated effect of inequality on voting decreased. This is consistent with the idea that when it is possible to form a relatively small electoral majority based on ethnic groups, inequality has little effect on voting outcomes because there are incentives for ethnic politics at almost any level of inequality. As societies become more homogeneous, inequality should become more salient, with greater inequality tipping politics in the direction of ethnic rather than class coalitions. Thus, the effect of inequality on ethnic voting should be positive, but it should decline as the ethnic diversity of society increases, disappearing when society is sufficiently diverse that it's difficult for class politics to prevail at any level of inequality.

If patterns of redistribution reflect these voting patterns, then we should see the same type of interaction between inequality and ethnic diversity. When ethnic polarization is relatively low, inequality should have a relatively strong *negative* relationship with redistribution, with more inequality leading to less redistribution. As ethnic diversity increases, the relationship between inequality and redistribution should weaken.

This chapter examines whether these relationships exist in the data. I first examine whether the level of redistribution across democracies correlates with inequality and ethnic diversity in the way predicted by the theory. I then consider the "redistributive cost of democracy" that is central in theories of strategic democratization. Theoretical research on strategic decisions by elites to undertake democratic transitions often begins by asking how elite expectations regarding redistribution under democracy are affected by the level of inequality in society. This research assumes that if democracy occurs, class politics will emerge, which implies that under democracy, redistribution will be highest – and thus autocratic elites will lose the most – when inequality is highest. The theory presented here paints a different picture because inequality can trigger ethnic politics, which leads to less redistribution. Thus, the expectations about the redistributive effects of democracy should depend on the interaction of ethnic diversity and inequality. I explore these expectations by pooling democratic and nondemocratic countries and estimating models of democratic transitions.

9.1 INEQUALITY, ETHNIC DIVERSITY, AND REDISTRIBUTION IN DEMOCRATIC SYSTEMS

Recall that Chapter 7 described a measure of redistribution that is based on the relationship between gross inequality (before taxes and transfers) and net inequality (after taxes and transfers). Solt (2009) provides time-varying measures of both variables, allowing us to measure redistribution as the proportion of inequality that is removed via taxes and transfers:

$$Redistribution = \frac{\text{Gross Gini} - \text{Net Gini}}{\text{Gross Gini}}.$$

I begin by using *Redistribution* as the dependent variable, focusing on all democratic countries in the Solt data set. Because it would be very difficult for a government in a newly formed democracy to influence redistribution

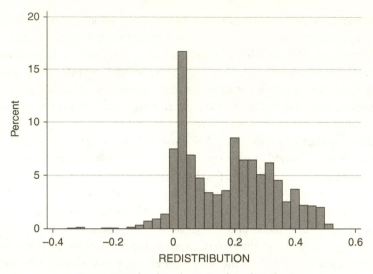

FIGURE 9.1. The distribution of *Redistribution*.

immediately, I include a country-year in the data set only if the country has been continuously democratic for at least five years. This results in an unbalanced panel with up to 1,538 observations (i.e., country-years) from eighty-two countries from 1965 through 2009. At the minimum, there is one observation for a country, at a maximum there are forty-three observations, and on average there are nineteen years per country.

Redistribution has a mean of 0.18 and a standard deviation of 0.15. Figure 9.1 presents a histogram showing the distribution of the dependent variable. Many of the country-years have relatively low levels of redistribution, with roughly 17 percent of observations showing a reduction in inequality of about 3 percent. The variable takes a negative value for a number of country-years, indicating that government policy is actually regressive, exacerbating inequality. The observations that take the largest negative values (i.e., most regressive) come from Fiji, Botswana, and, especially Thailand (which provides all the observations on *Redistribution* that are less than −0.15). The observations that are largest positive values (i.e., most redistributive) come from the Scandinavian countries – Sweden, Denmark, Finland, and Norway – as well as from Germany.

I estimate random effects models with lagged dependent variables, dummy variables for each year, and robust standard errors clustered by country. It is crucial to include the lagged dependent variable because

Gini is at once a key right-hand-side variable and a component of *Redistribution*. Moreover, there exist macroeconomic factors in the world economy that are correlated across countries and that have a systematic effect on *Gini* and thus on *Redistribution*. The lagged dependent also reduces concern about the possible influence of omitted right-hand-side variables. Given issues that arise with lagged dependent variables in panel data, I estimate the model using a variety of lag structures, reducing concerns about bias and inefficiency. Of course, the lagged dependent variables and the year dummies explain a substantial amount of variation in *Redistribution*, ensuring that the estimated magnitudes of all right-hand-side variables will be quite small. To diminish concerns about reverse causality, I use one-year lags of all right-hand-side control variables. All other variables are the same as those in Chapter 7.[1]

Table 9.1 presents the results. Model 1 includes only the direct effects of *Gini* and *EP* (not their interaction) and one lag of the dependent variable. The coefficients for *Gini* and *EP* both have the expected negative signs and both are very precisely estimated. Model 2 adds a second lag of the dependent variable, and the results are quite stable. Model 3 adds a third lag of the dependent variable, and again the results are quite stable. The results, then, are not particularly sensitive to the number of lags of the dependent variable, and in what follows I focus on models that include the first and second lag.

Model 4 includes the interaction of *Gini* and *EP*. The main effects of these variables continue to be negative and very precisely measured, and the interaction is positive and also precisely measured. Of the control variables, only *Population* has a coefficient that is measured with some precision (significant at 0.10). The general small magnitude and imprecision of most coefficient estimates is of course due in large part to the inclusion of two lags of the dependent variable and indicator variables for each year. Model 5 is the same as model 4, but using the EHII measure of Gini. Again, the results with this different measure of inequality are similar to those from using the SWIID Gini.

Figure 9.2 plots the estimated marginal effect of inequality across different values of EP (ranging from the 10th to the 90th percentile of this variable). The top panel in the figure is from model 4. There is a negative and precisely estimated coefficient for *Gini* at lower levels of *EP*. As *EP* increases, the estimated effect of *Gini* remains negative but grows smaller in absolute value, moving toward 0 and becoming positive

---

[1] To ease interpretation, in this chapter I divide Resources by 1,000.

TABLE 9.1. *Inequality, ethnic diversity, and redistribution I*

	1	2	3	4	5
Gini (SWIID)	-0.0345***	-0.0318***	-0.0327***	-0.1086***	-0.0275*
	(0.0060)	(0.0061)	(0.0061)	(0.0348)	(0.0147)
EP	-0.0056***	-0.0051***	-0.0050**	-0.0655***	
	(0.0021)	(0.0019)	(0.0020)	(0.0208)	
GDP	0.0019***	0.0016**	0.0019***	0.0009	0.0012
	(0.0007)	(0.0007)	(0.0007)	(0.0009)	(0.0012)
Pop	-0.0003	-0.0003	-0.0004	-0.0007*	-0.0005
	(0.0004)	(0.0003)	(0.0003)	(0.0004)	(0.0005)
Natural Resources	-0.0011	-0.0016	-0.0019	-0.0025	-0.0015
	(0.0030)	(0.0031)	(0.0032)	(0.0032)	(0.0038)
Redistribution (t − 1)	0.9707***	1.0896***	1.0691***	1.0890***	1.0312***
	(0.0075)	(0.1099)	(0.0912)	(0.1040)	(0.1066)
Redistribution (t − 2)		-0.1153	0.1344	-0.1081	-0.0747
		(0.1089)	(0.1250)	(0.1046)	(0.1049)
Redistribution (t − 3)			-0.2334***		
			(0.0656)		

Gini (SWIID)*EP				0.1471***	
				(0.0482)	
Gini (EHII)					−0.1044***
					(0.0306)
Gini (EHII)*EP					0.0591
					(0.0379)
Constant	0.0011	0.0012	−0.0012	0.0409**	0.0383**
	(0.0066)	(0.0059)	(0.0056)	(0.0190)	(0.0185)
N	1565	1538	1511	1538	1221
Number of countries	82	82	82	82	71
Within R^2	0.82	0.82	0.83	0.83	0.81
Between R^2	0.99	0.99	0.99	0.99	0.99
Overall R^2	0.98	0.98	0.98	0.98	0.98

Note: The dependent variable is *Redistribution*, and the table presents results from random effects models with robust standard errors clustered by country. In addition to the lagged dependent variables, all models also include a dummy variable for each year. * $p < .10$, ** $p < .05$, *** $p < .01$.

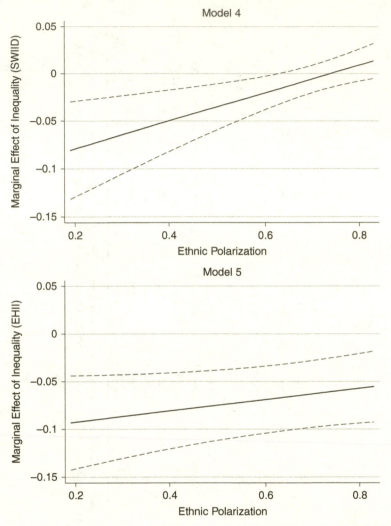

FIGURE 9.2. The estimated marginal effect of *Gini* at different levels of ethnic polarization.
Note: Results are from Table 9.1.

(but not significant) at the highest levels of inequality. Thus, as in the previous chapter, the data are consistent with a story where at lower levels of ethnic polarization, redistributive class politics can emerge most easily when inequality is low to begin with, but at a higher level of ethnic polarization, it is more difficult for class politics to emerge at any level of inequality. The bottom panel, based on the EHII data, tells a related but somewhat different story. Again, we find that inequality is associated with less redistribution, and that the estimated negative effect diminishes as ethnic polarization increases. But the interaction is weaker in size (though it still declines by about 50 percent when going from the largest to smallest *EP* in the plot), and the average negative effect of *Gini* across *EP* is larger when using the EHII data than when using the SWIID Gini.

Table 9.2 presents additional tests of the robustness of model 4. The first three models consider different control variables. Although all of the included countries are fairly democratic, there is a difference between countries that have a Polity2 score of 6 and those that have a score of 10. Model 6 therefore adds *Polity2* to the model. Although the coefficient for *Polity2* is very imprecisely measured and this variable does not seem to belong in the model, the results for the variables of interest are quite similar to those in model 4. Model 7 adds the dummy variable for PR, an institution that has often been associated with more redistribution. Again, the variable does not seem to belong: the coefficient is very imprecisely estimated and has the opposite sign of that predicted by existing research. Its inclusion does not, however, influence the results for inequality and ethnic diversity. And model 8 adds a control for the trade openness using a measure of trade as a percentage of GDP. Trade openness can put constraints on redistribution and can influence market inequality. Again, the coefficient on this variable is not at all precisely estimated and its inclusion does not influence the results of central interest.

The next three models reestimate model 4, but using different subsets of data. The data set includes a wide variety of countries, including some that are quite poor and that might have limited means to redress inequality in a way that is captured by *Redistribution*. Model 9 therefore reestimates model 4, but excluding the bottom decile of observations as ranked by GDP per capita.[2] When the poorest countries are excluded, we again find similar results to those in model 4, with the negative coefficients on *Gini* and *EP* and a positive coefficient on their interaction, with all coefficients precisely estimated. The coefficients of all three variables are larger in absolute magnitude than those in previous models, but the net effect Gini is similar across the range of *EP* in models 4 and 9.

---

[2] With this restriction, there are observations from Benin, Bangladesh, Bolivia, Ghana, Honduras, Indonesia, India, Sri Lanka, Moldova, Madagascar, Mali, Mongolia, Mauritius, Malawi, Nicaragua, Pakistan, Philippines, and Senegal are removed from the data set.

TABLE 9.2. Inequality, ethnic diversity and redistribution II

	(6)	(7)	(8)	(9)	(10)	(11)	(12)
Gini (SWIID)	−0.1101***	−0.1181***	−0.1095***	−0.1746***	−0.1223***	−0.1424**	−0.1384**
	(0.0355)	(0.0391)	(0.0348)	(0.0576)	(0.0454)	(0.0621)	(0.0576)
EP	−0.0673***	−0.0678***	−0.0672***	−0.1317***	−0.0607**	−0.1083***	−0.1013***
	(0.0219)	(0.0233)	(0.0211)	(0.0365)	(0.0253)	(0.0377)	(0.0359)
Gini*EP	0.1520***	0.1546***	0.1502***	0.2936***	0.1437**	0.2538***	0.2360***
	(0.0509)	(0.0537)	(0.0486)	(0.0867)	(0.0590)	(0.0944)	(0.0899)
Polity 2	0.0007						
	(0.0008)						
PR		−0.0009					
		(0.0014)					
Trade (% of GDP)			0.0000				
			(0.0000)				
GDP	0.0004	0.0010	0.0008	0.0071**	0.0000	0.0014	
	(0.0010)	(0.0009)	(0.0009)	(0.0030)	(0.0013)	(0.0029)	
Pop	−0.0007*	−0.0006	−0.0004	−0.0027**	−0.0012*	−0.0003	
	(0.0004)	(0.0004)	(0.0006)	(0.0012)	(0.0007)	(0.0005)	
Natural Resources	−0.0023	−0.0026	−0.0015	0.0004	−0.0261***	−0.0028	
	(0.0031)	(0.0034)	(0.0031)	(0.0036)	(0.0081)	(0.0029)	

	All avail.	All avail.	All avail.	Non poor	Not Neo-Europe	Neo Europe	Neo Europe
Redistribution $(t-1)$	1.0878***	1.0767***	1.0884***	1.0408***	0.8953***	1.2948***	1.2941***
	(0.1044)	(0.1060)	(0.1041)	(0.1040)	(0.1370)	(0.0485)	(0.0471)
Redistribution $(t-2)$	−0.1076	−0.0965	−0.1082	−0.0981	0.0612	−0.3113***	−0.3091***
	(0.1047)	(0.1068)	(0.1046)	(0.1030)	(0.1379)	(0.0464)	(0.0441)
Constant	0.0397**	0.0450**	0.0404**	0.0091	0.0509*		
	(0.0185)	(0.0211)	(0.0189)	(0.0408)	(0.0269)		
Constant						0.0000	0.0687***
						(.)	(0.0233)
N	1538	1434	1514	1384	793	745	798
No. of countries	82	82	81	69		60	22
Countries included	All avail.	All avail.	All avail.	Non poor	Not Neo-Europe	Neo Europe	Neo Europe

Note: The dependent variable is *Redistribution*, and the table presents results from random effects models with robust standard errors clustered by country. The Gini measure is from SWIID. R^2 results are essential identical to those in Table 9.1. In addition to the lagged dependent variables, all models also include a dummy variable for each year. RHS variables are lagged one year. * $p < .10$, ** $p < .05$, *** $p < .01$.

The richest "NeoEuropean" have a long tradition of redistributive welfare states, and indeed, the mean of *Redistribution* in these countries is 0.29, almost four times the average of 0.08 we find in the other countries. In addition, the NeoEuropean countries have on average a lower level of ethnic polarization: the mean of *EP* is 0.41 in NeoEurope countries and is 0.56 in countries that are not included in NeoEurope. Controlling for country wealth in the democracies included here should capture some of this effect, but models 10 and 11 present results based on dividing the data into two data sets. Model 10 estimates model 4, but *without* the NeoEurope countries. The results are very similar to those in model 4: even in countries that are not known for large welfare states, redistribution is decreasing with inequality, and the magnitude of this effect decreases with ethnic polarization. The results also show that countries with more natural resources have less redistribution. Indeed, the coefficient for *Natural Resources* is very precisely estimated, which was not the case in the models where all data are pooled. Thus, the theoretical argument suggesting that exogenous resources could depress class politics finds support in the redistribution data, but only in the non-NeoEuropean countries, and not in the voting data. As noted, *Natural Resources* is a weak measure of the government dependence on natural resources because it does not separate resource revenue that goes to the government from resource revenue that goes to private companies.

Model 11 presents results from estimating model 4 using only the NeoEurope countries. Again, we find similar results in the two sets of countries, although the interaction term is larger than in model 4. There are only 22 countries in the set of NeoEuropean countries, which can make the results especially sensitive to specification. Indeed, we find in model 11 that the only macrovariables that have coefficients that are at all precisely estimated are those related to inequality and ethnic diversity. Model 12 therefore reestimates model 9, but with only the inequality and diversity variables (along with the lags and the year indicators). The results for the variables of core interest are very similar to those of other models.

How large are the estimated effects in these models? As noted previously, the two lags of the dependent variable explain a very large proportion of the variation in the dependent variable, ensuring the substantive effects of all other variables will be small. We can nonetheless get some sense of the size, both nominally and relatively. Suppose *EP* takes a value such that the estimated coefficient for *Gini* is −0.08, which is within the range of significance in all the panels of Figure 9.2. If we moved from a country where *Gini* is 0.33 to one where *Gini* is 0.55 (a move from the 10th to 90th percentile), this would be associated with an estimated increase in *Redistribution* of around 0.02. Recall the mean of *Redistribution* is 0.18 with a standard deviation of 0.15. While the structure of the model ensures this modest effect, it is useful to compare it with other variables. This effect of 0.02 is roughly three times the size of the effect of the NeoEurope indicator variable in model 8. There is no other variable that is consistently estimated with precision across models in Table 9.1. *GDP* has a positive and precisely estimated coefficient in only one model that includes the interaction of *Gini* and *EP* (model 7, which excludes the poorest countries). In that model, *GDP* (which recall is measured as the log of GDP per capita) has a coefficient of 0.007. Thus, in this set of countries, if *GDP* moved from its value at the 10th percentile (8.6) to its value at its 90th percentile (10.4), *Redistribution* would increase by 0.01, or by about half the effect found in the example for *Gini*. Thus, not only is *GDP* rarely significant, but also when it is, the effect is quite small even compared to the effect of *Gini*. *Population* is the other variable that is most often estimated with some precision – it is negative and statistically significant at the 0.10 level (or better) in five of the seven models where it is included with the interaction of *Gini* and *EP*. In model 4, the coefficient for *population* is −0.0007. If *Population* (which is measured by its log) moved from its value at the 10th percentile (7.7) to its value at its 90th percentile (11.4), *Redistribution* would decrease by 0.003, or roughly one-hundredth the size of the effect of *Gini* described previously. Thus, although the effect of *Gini* is not large in nominal terms, as expected given the inclusion of two lagged dependent variables, the results are nonetheless impressive both with respect to the robustness of the parameter estimates for *Gini* at different levels of ethnic diversity and with respect to the size of the estimated effect relative to the size of other coefficients.

The analysis presented to this point is largely consistent with the theoretical framework. The model suggests that redistribution should decrease with inequality and ethnic diversity, but that the effect for each of these variables should be mediated by the value of the other. We find evidence of a precisely estimated negative relationship between redistribution and inequality. The analysis also shows a negative and precisely estimated relationship between redistribution and ethnic diversity. Finally, we find that the estimated negative effect of inequality diminishes – that is, moves toward zero – as ethnic diversity increases. These results are robust across a range of models that include different control variables. And they are robust when we estimate the model only on specific sets of countries, including when we separate out the advanced democracies from the rest of the countries.

Ethnic Voting and Redistribution

The theoretical argument suggests that ethnic politics should emerge when the conditions for class politics are weak, that is, when inequality is large given the level of ethnic diversity. The argument also suggests that when ethnic politics emerges, redistribution should decline. In the previous chapter, we found that when the theoretical conditions for class politics are weak, the ethnification of party systems is strong. In the previous section, we found that when the theoretical conditions for class politics are weak, redistribution is lower. But if the politicization of ethnicity in elections is what leads to lower levels of redistribution, it is useful to consider whether the level of redistribution is related to the ethnification of party systems.

Table 9.3 explores this relationship. The central right-hand-side variable of interest is Party Voting Polarization (*PVP*), which was described in Chapter 8. Recall *PVP* takes a higher value when political parties have a more clear ethnic basis of support. Thus, if ethnification of party systems leads to less redistribution, *PVP* should have a negative coefficient. As I have measures of ethnic voting for a relatively limited set of elections, the amount of data for this test is quite small, with many countries having only one observation. I therefore estimate OLS models with robust standard errors.

Model 1 adds *PVP* to a baseline model with *EP*, *Gini*, and other basic controls. Although *PVP* is obviously endogenous to inequality and ethnic diversity, I include the direct effects of these variables as well, which of course creates collinearity in the right-hand-side regressors. *PVP* has a negative coefficient and it is estimated precisely (the *p*-value is .04). *Ethnic Polarization* and *Gini* have the expected negative coefficients, but only the coefficient for *EP* is precisely estimated. Since the coefficient for *Gini* is measured with considerable error, model 2 reestimates model 1, but without *Gini*. The results change little. Since *PVP* is endogenous to *EP*, model 3 reestimates model 2, but without *EP*. The coefficient for *PVP* increases substantially in size and is estimated quite precisely. Model 4 adds a control for the electoral law and model 5 adds a control for the level of democracy. While the coefficient for *Polity2* is not precisely estimated, the coefficient for *PR* is negative and significant. The results for *PVP* are unaffected by the inclusion of either variable. Finally, model 6 reestimates model 5, but including indicator variables for each year. Again, the results for *PVP* are robust. We find, then, that greater ethnic voting is associated with less redistribution. If *PVP* went from its minimum to its maximum, *Redistribution* would decrease by 0.08, which is roughly one half its mean and two-thirds of its standard deviation.

Education as a Gini Measure of "Redistribution"

The Solt data on redistribution have the advantage of directly measuring the extent to which policy reduces inequality. But as noted previously, the Solt measures of the Gross Gini (or Market Gini) and the Net Gini are often based on the imputation of missing data, a particular concern in countries for which reliable surveys of income before and after taxes and transfers do not exist. Although the concern is likely less pronounced in many of the countries in this data set because they are reasonably established democracies, it is nevertheless useful to consider an alternative measure of redistribution. To this end, I consider educational achievement as a way to measure redistributive efforts by governments. When few students are educated, children of the rich will typically find a way to educate their children, but as government efforts to educate children increase, richer individuals will bear much of the cost and the least well-off will increasingly benefit. Thus, it is reasonable to expect that the higher the level of educational achievement, the greater the level of redistribution.

Using the set of democratic countries and years in this study, Figure 9.3 shows the distribution of two measures of educational achievement that are published by the World Bank. On the top is primary school enrollment, which is measured as the "Total enrollment in primary education, regardless of age, expressed as a percentage of the population of official primary education age."[3] For these countries, there is little variation in primary school enrollment, with the vast majority of countries achieving quite high levels. On the bottom is the distribution of secondary education enrollment levels. Here there is considerable variation. Thus, if we want to consider educational enrollment as a measure of redistribution, it makes sense to focus on secondary school.

---

[3] See http://data.worldbank.org/indicator/SE.PRM.ENRR. Values can exceed 100 percent because the numbers can include overaged and underaged students due to early or late school entrance and grade repetition.

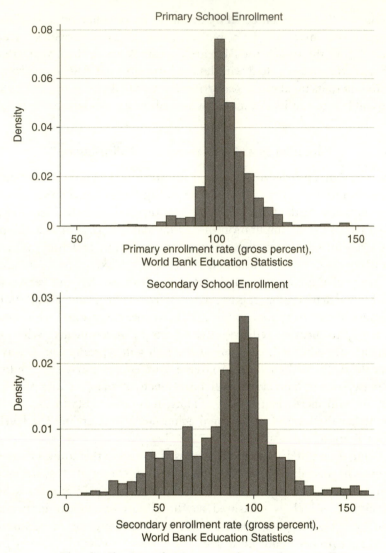

FIGURE 9.3. The distribution of primary and secondary enrollment across democracies.

Solon (2004), it is useful to note, provides a nice discussion of why secondary schooling provides a useful measure of redistributive policies.

Model 1 in Table 9.4 estimates the basic empirical model (based on model 4 in Table 9.1) using *secondary school enrollment* as the dependent variable. There are fewer observations than was the case

TABLE 9.3. *Ethnic parties and redistribution*

	1	2	3	4	5	6
PVP	−0.2177**	−0.2131*	−0.3034**	−0.3145***	−0.2699**	−0.2783**
	(0.1014)	(0.1132)	(0.1197)	(0.1174)	(0.1181)	(0.1160)
Ethnic Polarization	−0.1215***	−0.1317***				
	(0.0440)	(0.0467)				
Gini	−0.0312					
	(0.1295)					
GDP	0.0564***	0.0745***	0.0748***	0.0806***	0.0626***	0.0896***
	(0.0112)	(0.0070)	(0.0078)	(0.0077)	(0.0125)	(0.0088)
Pop	−0.0133**	−0.0124**	−0.0119**	−0.0182***	−0.0136**	−0.0193***
	(0.0054)	(0.0050)	(0.0054)	(0.0064)	(0.0058)	(0.0065)
Natural Resources	−0.2736	−0.2572	−0.2075	−0.4606**	−0.1900	−0.6080**
	(0.1920)	(0.1984)	(0.1684)	(0.2300)	(0.1630)	(0.2390)
NeoEurope	0.0559					
	(0.0348)					
PR				−0.0610**		−0.0810***
				(0.0246)		(0.0234)
Polity2					0.0129	
					(0.0108)	
Constant	−0.3019***	−0.4500***	−0.5222***	−0.5470***	−0.5342***	−0.5693***
	(0.0912)	(0.0612)	(0.0706)	(0.0649)	(0.0717)	(0.0895)
R^2	.63	.61	.57	.60	.58	.67
N	74	74	74	74	74	74
Year indicators?	No	No	No	No	No	Yes

Note: The dependent variable is *Redistribution*, and the table presents results from OLS models with robust standard errors.
* $p < .10$, ** $p < .05$, *** $p < .01$.

TABLE 9.4. *Secondary school enrollment*

	1	2	3	4	5	6
Gini (SWIID)	-1.898 (2.306)	-3.091 (4.427)	-4.417 (4.436)	0.262 (6.065)	-11.563*** (3.581)	
Ethnic Polarization	-0.631 (1.490)	-2.960 (2.854)	-3.515 (2.809)	-0.051 (3.490)	-7.717** (3.095)	-0.311 (3.499)
Gini (SWIID)*EP	1.400 (3.431)	6.532 (6.792)	7.314 (6.683)	-0.984 (8.505)	18.482*** (7.155)	
Gini (EHII)						-2.428 (5.426)
Gini (EHII)*EP						2.058 (8.092)
GDP per capita	0.536** (0.231)	1.089*** (0.363)	1.157*** (0.359)	-0.182 (0.556)	0.759* (0.450)	0.664*** (0.257)
Population	-0.038 (0.046)					
Natural resources per capita	0.000007 (0.00004)					
Secondary enrollment rate $(t-1)$	1.078*** (0.050)	1.076*** (0.048)	1.075*** (0.048)	1.070*** (0.050)	1.152*** (0.071)	1.149*** (0.078)
Secondary enrollment rate $(t-2)$	-0.122*** (0.045)	-0.145*** (0.039)	-0.153*** (0.039)	-0.122*** (0.043)	-0.213*** (0.070)	-0.191** (0.077)
Year			0.026** (0.011)	0.013 (0.019)	0.051*** (0.019)	0.022* (0.013)
Constant	0.000 (.)	-2.025 (3.155)	-52.371** (22.489)	-17.957 (33.554)	-97.847*** (36.919)	-45.465* (25.039)
Countries	All	All	All	NeoEur.	Non-NeoEur.	Non-NeoEur
N	1131	1208	1208	605	603	473
Year indicators	Yes	No	No	No	No	No

Note: The dependent variable is gross secondary school enrollment. Results from random effects models with robust standard errors (in parentheses) clustered by country. * $p < .10$, ** $p < .05$, *** $p < .01$.

in the *Redistribution* equation, with roughly 1,100 observations from 76 countries, compared with more than 1,500 observations from 82 countries in Table 9.1. The coefficient for *Gini* and *EP* have the expected negative signs and their interaction has the expected positive sign, but all three coefficients are measured with considerable error. The one variable that has a large and precisely estimated coefficient is *GDP*, with richer countries having higher secondary enrollment rates. Because the other variables are never precisely estimated, in the models that follow, *GDP* is the only control variable I include on the right-hand side.

In model 1, the year indicator variables are estimated with considerable error, with only one year having a coefficient that is estimated at all accurately. Model 2 therefore estimates the model with no time controls (other than the two lags of the dependent variable) and model 3 estimates the model with a *Year* variable (to explore the possibility that education enrollment levels may be increasing over time). In both models, the coefficients for *Gini*, *EP* and their interaction are not precisely estimated, while *GDP* continues to have a positive and precisely estimated coefficient, as does *Year* in model 3.

Because the mean of the dependent variable for NeoEuropean countries is much higher than the mean for other countries, it is doubtful that the theory can explain variation in enrollment rates among NeoEuropean countries because these countries typically do a very good job of educational enrollment. Model 4 therefore reestimates model 3 using only the NeoEurope countries, while model 5 does so using the non-NeoEuropean democracies. In model 4, the p-values of the coefficients on the three variables of interest are all over .9. Thus, these variables have absolutely no explanatory power when the dependent variable is secondary school enrollment. Indeed, the only variables that are precisely estimated are the lags of the dependent variable. By contrast, in model 5, for the non-NeoEuropean countries, all of the variables are quite precisely estimated and have the expected sign. Figure 9.4 shows the marginal effect of *Gini* at different levels of *EP*. At lower level of ethnic polarization, there is a reasonable strong negative estimated effect of inequality on secondary school enrollment. But as ethnic diversity increases, this effect diminishes, and at a sufficiently high level of ethnic diversity, there is no statistically significant effect of the Gini. Thus, the results for *secondary school enrollment* are very similar to those found for *Redistribution* in the non-NeoEuropean countries (which were shown in Figure 9.2). This result is not, however, robust to the use of the EHII data, as can be seen

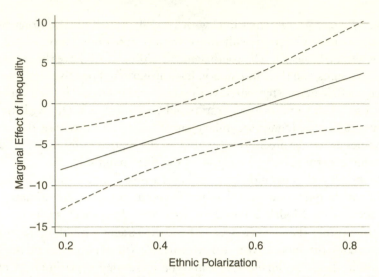

FIGURE 9.4. The marginal effect of Gini on secondary enrollment at different levels of ethnic diversity.

in model 6. Although all of the coefficients of theoretical interest have the expected sign, none are estimated precisely in this smaller data set.

9.2 INEQUALITY AND DEMOCRATIC TRANSITIONS

The empirical analysis in this chapter has focused on how the conditions for class politics are related to redistribution in democracies. We have found that conditional on the level of ethnic diversity, democracies redistribute less when inequality is high. As noted in Chapter 5, the argument also has implications for studying the redistributive cost of democracy, and thus for furthering our understanding of democratic transitions. Because inequality discourages class politics when ethnic polarization is sufficiently large, the effect of inequality on democratic transitions should depend on ethnic polarization levels. When ethnic polarization is low, higher levels of inequality should be associated with a lower likelihood of transition to democracy. When ethnic polarization is high, making class politics quite difficult under democracy, inequality should have little impact on strategic decisions to democratize because the level of inequality should not influence outcomes under democratic competition.

To explore whether these patterns exist in the data, I estimate models of democratization using data from Cheibub, Gandhi, and Vreeland (2010). Countries enter the data set when they are autocratic and they leave the data set when they become democratic using the measure of Cheibub et al. For ease of interpretation, I begin by estimating simple linear probability models with robust standard errors clustered by country, and I lag all right-hand-side variables by one year. I control for GDP per capita (logged), population (logged) and natural resources. Given the sparseness of observations where transitions occur. I use the SWIID measure of market Gini. The empirical models are in Table 9.5.

Model 1 includes the direct effects of *Gini* and *EP*. Although the coefficient for *Gini* has the expected negative sign, it is not at all precisely estimated. The coefficient for *EP* is positive, but it too has a large standard error. Only *Natural Resources* has a precisely estimated coefficient, and higher levels of natural resources are associated with lower levels of democratization. Model 2 includes the quadratic term for the Gini variable to test the nonlinear implication from Acemoglu and Robinson's theory. Both variables measuring the Gini have coefficients with very large standard errors. These models, then, provide little support for theories that invoke the class-based tax-and-transfer models of democratic competition to link inequality to democratic transitions.

Model 3 adds the interaction of *Gini* and *EP*. In this specification, we see a negative and precisely estimated coefficient for *Gini*, and a positive and relatively precisely estimated coefficient for the interact. The top panel in Figure 9.5 plots the coefficient and 95-percent confidence interval for *Gini* at different levels of *EP*. At relatively low levels of *EP*, the coefficient is negative and quite precisely estimated. As *EP* increases, the coefficient moves toward 0.

Models 4 to 8 test the robustness of the results. Model 4 excludes *GDP* and *Population*, both of which are not remotely significant in model 3. The results for inequality and ethnic polarization are essentially the same. Model 5 reestimates model 4 using a different measure of the Gini: the average of Gini during the prior five years (as opposed to the simple lag of *Gini*). The results are very similar to those in model 4. Model 6 reestimates model 5, but includes an indicator variable for each year. Again, the results are largely consistent with those in model 5. The bottom panel in Figure 9.5 plots the coefficient on *Gini* from model 6, and the substantive implications are virtually identical to those that are depicted in the top

TABLE 9.5. *Inequality, ethnic diversity and transitions to democracy*

	1	2	3	4	5	6	7	8
Gini (SWIID)	-0.0520	-0.3062	-0.2315*	-0.2235**				
	(0.0485)	(0.4002)	(0.1182)	(0.1089)				
EP	0.0303	0.0319	-0.1119	-0.1108	-0.1909	-0.2342	-5.5908*	-8.3031
	(0.0232)	(0.0230)	(0.0910)	(0.0881)	(0.1343)	(0.1635)	(3.0126)	(5.1586)
Gini²		0.2679						
		(0.4048)						
*Gini*EP*			0.3187	0.3183				
			(0.2005)	(0.1961)				
Gini (5-year average)					-0.2909*	-0.3154	-9.4194**	-12.0893*
					(0.1592)	(0.1839)	(4.0100)	(6.4826)
*Gini (5-year average)*EP*					0.4127	0.4881	12.7612**	18.4121*
					(0.2640)	(0.3169)	(6.2418)	(10.8685)
GDP	0.0023	0.0020	0.0011					
	(0.0066)	(0.0065)	(0.0065)					
Population	0.0008	0.0007	0.0002					
	(0.0034)	(0.0034)	(0.0035)					
Natural Resources	-0.1859**	-0.1800**	-0.1747**	-0.1642**	-0.1132**	-0.1040	-20.7262***	-23.3903***
	(0.0847)	(0.0841)	(0.0839)	(0.0702)	(0.0548)	(0.0637)	(7.8679)	(9.0482)
Constant	0.0200	0.0810	0.1141	0.1194**	0.1694**	0.1448	0.9953	2.6751
	(0.0769)	(0.1228)	(0.0966)	(0.0495)	(0.0821)	(0.0904)	(1.9040)	(3.1419)
R²	0.004	0.005	0.006	0.005	0.006	0.04	0.035	0.078
N	1398	1398	1398	1424	1747	1747	1747	1225

Note: There are 104 countries in each model. The dependent variable is an indicator taking the value 1 if a country is democratic (see text for further details). Models 1 to 6 are linear probability models and models 7 and 8 are logit models. Robust standard errors clustered by country are in parentheses. The pseudo R-squared is given for models 7 and 8. Models 6 and 8 contain year indicator variables. * $p < .10$, ** $p < .05$, *** $p < .01$.

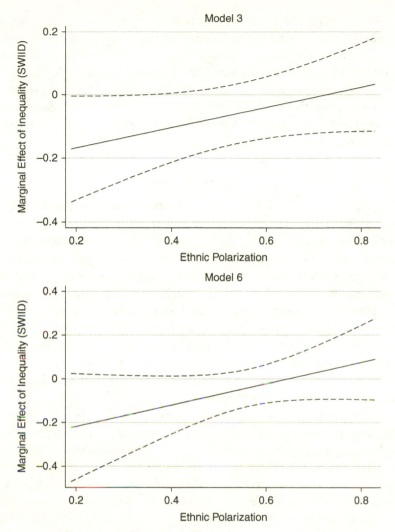

FIGURE 9.5. The estimated marginal effect of *Gini* on transitions to democracy at different levels of ethnic polarization.

Note: Results are from Table 9.5.

panel. Finally, models 7 and 8 reestimate models 5 and 6 using logit.[4] The coefficients are even more precisely estimated than those using the linear probability models.

[4] Model 8 has fewer observations because when year indicators are included, those years with no conflict are perfectly predicted and thus are dropped in the logit models.

The evidence presented here is therefore consistent with previous arguments that autocratic elites are less likely to democratize when economic inequality is high, but this is true only when ethnic polarization is sufficiently low. When ethnic polarization is large enough, inequality has no association with transitions to democracy. Thus, if we wish to think about the strategic incentives of elites to democratize, it is useful to relax the assumption that only class-based politics can unfold if democratization occurs.

9.3 SUMMARY

The evidence in this chapter is largely consistent with the theoretical model. Inequality and ethnic polarization are associated with lower levels of redistribution, but the strength of these associations depends on the interaction of inequality with ethnic polarization. When ethnic polarization is sufficiently low, more inequality is associated with less redistribution. When ethnic polarization is sufficiently high, the relationship between inequality and redistribution weakens. These patterns exist when pooling all data and when older democracies are separated from newer ones. The empirical analysis also reveals that ethnic voting itself is associated with lower levels of redistribution, suggesting that the voting patterns revealed in Chapter 8 are directly related to the redistributive outcomes measured in this chapter.

Given these patterns in the data, we should expect a different relationship between inequality and democratization than has been traditionally posited in the literature, one that is conditional on the level of ethnic polarization. The last section of this chapter provides evidence that an association between inequality and democratic transitions does not exist in the data unless we consider the interaction of inequality and ethnic polarization. When ethnic polarization is sufficiently low, higher inequality is associated with lower probabilities of transition, as previous research argues should be the case. But when ethnic polarization is sufficiently high, there is no relationship between the level of inequality and the probability of democratic transitions.

10

Conclusion

Inequality and the Politics of Exclusion

This book argues that social structure influences whether ethnic or class identities become the targets of distributive benefits in democratic electoral competition. The argument is based on the premise that voters will support parties that can credibly commit to offering the greatest material gain, and that political parties form in an effort to gain rents (by winning) or influence policy (in losing). Parties that represent the smallest majorities have an advantage because they can offer more to their supporters. As a consequence, when inequality is sufficiently low, class politics has an advantage (because low inequality is associated with a smaller number of voters receiving distributive benefits under class politics) and when ethnic polarization is high, ethnic politics has an advantage (because high ethnic polarization is associated with a smaller number of voters receiving distributive benefits under ethnic politics). But what it means for inequality or ethnic polarization to be low depends on the value of the other variable: a particular level of inequality may be "high" in a country with low ethnic polarization and may be "low" in a country with high ethnic polarization. For this reason, to understand how social structure influences electoral politics, we need to consider the interaction of inequality and ethnic diversity. Chapter 4 suggests that this theoretical intuition is robust to a number of alternative assumptions about the nature of the electoral law, the source of government revenues and the number of ethnic groups. Chapter 5 also suggests that the intuition would be robust if we assumed that the class-based element of electoral competition unfolded along the lines of median voter models if class-based parties could imperfectly target benefits at the median voter.

A variety of evidence has been brought to bear in Chapters 7 through 9 regarding the predicted role of social structure. If social structure affects electoral competition in the way implied by the theory, the conditions leading to class versus ethnic politics should influence the relationship between individual income and voting behavior. The evidence in Chapter 7 finds this pattern in the data. In countries with lower levels of inequality, voters sort themselves by income, with lower income voters supporting more left-leaning parties that favor redistribution and higher income voters supporting parties that oppose redistribution. In higher inequality countries, income is a much less useful predictor of how voters will choose. This relationship, however, is conditioned by the level of ethnic polarization, with the relationship between inequality and voting behavior much stronger in the less ethnically diverse countries. The chapter shows that these patterns are robust to different ways of measuring inequality, to the inclusion of a variety of different controls, to the separation of data into established and new democracies, and to the use of attitudes toward inequality (rather than vote choice) as the outcome variable.

As discussed in Chapter 3, ethnicity and class are hardly the only identities that can be used for targeting in electoral politics, but these identities are prevalent across almost all countries and they do (largely) satisfy the criteria discussed in that chapter for a group to be a credible target for inclusion or exclusion. The theoretical model therefore labels the two group identities as class and ethnicity, and if this labeling is useful, the conditions that mitigate against class politics should encourage ethnic politics. Chapter 8 also finds this pattern in the data. Ethnification of party systems (the degree to which party systems have a clear ethnic basis of support) increases with inequality and ethnic polarization, but the estimated effect of each variable depends on the other. Higher levels of inequality are associated with higher levels of ethnic voting, for example, but the magnitude of this relationship declines as ethnic polarization increases. Again, the patterns are robust to the inclusion of different controls, to different measures of inequality, to different measures of party system ethnification, and to the separation of the data into old and new democracies. In addition, consistent with the model, the results are quite similar in plurality rule and proportional electoral systems. Thus, when the theory is evaluated with respect to its empirical implications for electoral behavior, there is consistent evidence that inequality, ethnic diversity, and their interaction are related to the salience of class and ethnic identity in elections.

The theory suggests that this relationship between social structure and electoral behavior exists because social structure influences the types of policies to which parties can credibly commit. If such commitment is relevant to the link between social structure and voting patterns, one should expect that social structure is also related to outcomes from the governing process. The model suggests that when class politics prevails, redistribution should be relatively large (because no rich receive benefits and all nonrich receive benefits), whereas when ethnic politics prevails, redistribution should be lower (because rich members in the winning ethnic group receive benefits and nonrich members of the excluded group receive no benefits). Although I do not have broad cross-national data on which members of ethnic groups receive benefits, Chapter 2 describes a range of evidence in other studies regarding how politicians target members of ethnic groups.

In Chapter 9, I examine the relationship between social structure and redistribution. The evidence suggests that inequality is associated with less redistribution, but that the magnitude of this negative effect diminishes as ethnic polarization increases. The patterns are robust to different measures of redistribution, to different measures of inequality, to the inclusion of different controls, and to the separation of data into the wealthy and less wealthy sets of countries. In addition, the chapter provides evidence that redistribution is lowest in countries where ethnic voting is highest.

These patterns of redistribution in democratic systems suggest a final, less direct implication of the model. If one assumes that rich autocratic elites consider the redistributive consequences of democracy in deciding whether to allow democratization, then the theory provides a new argument about how inequality, a variable that is central in the literature, should condition these expectations. In particular, the negative effect of inequality on transitions should diminish as ethnic polarization increases (because ethnic polarization discourages class politics). Chapter 9 provides evidence for this relationship.

As discussed in Chapter 6, I do not provide a clear evidence of any causal relationships in my empirical research. My hope, however, is that the reader will take seriously the causal logic of the theory because I have presented patterns in the data that are consistent with a range of distinct empirical implications of the theory. These implications concern a constellation of relationships about which we did not have strong prior beliefs, and the implications are related to outcomes – class voting, ethnic voting, redistribution, and democratic transitions – that are not typically studied together.

If one does believe the story here, it is rather discouraging. As discussed in Chapter 2, inequality can be viewed as intrinsically unjust, and it has also been connected to a range of negative outcomes, including lower economic growth, lower social mobility, and higher crime. And ethnic politics can also be viewed as intrinsically unjust, and it has been associated with a range of negative outcomes, including lower economic growth, lower public goods provision, and higher levels of violence. Thus, if there are conditions that at once encourage ethnic politics and discourage the sort of class politics that most effectively addresses inequality, this is a bad situation indeed. Alas, a central one of these conditions seems to be inequality itself, with more unequal countries exhibiting the traits of ethnic rather than class politics. It is therefore important to ask what might be done to avoid the "trap" implied by the theory and evidence here.

There is one element of social structure that I have not discussed and that may mute the negative implications of the argument, which is the relationship between ethnicity and class. To take an extreme example, if it turns out that all the nonrich are from the majority group and all the rich are from the minority group, then ethnic politics and class politics would converge to the same thing and we would not care about the distinction between the two. There is evidence that ethnic politics, at least in majoritarian systems, are most likely to emerge when ethnicity and income are related (Huber and Suryanarayon 2016), and that the consequences of ethnic diversity are most severe when there is inequality between groups (Baldwin and Huber 2010; Alesina, Michalopoulos, and Papaioannou 2013). One might view the "ethnic politics" in Malaysia that were described in Chapter 1, for example, as a form of class politics because the Bumiputera are on average quite poor whereas the Chinese and (to a lesser extent) the Indians are quite rich. If "ethnic politics" implies redistribution to a poor majority group, this would be quite a different normative situation than if income were correlated more weakly with group.

Although an "ethnic politics" that supports a poor majority clearly is less problematic for inequality than other forms of ethnic politics, it is important to bear in mind the limits of such situations. There are always nontrivial numbers of rich members in the nonrich group and of nonrich members in the rich groups, even when ethnicity correlates with income. And it is often the rich within that targeted groups that benefit disproportionately from group-specific policies (e.g., Sowell 2004). In Malaysia, for example, the rich Bumiputera often disproportionately benefit from New Economic Program (NEP) policies. Reservation policies in India benefit those in lower castes who are best able to compete for public sector positions. Affirmative action in the United States typically benefits the best educated blacks. Similar policies benefit the most well-off in minority groups in Brazil. This is relatively unsurprising, as the elites within minority groups are not only the best able to advocate for policies that benefit them; they are also the best able to take advantage more generally of the opportunities that come with the freedoms of democracy. This might be particularly important when group leaders such as tribal chiefs can directly and indirectly influence policy outcomes through their interactions with legislators and their constituents (Baldwin 2013, 2015).

Setting aside the issue of how group and class are related, there are two challenges that must be addressed in efforts to redress inequality. The first is to understand what policies contribute to inequality and what policies will therefore actually reduce it. This has been a key focus in economics, and in response to rising inequality, there has been vigorous debate about such policies in recent years. Two recent contributions, Stiglitz (2015) and Atkinson (2015), for example, emphasize things such as reinforcing the strength of unions, changing the way trade agreements are structured, maintaining strong competition within industries, stronger regulation of the financial industry, higher minimum wages, and the use of government employment. There are of course many other proposals, and disagreement about the effects of particular policies, but what these approaches typically share in common is their focus on what policies might work best.

The second challenge concerns how political incentives shape opportunities to adopt the best policies. One can know precisely what policies will reduce inequality, but if political incentives lead to the adoption of other polices, such policy knowledge is of little value for changing outcomes. The analysis in this book has little to say about the first challenge, but it can potentially aid in the second. Policies that address inequality fall in the domain of distributive politics: they concern who gets what. In the language of the argument I've been making here, policies that emerge from "class politics" will do the most to reduce inequality, so the second challenge associated with efforts to address inequality involves understanding how to encourage class politics in electoral competition.

The central theme of this book has been that class politics can be difficult to sustain because it is often fairly easy to divide the nonrich against each other, with some nonrich forming electoral coalitions with the rich at the expense of others who are nonrich. It is important to bear in mind that voters in the theory are choosing to advance their material interests, so when nonrich voters align themselves electorally with the rich, they do so to make themselves better off. I emphasize this point because it directs attention to different conditions regarding how to foster class politics than does research that emphasizes the possibility that the nonrich may support non-redistributive policies because they care about some "second dimension" of policy, such as religion, nationalism, gun rights, or ethnic enmity. This "second dimension" perspective might lead us to embrace political arrangements that isolate policymaking on a divisive second dimension from policymaking on class issues. For example, if religious issues (such as abortion or gay marriage), or issues related to gun control (an important one in the United States) are largely the domain of the courts, then it is less likely that these issues can divert political competition from core issues such as class. Or if the electoral law allows a wide range of parties to form, such as when there is high district magnitude proportional representation, then voters might not be forced to choose between, say, their "gun party" and their "class party." This could be true because a party could form that appealed to their preference on both issues.

My aim is not to dispute the relevance of "second dimensions," but rather to offer a different take on what divides the nonrich from each other, one that focuses on material interest. This perspective can generate different ideas about how to create incentives for class politics, and to see where the differences comes from, it is important to keep in mind that the distributive framework advanced here requires clearly identifiable group boundaries that can serve as the basis for inclusion and exclusion. These boundaries are what allows groups to be used in electoral competition to divide the nonrich against each other. Thus, the theoretical framework suggests that one pathway to encouraging the type of political competition that will emphasize class politics is to weaken group boundaries.

There are several types of policies that might contribute to this end. One is to adopt policies that blur the group boundaries themselves, so that it is less clear to voters what a credible commitment to a particular group might entail. This might be done by encouraging intergroup marriage if group boundaries tend to be reinforced by attributes with which one is born, such as race. To this end, sociologists have emphasized that intergroup marriage can be reinforced by national service, attending university, and migration to urban areas, among others (e.g., Heaton and Jacobson 2000).

Another policy would involve adopting an educational model that is common to all students. Such a strategy need not follow a French model of assimilation to a specific national culture. The curriculum's content could take a variety of forms, including one that celebrated pluralism. But it should not delegate educational curriculum to subgroups that would give different, group-specific perspectives to children from different subgroups.

Part of the educational curriculum could involve language training. In multilingual societies, if there exists a common language that all children must learn, or if children are strongly encouraged or even required to learn more than one language, the extent to which politicians could use language identity for distributive commitments would diminish. And to the extent that groups tend to live in specific geographical regions, policies that encourage migration within a country could make it more difficult for parties to credibly commit to specific groups.

These types of policies have of course been discussed and debated in research on governance in multiethnic societies. The overwhelming focus in such studies, however, has been on issues of political stability and violence. The point here is to underline that these policies can also be evaluated on a different dimension. By affecting the porosity and salience of group boundaries, policies affecting marriage, national service, access to universities, education, language, and migration can also have an impact on the conditions under which inequality-reducing class politics can emerge.

If one embraces the idea that weaker group boundaries can foster class politics, then we should also consider trade-offs that come with policies that target specific groups precisely to redress inequality. One is affirmative action policies aimed at minority groups that are typically less well-off. Such policies are the result of explicit ethnic targeting, and to the extent that they reinforce group over class identities, they can discourage class-based politics that can help all of the nonrich. Thus, if our concern in affirmative action debates is about inequality (and there are of course reasons to embrace affirmative action for reasons unrelated to inequality), it is important that the affirmative action policies grapple with two issues. The first is to determine whether the policies truly help the nonrich, rather than the rich in the targeted group. The second is whether there are mechanisms in the policies themselves that establish criteria for evaluating the outcomes of affirmative action policies and bring them to an end if the goals of the program are achieved or if the program is proving inadequate for achieving the desired ends. Such evaluation and "sunsetting" is important from the perspective of inequality reduction if affirmative action programs help a disadvantaged group but discourage class-based politics that help the nonrich. A similar concern might exist for institutional arrangements that reserve seats for specific groups, such as seats reserved for particular castes in India. To the extent that such arrangements discourage class-based appeals, they can create a trade-off between helping a disadvantaged group and encouraging electoral competition that emphasizes broad-based approaches that help the least well-off.[1]

A similar issue arises around policies regarding unions. Although unions are obviously not ethnic groups, they can create an electoral dynamic of inclusion and exclusion among the nonrich. This occurs through conflict between "insiders" (individuals whose jobs and wages are heavily protected by government policy) and "outsiders" (individuals who are unemployed or who work in the informal sector). To the extent that rigid union membership allows distributive coalitions that include rich and nonrich insiders at the expense of nonrich outsiders, it will be more difficult for true class-based politics to emerge. This issue might be particularly acute in less developed democracies, but we also see it clearly in more advanced countries. In recent US politics, for example, there are divisions between union members who seek support for gas pipelines (and the jobs they create) and environmentalists (who can create jobs in other energy-related sectors).

Any policy idea to address inequality directly (e.g., by regulating the financial sector) or indirectly (e.g., by influencing the porosity of group boundaries) face the political reality that policy adoption in democracies requires support of political majorities, and such majorities, the winners of electoral competition, will often prefer not to adopt policies that undercut their ability to win. It is therefore useful to consider whether there are institutional choices, especially constitutional ones, that might encourage class-based politics independent of the pull-and-tug of particular electoral campaigns. One possibility that comes from outside the model concerns the electoral law. Although the analysis here suggests that empirical patterns related to group size are present in both proportional and majoritarian systems, Huber (2012) and much of the

---

[1] It is interesting to note, however, that there is evidence that India's reservation system has encouraged multiethnic parties (e.g., Dunning and Nilekani 2013).

analysis in Chapter 8 also find a consistent negative relationship between between proportional representation and ethnic voting. This may be true because when party entry costs are low, multiple parties competing for support from the same group can divide the members of the same group against each other (Huber 2012). What the analysis here suggests is that electoral competition based more on class likely follows from this weakening of ethnic identity. Thus, if ethnic and class politics emerge under complementary conditions, proportional electoral laws could be a valuable way of encouraging electoral competition that focuses on reducing inequality.

It is also important to consider other ways that constitutional arrangements can encourage class-based politics while discouraging a group-based politics of exclusion. The theoretical model suggests one way to do this is to design electoral competition so that it unfolds in relatively homogenous electorates. If group members tend to live together in specific geographic regions, then particular forms of federalism could be helpful. First, important political rights could be delegated to subnational units to adopt policies that affect the distribution of income. Since the subnational units would be relatively homogeneous, this could encourage a class-based politics at the subnational level that would be impossible at the national level. This, however, would be insufficient for reducing inequality because of the substantial inequality that often exists across regions. Some regions might have every incentive to have class politics, but if too many people are poor, they may resort to ethnic politics and they may have little economic means for addressing inequality. But this issue could be addressed by adopting a German-style constitutional mandate for fiscal equalization across the German Länder (i.e., states). In Germany, the Constitutional Court has interpreted a clause in the constitution requiring equivalent living conditions across the Länder to require a system of transfers from richer states to poorer ones. Although one must pay attention to ensuring such a system does not encourage profligate fiscal policy at the subnational level,[2] a constitutional structure that delegates subnational autonomy with equalization across states could be one way to encourage electoral competition on class-based issues. It is perhaps instructive to note, for example, that among ethnically diverse countries in the advanced democracies, Switzerland has the lowest level of inequality after taxes and redistribution, and Switzerland has strong fiscal and political autonomy at the cantonal level, along with a policy of

---

[2] See discussion in Rodden (2006).

fiscal equalization across cantons. It is probably also important, however, that Switzerland has substantial economic heterogeneity among each of its language groups.

In this book, I have emphasized that voters and parties have incentives to build the smallest possible winning electoral coalitions, and to therefore exclude as many individuals as possible from government benefits. This framework has led to the idea that in some contexts, inequality itself will discourage attention to inequality by elected officials. Whether this specific framework is viewed as valuable, and whether the policy and institutional prescriptions that follow from the framework are substantively useful, I hope that the effort at least reinforces the idea that if we care about inequality and its adverse consequences, it's insufficient to identify the regulatory or other policies that can redress inequality. We also need to identify the conditions under which incentives in electoral competition will encourage a focus by elected officials on the issue of inequality. Understanding and then shaping such electoral conditions provides one of the most effective ways forward for influencing whether policy prescriptions for redressing inequality will ever be adopted.

References

Acemoglu, Daron, and James Robinson. 2000. "Inequality, Growth and Development: Democratization or Repression?" *European Economic Review* 44: 683–693.

———. 2005. *Economic Origins of Dictatorship and Democracy.* Cambridge: Cambridge University Press.

———. 2008. "Persistence of Power, Elites, and Institutions." *American Economic Review* 98: 267–293.

Ager, Philipp, and Markus Brückner. 2013. "Cultural Diversity and Economic Growth: Evidence from the US During the Age of Mass Migration." *European Economic Review* 64 (November): 76–97.

Aghion, Philippe, and Patrick Bolton. 1997. "A Theory of Trickle-Down and Development." *Review of Economic Studies* 64: 151–172.

Alesina, Alberto, and George-Marios Angeletos. 2005. "Fairness and Redistribution." *American Economic Review* 95: 913–935.

Alesina, Alberto, Reyza Baqir, and William Easterly. 1999. "Public Goods and Ethnic Divisions." *Quarterly Journal of Economics* 114(4): 1243–1284.

Alesina, Alberto, Arnaud Devleeschauwer, William Easterly, Sergio Kurlat, and Romain Wacziarg. 2003. "Fractionalization." *Journal of Economic Growth* 8: 155–194.

Alesina, Alberto, and Edward Glaeser. 2003. *Fighting Poverty in the US and Europe: A World of Difference.* Oxford: Oxford University Press.

Alesina, Alberto, and Eliana La Ferrara. 2002. "Who Trusts Others?" *Journal of Public Economics* 85: 207–234.

———. 2005. "Ethnic Diversity and Economic Performance." *Journal of Economic Literature* 43(3): 762–800.

Alesina, Alberto, Stelios Michalopoulos, and Elias Papaioannou. 2013. "Ethnic Inequality." *NBER Working Papers,* 18512, revised on July 1, 2013. Cambridge, MA: National Bureau of Economic Research.

Alesina, Alberto, and Dani Rodrik. 1994. "Distributive Politics and Economic Growth." *Quarterly Journal of Economics* 109: 465–490.

References

Alesina, Alberto, and Enrico Spolaore. 1997. "On the Number and Size of Nations." *Quarterly Journal of Economic* 112(4): 1027–1056.

Alwy, Alwiya, and Susanne Schech. 2004. "Ethnic Inequalities in Education in Kenya." *International Education Journal* 5(2): 266–274.

Arbatli, Cemal Eren, Quamrul Ashraf, and Oded Galor. 2015. "The Nature of Civil Conflict." NBER Working Paper 21079. Cambridge, MA: National Bureau of Economic Research.

Arneson, Richard. 1989. "Equality of Opportunity for Welfare." *Philosophical Studies: An International Journal for Philosophy in the Analytic Tradition* 56(1): 77–93.

Atkinson, Anthony B. 1970. "On the Measurement of Inequality." *Journal of Economic Theory* 2(3): 244–263.

1975. *The Economics of Inequality*. Oxford: Clarendon Press.

2015. *Inequality: What Can Be Done?* Cambridge, MA: Harvard University Press.

Austen-Smith, David, and Michael Wallerstein. 2006. "Redistribution and Affirmative Action." *Journal of Public Economics* 90: 1789–1823.

Baldwin, Kate. 2013. "Why Vote with the Chief? Political Connections and Public Goods Provision in Zambia." *American Journal of Political Science* 57(4): 794–809.

2015. *The Paradox of Traditional Leaders in Democratic Africa*. New York: Cambridge University Press.

Baldwin, Kate, and John D. Huber. 2010. "Economic versus Cultural Differences: Forms of Ethnic Diversity and Public Goods Provision." *American Political Science Review* 104(4):644–662.

Banerjee, Abhijit, and Andrew Newman. 1993. "Occupational Choice and the Process of Development." *Journal of Political Economy* 101(2): 274-298.

Bates, Robert H. 1983. "Modernization, Ethnic Competition and the Rationality of Politics." In *State versus Ethnic Claims: African Policy Dilemmas*, eds. D. Rothchild and V. A. Olunsorola (pp. 152–171). Boulder, CO: Westview Press.

Beck, Thorsten, George Clarke, Alberto Groff, Philip Keefer, and Patrick Walsh. 2001. "New Tools in Comparative Political Economy: The Database of Political Institutions." *World Bank Economic Review* 15(1): 165–176.

Becker, Gary S. 1968. "Crime and Punishment: An Economic Approach." *Journal of Political Economy* 76(2): 169–217.

Bénabou, Roland. 1996. "Inequality and Growth." *NBER Macroeconomics Annual*, eds. Ben Bernanke and Julio Rotemberg (pp. 11–74). Cambridge, MA: National Bureau of Economic Research.

2000. "Unequal Societies: Income Distribution and the Social Contract." *American Economic Review* 90: 96–129.

Birnir, Jóhanna Kristõn. 2007. *Ethnicity and Electoral Politics*. New York: Cambridge University Press.

Boix, Carles. 2003. *Democracy and Redistribution*. New York: Cambridge University Press.

Bourguignon, François, Francisco H. G. Ferreira, and Marta Menéndez. 2007. "Inequality of Opportunity in Brazil." *Review of Income and Wealth* 53(4): 585–618.

Bourguignon, François, and Thierry Verdier. 2000. "Oligarchy, Democracy, Inequality, and Growth." *Journal of Development Economics* 62(2): 231–285.

Braithwaite, John. 1979. *Inequality, Crime, and Public Policy.* New York: Routledge.

Brancati, Dawn. 2008. *Peace by Design: Managing Intrastate Conflict through Decentralization.* New York: Oxford University Press.

Burgess, Robin, Remi Jedwab, Edward Miguel, Ameet Morjaria, and Gerard Padro i Miquel. 2015. "The Value of Democracy: Evidence form Road Building in Kenya." *American Economic Review* 105(6): 1817–1851.

Chandra, Kanchan. 2004. *Why Ethnic Parties Succeed: Patronage and Ethnic Headcounts in India.* Cambridge: Cambridge University Press.

Cheibub, José Antonio, Jennifer Gandhi, and James Raymond Vreeland. 2010. "Democracy and Dictatorship Revisited." *Public Choice* 143(2-1): 67–101.

Cohen, Gerry. 1989. "On the Currency of Egalitarian Justice." *Ethics* 99(4): 906–944.

Corak, Miles. 2013. "Income Inequality, Equality of Opportunity, and Intergenerational Mobility." *Journal of Economic Perspectives* 27(3): 79–102.

Cusack, Thomas. 1997. "Partisan Politics and Public Finance: Changes in Public Spending in the Industrialized Democracies, 1955-89." *Public Choice* 91: 375-395.

Deaton, Angus S. 2010. "Instruments, Randomization, and Learning about Development." *Journal of Economic Literature* 48(2): 424–455.

de la O, Ana L., and Jonathan A. Rodden. 2008. "Does Religion Distract the Poor? Income and Issue Voting Around the World." *Comparative Political Studies* 41: 437–476.

De Maio, Fernando G. 2007. "Income Inequality Measures." *Journal of Epidemiology and Community Health* 61(10): 849–852.

Doyle, Michael, and Nicholas Sambanis. 2006. *Making War and Building Peace.* Princeton, NJ: Princeton University Press.

Dunning, Thad, and Lauren Harrison. 2010. "Cross-cutting Cleavages and Ethnic Voting: An Experimental Study of Cousinage in Mali." *American Political Science Review* 104(1): 21–39.

Dunning, Thad, and Janhavi Nilekani. 2013. "Ethnic Quotas and Political Mobilization: Caste, Parties and Distribution in Indian Village Councils." *American Political Science Review* 107(1): 35–56.

Dworkin, Ronald. 1981a. "What Is Equality? Part 1: Equality of Welfare." *Philosophy and Public Affairs* 10(3): 185–246.
    1981b. "What Is Equality? Part 2: Equality of Resources." *Philosophy and Public Affairs* 10(4): 283–345.

Easterly, William. 2001. "Can Institutions Resolve Ethnic Conflict?" *Economic Development and Cultural Change* 49(4): 687–706.

Easterly, William, and Ross Levine. 1997. "Africa's Growth Tragedy: Policies and Ethnic Division." *Quarterly Journal of Economics* 112: 1203–1250.

Enamorado, Ted, Luis-Felipe López-Calva, Carlos Rodríguez-Castelán, and Hernán Winkler. 2014. "Income Inequality and Violent Crime Evidence from

Mexico's Drug War." Policy Research Working Paper 6935. Washington, DC: The World Bank.

Esteban, Joan, Laura Mayoral, and Debraj Ray. 2012. "Ethnicity and Conflict: An Empirical Study." *American Economic Review* 102(4): 1310–1342.

Esteban, Joan Maria, and Debraj Ray. 2000. "Wealth Constraints, Lobbying, and the Efficiency of Public Allocation." *European Economic Review* 44: 694–705.

Esteban, Joan, and Debraj Ray. 2011. "A Model of Ethnic Conflict." *Journal of the European Economic Association* 9(3): 496–521.

Fearon, James D. 1999. "Why Ethnic Politics and 'Pork' Tend to Go Together." Unpublished Manuscript, Stanford University.

Fearon, James. 2003. "Ethnic and Cultural Diversity by Country." *Journal of Economic Growth* 8(2): 195–222.

Fearon, James, Macartan Humphreys, and Jeremy M. Weinstein. 2015. "How Does Development Assistance Affect Collective Action Capacity? Results from a Field Experiment in Post-Conflict Liberia." *American Political Science Review* 109: 450–469.

Fearon, James D., and David D. Laitin. 1996. "Explaining Interethnic Cooperation." *American Political Science Review* 90(4): 715–35.

Feddersen, Timothy J., Itai Sened, and Stephen G. Wright. 1990. "Rational Voting and Candidate Entry under Plurality Rule." *American Journal of Political Science* 34(4): 1005–1016.

Fernàndez, Raquel, and Gilat Levy. 2008. "Diversity and Redistribution." *Journal of Public Economics* 92: 925–943.

Ferreira, Francisco, and Jèrèmie Gignoux. 2011. "The Measurement of Inequality of Opportunity: Theory and an Application to Latin America." *Review of Income and Wealth* 57(4): 622–657.

Ferreira, Francisco H. G., Christoph Lakner, and Maria Ana Lugo Berk Özler. 2014. "Inequality of Opportunity and Economic Growth A Cross-Country Analysis." Policy Research Working Paper 6915. Washington, DC: The World Bank.

Franck, Raphael, and Ilia Rainer. 2012. "Does the Leader's Ethnicity Matter? Ethnic Favoritism, Education and Health in Sub-Saharan Africa." *American Political Science Review* 106(2): 294–325.

Freeman, Richard. 1999. "The Economics of Crime." In *Handbook of Labor Economics, 3c*, eds. O. Ashenfelter and D. Card, pp. 3529–71 Philadelphia: Elsevier.

Galbraith James K., Béatrice Halbach, Aleksandra Malinowska, Amin Shams, and Wenjie Zhang. 2014. "The UTIP Global Inequality Data Sets 1963–2008: Updates, Revisions and Quality Checks." UTIP Working Paper 68, The University of Texas at Austin.

2015. "A Comparison of Major World Inequality Data Sets: LIS, OECD, SILC, WDI and EHII." UTIP Working Paper 69, The University of Texas at Austin.

Galor, Oded, and Joseph Zeira. 1993. "Income Distribution and Macroeconomics." *Review of Economic Studies* 60: 35–52.

Garrett, Geoffrey, and Peter Lange. 1991. "Political Responses to Interdependence: What's "Left" for the Left?" *International Organization*: 45: 539–564.

Genicot, Garance, and Debraj Ray. 2014. "Aspirations and Inequality." NBER Working Paper 19976. Cambridge, MA: National Bureau of Economic Research.

Gilens, Martin, 1999. *Why Americans Hate Welfare: Race, Media, and the Politics of Anti-Poverty Policy*. Chicago: University of Chicago Press.

Greif, Avner. 1993. "Contract Enforceability and Economic Institutions in Early Trade: The Maghribi Traders' Coalition." *American Economic Review* 83(3): 525–548.

Haber, Stephen, and Victor Menaldo. 2011. "Do Natural Resources Fuel Authoritarianism? A Reappraisal of the Resource Curse." *American Political Science Review* 105(1): 1–26.

Habyarimana, James, Macartan Humphreys, Daniel Posner, and Jeremy Weinstein. 2007. "Why Does Ethnic Diversity Undermine Public Goods Provision?" *American Political Science Review* 101(4): 709–725.

2009. *Coethnicity: Diversity and Dilemmas of Collective Action*. New York: Russell Sage Foundation.

Hagiopan, Frances. 2007. "Parties and Voters in Emerging Democracies." In *The Oxford Handbook of Comparative Politics*, eds. Carles Boix and Susan Stokes, pp. 582–603. Oxford: Oxford University Press.

Heaton, Tim B., and Cardell K. Jacobson. 2000. "Intergroup Marriage: An Examination of Opportunity Structures." *Sociological Inquiry* 70(1): 30–41.

Horowitz, Donald L. 1985. *Ethnic Groups in Conflict*. Berkeley: University of California Press.

2001. *The Deadly Ethnic Riot*. Berkeley: University of California Press.

Huber, John D. 2012. "Measuring Ethnic Voting: Do Proportional Electoral Laws Politicize Ethnicity." *American Journal of Political Science* 56(4): 986–1001.

Huber, John D., and Piero Stanig. 2011. "Church-State Separation and Redistribution." *Journal of Public Economics* 95: 828–836.

Huber, John D., and Pavithra Suryanarayon. 2016. "Ethnic Inequality and the Ethnification of Political Parties: Evidence from India." *World Politics* 68(1): 149–188.

Huber, John D., and Michael M. Ting. 2013. "Redistribution, Pork and Elections." *Journal of the European Economic Association* 11(6): 1382–1403.

Humphreys, Macartan, and Alan M. Jacobs. 2015. "Mixing Methods: A Bayesian Approach." *American Political Science Review* 109(4): 653–673.

Ioannidis, John P. A. 2005. "Why Most Published Research Findings Are False." *PLoS Medicine* 2(8, e124): 696–701.

Iversen, Torben, and David Soskice. 2006. "Electoral Institutions and the Politics of Coalitions: Why Some Democracies Redistribute More Than Others." *American Political Science Review* 100(2): 165–181.

Jablonski, Ryan. 2014. "How Aid Targets Votes: The Impact of Electoral Incentives on Foreign Aid Distribution." *World Politics* 66(2): 293–330.

Kasara, Kimuli. 2007. "Tax Me if You Can: Ethnic Geography, Democracy, and the Taxation of Agriculture in Africa." *American Political Science Review* 101(1): 159–172.

Kawachi, I., P. B. Kennedy, and R. G. Wilkinson (eds.). 1999. *The Society and Population Health Reader. Income Inequality and Health*. New York: The New Press.

Kearney, Melissa S., and Phillip B. Levine. 2014. "Income Inequality, Social Mobility, and the Decision to Drop Out of High School." NBER Working Paper No. 20195. Cambridge, MA: National Bureau of Economic Research.

Kenworthy, Lane, and Jonas Pontusson. 2005. "Rising Inequality and the Politics of Redistribution in Affluent Countries." *Perspectives on Politics* 3(3): 449–471.

Khwaja, A. 2009. "Can Good Projects Succeed in Bad Communities?" *Journal of Public Economics* 93(August): 899–916.

King, Gary, Robert O. Keohane, and Sidney Verba. 1994. *Designing Social Inquiry: Scientific Inference in Qualitative Research*. Princeton, NJ: Princeton University Press.

Kitschelt, Herbert, and Steven I. Wilkinson (eds.). 2007 *Patrons or Policies: Patterns of Democratic Accountability and Political Competition*. New York: Cambridge University Press.

Kramon, Eric, and Daniel N. Posner. 2016. "Ethnic Favoritism in Education in Kenya." *Quarterly Journal of Political Science* 11(1): 1–58.

Laitin, David D. 1998. *Identity in Formation: The Russian-Speaking Populations in the New Abroad*. Ithaca, NY: Cornell University Press.

La Porta, Rafael, Florencio Lopez-de-Silanes, Andrei Shleifer, and Robert Vishny. 1999. "The Quality of Government." *Journal of Law, Economics, and Organization* 15(1): 222–279.

Laslier, Jean-Franqis, and Nathalie Picard. 2002. "Distributive Politics and Electoral Competition." *Journal of Economic Theory* 103: 106–130.

Levy, Gilat. 2004. "A Model of Political Parties." *Journal of Economic Theory* 115(2): 250–277.

Lupu, Noam, and Jonas Pontusson. 2011. "The Structure of Inequality and the Politics of Redistribution." *American Political Science Review* 105(2): 316–336.

Luttmer, Erzo. 2001. "Group Loyalty and the Taste for Redistribution." *Journal of Political Economy* 109(3): 500–528.

McCarty, Nolan, Keith T. Poole, and Howard Rosenthal. 2006. *Polarized America: The Dance of Ideology and Unequal Riches*. Cambridge, MA: MIT Press.

Meltzer, Allan H., and Scott F. Richard. 1981. "A Rational Theory of the Size of Government." *Journal of Political Economy*: 89: 914–927.

Miguel, Edward, and Mary Kay Gugerty. 2005. "Ethnic Diversity, Social Sanctions, and Public Goods in Kenya." *Journal of Public Economics* 89 (December): 2325–2368.

Moene, Karl Ove, and Michael Wallerstein. 2003. "Earnings Inequality and Welfare Spending." *World Politics* 55(4): 485–516.

Montalvo, José G., and Marta Reynal-Querol. 2005. "Ethnic Polarization, Potential Conflict and Civil War." *American Economic Review* 95(3): 796–816.

Myerson, Roger B. 1993. "Incentives to Cultivate Favored Minorities under Alternative Electoral Systems." *American Political Science Review* 87: 856–869.

Offe, Claus. 1992. "Strong Causes, Weak Cures." *East European Constitutional Review* 1: 21–23.

Page, Scott E. 2008. *The Difference: How the Power of Diversity Creates Better Groups, Firms, Schools, and Societies*. Princeton, NJ: Princeton University Press.

Penn, Elizabeth Maggie. 2008. "Citizenship versus Ethnicity: The Role of Institutions in Shaping Identity Choice." *Journal of Politics* 70(4): 956–973.

Pepinsky, Thomas B. 2009. "The 2008 Malaysian Elections: An End to Ethnic Politics?" *Journal of East Asian Studies* 9(1): 87–120.

Perotti, Roberto. 1996. "Growth, Income Distribution, and Democracy: What the Data Say." *Journal of Economic Growth* 1: 149–188.

Persson, Torsten, and Guido Tabellini. 1994. "Is Inequality Harmful for Growth?" *American Economic Review* 84: 600–621.

2002. *Political Economics: Explaining Economic Policy*. Cambridge, MA: MIT Press.

Piketty, Thomas. 2014. *Capital in the 21st Century*. Cambridge, MA: Harvard University Press.

Posner, Daniel N. 2004. "The Political Salience of Cultural Difference: Why Chewas and Tumbukas Are Allies in Zambia and Adversaries in Malawi." *American Politcal Science Review* 98(4): 529–545.

2005. *Institutions and Ethnic Politics in Africa*. Cambridge: Cambridge University Press.

Prat, Andrea. 2002. "Should a Team Be Homogeneous?' A Comparative Exploration." *European Economic Review* 46(7): 1187–1207.

Ramcharan, Rodney. 2010. "Inequality and Redistribution: Evidence from U.S. Counties and States, 1890–1930." *The Review of Economics and Statistics* 92(4): 729–744.

Rawls, John. 1971. *A Theory of Justice*. London: Belknap.

Reynal-Querol, Marta. 2002. "Ethnicity, Political Systems, and Civil Wars." *Journal of Conflict Resolution* 46(1): 29–54.

Rodden, Jonathan. 2006. *Hamilton's Paradox: The Promise and Peril of Fiscal Federalism*. New York: Cambridge University Press.

Roemer, John. 1993. "A Pragmatic Theory of Responsibility for the Egalitarian Planner." *Philosophy and Public Affairs* 22(2): 146–166.

1998. *Equality of Opportunity*. Cambridge, MA: Harvard University Press.

Roemer, John E., et al. 2003. "To What Extent Do Fiscal Regimes Equalize Opportunities for Income Acquisition among Citizens?" *Journal of Public Economics* 87: 539–565.

Romer, Thomas. 1975. "Individual Welfare, Majority Voting, and the Properties of a Linear Income Tax." *Journal of Public Economics* 4(2): 163–185.

Shayo, Moses. 2009. "A Model of Social Identity with an Application to Political Economy: Nation, Class, and Redistribution." *American Political Science Review* 103(2): 147–174.

Shertzer, Allison. 2013. "Immigrant Group Size and Political Mobilization: Evidence from European Migration to the United States." NBER Working Paper 18827. Cambridge, MA: National Bureau of Economic Research.

Solon, Gary. 2004. "A Model of Intergen erational Mobility Variation over Time and Place." In *Generational Income Mobility in North America and Europe*, ed. Miles Corak, pp. 38–47. New York: Cambridge University Press.

Solt, Frederik. 2009. "Standardizing the World Income Inequality Database." *Social Science Quarterly* 90(2): 231–242.

Sowell, Thomas. 2004. *Affirmative Action around the World: An Empirical Study*. New Haven, CT: Yale University Press.

Stack, Steven. 1984. "Income Inequality and Property Crime: A Cross-National Analysis of Relative Deprivation Theory." *Criminology* 22: 229–256.

Stiglitz, Joseph E. 2015. *The Great Divide: Unequal Societies and What We Can Do about Them*. New York: W. W. Norton.

Stokes, Susan C., Thad Dunning, Marcelo Nazareno, and Valeria Brusco. 2013. *Brokers, Voters, and Clientelism: The Puzzle of Distributive Politics*. New York: Cambridge University Press.

Teik, Khoo Boo. 2005. "Ethnic Structure, Inequality and Governance in the Public Sector: Malaysian Experiences." Democracy, Governance and Human Rights Programme Paper No. 20, United Nations Research Institute for Social Development.

Thachil, Tariq. 2014a. "Elite Parties and Poor Voters: Theory and Evidence from India." *American Political Science Review* 108(2): 454–477.

2014b. *Elite Parties, Poor Voters: Social Services as Electoral Strategy in India*. New York: Cambridge University Press.

2014c. "Do Internal Migrants Divide or Unite Across Ethnic Lines? Ethnographic and Experimental Evidence from Urban India." Unpublished Manuscript, Yale University.

Voitchovsky, Sarah. 2009. "Inequality and Economic Growth." In *The Oxford Handbook of Economic Inequality*, eds. W. Salverda, B. Nolan, and T. Smeeding, pp. 549–74. Oxford: Oxford University Press.

Wilkinson. Steven I. 2004. *Votes and Violence: Electoral Competition and Ethnic Riots in India*. New York: Cambridge University Press.

Index

Sidney Tarrow, *Power in Movement: Social Movements and Contentious Politics*

Sidney Tarrow, *Power in Movement: Social Movements and Contentious Politics, Revised and Updated Third Edition*

Tariq Thachil, *Elite Parties, Poor Voters: How Social Services Win Votes in India*

Kathleen Thelen, *How Institutions Evolve: The Political Economy of Skills in Germany, Britain, the United States, and Japan*

Kathleen Thelen, *Varieties of Liberalization and the New Politics of Social Solidarity*

Charles Tilly, *Trust and Rule*

Daniel Treisman, *The Architecture of Government: Rethinking Political Decentralization*

Guillermo Trejo, *Popular Movements in Autocracies: Religion, Repression, and Indigenous Collective Action in Mexico*

Rory Truex, *Making Autocracy Work: Representation and Responsiveness in Modern China*

Lily Lee Tsai, *Accountability without Democracy: How Solidary Groups Provide Public Goods in Rural China*

Joshua Tucker, *Regional Economic Voting: Russia, Poland, Hungary, Slovakia and the Czech Republic, 1990–1999*

Ashutosh Varshney, *Democracy, Development, and the Countryside*

Yuhua Wang, *Tying the Autocrat's Hand: The Rise of The Rule of Law in China*

Jeremy M. Weinstein, *Inside Rebellion: The Politics of Insurgent Violence*

Stephen I. Wilkinson, *Votes and Violence: Electoral Competition and Ethnic Riots in India*

Andreas Wimmer, *Waves of War: Nationalism, State Formation, and Ethnic Exclusion in the Modern World*

Jason Wittenberg, *Crucibles of Political Loyalty: Church Institutions and Electoral Continuity in Hungary*

Elisabeth J. Wood, *Forging Democracy from Below: Insurgent Transitions in South Africa and El Salvador*

Elisabeth J. Wood, *Insurgent Collective Action and Civil War in El Salvador*

Daniel Ziblatt, *Conservative Parties and the Birth of Modern Democracy in Europe*